The Higher Objectives of Islamic Theology

AMERICAN ACADEMY OF RELIGION

REFLECTION AND THEORY IN THE STUDY OF RELIGION

SERIES EDITOR

Vincent Lloyd, Villanova University

A Publication Series of

The American Academy of Religion

and

Oxford University Press

OPTING FOR THE MARGINS
Postmodernity and Liberation in Christian Theology
Edited by Joerg Rieger

MAKING MAGIC
Religion, Magic, and Science in the Modern World
Randall Styers

THE METAPHYSICS OF DANTE'S *COMEDY*
Christian Moevs

PILGRIMAGE OF LOVE
Moltmann on the Trinity and Christian Life
Joy Ann McDougall

MORAL CREATIVITY
Paul Ricoeur and the Poetics of Possibility
John Wall

MELANCHOLIC FREEDOM
Agency and the Spirit of Politics
David Kyuman Kim

FEMINIST THEOLOGY AND THE CHALLENGE OF DIFFERENCE
Margaret D. Kamitsuka

PLATO'S GHOST
Spiritualism in the American Renaissance
Cathy Gutierrez

TOWARD A GENEROUS ORTHODOXY
Prospects for Hans Frei's Postliberal Theology
Jason A. Springs

CAVELL, COMPANIONSHIP, AND CHRISTIAN THEOLOGY
Peter Dula

COMPARATIVE THEOLOGY AND THE PROBLEM OF RELIGIOUS RIVALRY
Hugh Nicholson

SECULARISM AND RELIGION-MAKING
Markus Dressler and Arvind-Pal S. Mandair

FORTUNATE FALLIBILITY
Kierkegaard and the Power of Sin
Jason A. Mahn

METHOD AND METAPHYSICS IN MAIMONIDES' *GUIDE FOR THE PERPLEXED*
Daniel Davies

THE LANGUAGE OF DISENCHANTMENT
Protestant Literalism and Colonial Discourse in British India
Robert A. Yelle

WRITING RELIGION
The Making of Turkish Alevi Islam
Markus Dressler

THE AESTHETICS AND ETHICS OF FAITH
A Dialogue Between Liberationist and Pragmatic Thought
Christopher D. Tirres

VISIONS OF RELIGION
Experience, Meaning, and Power
Stephen S. Bush

STUDYING THE QUR'AN IN THE MUSLIM ACADEMY
Majid Daneshgar

SYNCRETISM AND CHRISTIAN TRADITION
Race and Revelation in the Study of Religious Mixture
Ross Kane

ASIAN AMERICANS AND THE SPIRIT OF RACIAL CAPITALISM
Jonathan Tran

THE HIGHER OBJECTIVES OF ISLAMIC THEOLOGY
Toward a Theory of Maqāṣid al-ʿAqīda
Mohammed Gamal Abdelnour

AMERICAN ACADEMY OF RELIGION

The Higher Objectives of Islamic Theology

Toward a Theory of Maqāṣid al-ʿAqīda

MOHAMMED GAMAL ABDELNOUR

OXFORD
UNIVERSITY PRESS

OXFORD
UNIVERSITY PRESS

Oxford University Press is a department of the University of Oxford. It furthers the University's objective of excellence in research, scholarship, and education by publishing worldwide. Oxford is a registered trade mark of Oxford University Press in the UK and certain other countries.

Published in the United States of America by Oxford University Press
198 Madison Avenue, New York, NY 10016, United States of America.

CIP data is on file at the Library of Congress

ISBN 978–0–19–764863–6

DOI: 10.1093/oso/9780197648636.001.0001

3 5 7 9 8 6 4 2
Printed by Integrated Books International, United States of America

وعند ذلك، فحقّ على الناظرِ المتأملِ، إذا وجد فيه نقصاً أن يُكمّل، وليحسن الظنّ بمَن حالَف الليالي والأيام، واستبدَل التعبَ بالراحةِ والسَّهَرَ بالمنام، حتى أهدَى إليه نتيجةَ عُمرِه، وَوَهَبَ له يتيمةَ دهرِه، فقد ألقى إليه مقاليدَ ما لديه، وطَوَّقَه طوقَ الأمانة التي في يديه، وَخَرَجَ عن عُهدة البيان فيما وَجَبَ عليه، وإنما الأعمال بالنيات، وإنما لكل امرىء ما نوى.

—الموافقات في أصول الشريعة (ت. 1388م)، أبو إسحاق الشاطبي

In the light of this, it is incumbent upon the mindful reader to complement any deficiency that he may find in it [the present book]. He should harbour a good thought about the one who allied with the nights and days and substituted weariness for ease and wakefulness for sleep till he was able to gift him the sum total of his life and present his entire precious time to him. He has now put the keys of all that he has in front of him, placed around his neck the trust that was in his own hand, and discharged himself of the duty of speaking up by stating what is incumbent upon him [to state]. Indeed, actions are but by intentions, and each person will have but that which he intended.

—Abū Isḥāq al-Shāṭibī (d. 1388 CE), *al-Muwāfaqāt fi uṣūl al-Sharīʿa*

Contents

Acknowledgments ix

Transliteration and Dating xi

Introduction xiii

Important Definitions and Clarifications xv

The Monograph's Epistemological Paradigm xvii

Key Arguments xxii

Structure of the Monograph xxiv

Important Caveats xxvi

CHAPTER 1: Historical Roots of *Maqāṣid al-ʿAqīda* 1

Maqāṣid al-ʿAqīda before al-Ghazālī 2

Maqāṣid al-ʿAqīda with al-Ghazālī 7

Maqāṣid al-ʿAqīda after al-Ghazālī 23

Muḥammad ʿAbduh's Contributions to *Maqāṣid al-ʿAqīda* 26

Explaining the Underdevelopment of *Maqāṣid al-ʿAqīda* 31

CHAPTER 2: Sources and Methods of *Maqāṣid al-ʿAqīda* 38

The Qur'ān and *Maqāṣid al-ʿAqīda* 38

The Sunna and *Maqāṣid al-ʿAqīda* 44

Maqāṣid al-ʿAqīda between Exotericism and Esotericism 46

CHAPTER 3: From *Maqāṣid al-Sharīʿa* to *Maqāṣid al-ʿAqīda* 53

"Interrogating" the Classical "Theory" of *Maqāṣid al-Sharīʿa* 53

"Generating" the Higher Objective(s) of Islamic Theology 56

The Nature of the Islamic Truth 63

CHAPTER 4: "Integrating" the "Tools" of *Maqāṣid al-Sharīʿa* into *Maqāṣid al-ʿAqīda* 68
Definition and Transmission 68
Al-Firqa al-Nājiya in *al-Ḍarūriyyāt*, *al-Ḥājiyyāt*, and *al-Taḥsīniyyāt* 77
Faith vis-à-vis Deeds in *al-Ḍarūriyyāt*, *al-Ḥājiyyāt*, and *al-Taḥsīniyyāt* 86
The Prophet Muḥammad in *al-Ḍarūriyyāt* and *al-Ḥājiyyāt* 90

CHAPTER 5: Why Does *Maqāṣid al-ʿAqīda* Matter? 97
The *Maqāṣidī*-Oriented Approach and Treating the Wahhabi-Shiite Conflict 103

Conclusions 110
The Way Forward 113

Notes 115
Bibliography 145
Index 161

Acknowledgments

THIS MONOGRAPH WAS drafted while I was a Fellow of the Centre of Islamic Studies at SOAS (2019/2020–2020/2021). Therefore, I thank Muhammad Abdel Haleem (head of the Centre), Mustafa Shah, and Abdul Hakim al-Matroudi, who provided me with an ideal environment in which I could collect and dissect the data of this monograph. I have benefited not only from their insights and friendships but also from their students, whom I too taught in the past five years. Also, I am grateful for Al-Azhar, my alma mater, and the British Council in Egypt (who funded my PhD project) for granting me a leave, allowing me to accept SOAS's fellowship. I am thankful also for the Philosophy Department at the University of York, especially Tom Stoneham and David Worsley, who not only allowed me to complete this manuscript by the time I joined their department but also engaged with its ideas by holding seminar series discussing its questions and potential.

In the writing process, I benefited greatly from discussions with Ebrahim Moosa, Gavin D'Costa, Joshua Ralston, Khaled Abou El Fadl, and Mona Siddiqui. Over the past five years, exchanges with this cohort have helped me refine the arguments and check the evidence presented here. I found the American Academy of Religion's series, Reflection and Theory in the Study of Religion, a great host for this manuscript. Hence, I extend my thanks to Vincent Lloyd, the series editor, for his encouragement and belief in the manuscript, and to Cynthia Read, of Oxford University Press, for overseeing the manuscript through the stages of review and production.

I have often been asked: How did you manage to finish your second book a few months after publishing your first, with Brill? To this I say that the ideas presented in this book were conceived during the writing of the first book. By the time I published the first, I already had material for the second. Also, I have been blessed with a cohort of friends who have read this manuscript from A to Z and offered some significantly detailed comments and suggestions that have considerably contributed to the quick completion of this book. These are Shoaib A. Malik, Claire Gallien, and Umran Khan. I am much obliged to them.

As always, Mai Bakr, my beloved wife, was the first attentive listener for all ideas presented in this book. I thank her for the endless patience with which she helped me refine my ideas from the earliest phases of thinking through the basic idea of the book to its final submission. On top of that, she was perfectly looking after our daughter, Leen, and our son, Abraham. May God bless her and them.

Transliteration and Dating

For rendering Arabic words in English, I have followed the IJMES transliteration system (*International Journal of Middle East Studies*), except in cases where I need to comply with sources of direct quotations. As for dating figures and authors, I use the Gregorian calendar. Therefore, historical figures and classical authors are identified by their death dates using the Gregorian years only.

Introduction

This monograph takes the well-known *ḥadīth* of Angel Gabriel (*ḥadīth Jibrīl*)[1] as its starting point. In this *ḥadīth*, Gabriel asks Prophet Muḥammad about the three key dimensions of Islam: *islām* (submission), *īmān* (faith), and *iḥsān* (excellence). While the first dimension relates to the practical aspects of Islam, and the second refers to its creedal doctrines, the third refers to its spiritual realm. *Islām* in this *ḥadīth* is described with its five pillars (testimony of faith, prayer, charity, fasting, and pilgrimage). *Īmān* is described with its six articles (faith in God, His angels, His books, His messengers, the Last Day, and Predestination). *Iḥsān* is described as worshiping God as if you see Him, and if you do not see Him, then, to know that He sees you. From those dimensions, respectively, Islamic law (*Fiqh/Sharīʿa*), Islamic theology (*ʿAqīda/Kalām*), and Sufism (*Taṣawuf*) emerged as integral disciplines of the Islamic tradition.

Due to the centrality of this *ḥadīth* to the Islamic tradition and the holistic picture that it draws about it,[2] I appeal to it to essentially propose a value-based structure of the Islamic tradition. This value-based structure can be summarized in three cardinal values: Truth, Justice, and Beauty. I argue that while Islamic law's primary objective is the pursuit, preservation, and promotion of Justice, and Sufism's key objective is the pursuit, preservation, and promotion of Beauty, Islamic theology's cardinal objective is the pursuit, preservation, and promotion of Truth. I also contend that those three values lead to what the Qur'ān calls the "Good Life," as mentioned in Q. 16:97, which states, "Whoever does good, whether male or female, while he is a believer—We will surely cause him to live a Good Life, and We will surely give them their reward according to the best of what they used to do." Table I.1 summarizes this idea.

However, while the three disciplines of theology, law, and Sufism emerged primarily to serve those ethical values (Justice, Beauty, and Truth), those

The Higher Objectives of Islamic Theology. Mohammed Gamal Abdelnour, Oxford University Press.
 DOI: 10.1093/oso/9780197648636.001.0001

Table I.1 Three Cardinal Values of the Islamic Tradition

	Islamic Theology	Islamic Law	Sufism
Higher objective (*maqṣūd*)	Pursuit, preservation, and promotion of Truth	Pursuit, preservation, and promotion of Justice	Pursuit, preservation, and promotion of Beauty

disciplines often got distracted by other temporal concerns, leading to the underestimation of the values to be served. Fazlur Rahman (d. 1988) pointed out that Muslim theologians and philosophers failed "to develop a theory of knowledge that would do justice to religious facts and moral cognition." He proceeded to say that "when one scans the entire work of the Muslim philosophers, one is struck by the peculiar inattention shown to ethics."[3] In his *Reasoning with God*, Khaled Abou El Fadl observed that the Islamic law tradition, for practical reasons, often did not wrestle with questions of morality and ethics, due to the very nature and function of legal systems. This attitude contributed to a de facto divorce of Islamic ethics and morality from Islamic law, constituting a challenge that contemporary Muslims need to address.[4] Furthermore, in his *Jawāhir al-Qur'ān* (Jewels of the Qur'ān) al-Ghazālī (d. 1111) illustrated that much work has been done on *Fiqh* (Islamic law), such that it has exceeded its needed measures.[5] By implication, morality and ethics were largely overshadowed and were not actually given their due attention and space.

This overemphasis on and obsession with law (Justice) has largely contributed, in my view, to the stagnation of theology (Truth) and the marginalization of Sufism (Beauty). So discussions on the nature of "truth" in Islamic theology and how it relates to non-Islamic theories of truth are either absolutist or rudimentary. Additionally, Sufism has been relegated to the periphery of the tradition and given a backseat. Hence, elements of beauty in the tradition have largely been buried under layers of legalities, especially in modern Islam. The great Algerian philosopher Malek Bennabi (d. 1973) has observed this "imbalance" in modern Muslim discourse in his groundbreaking work, *Conditions of a Renaissance* (*Shurūṭ al-nahḍa*).[6] Similarly, Abou El Fadl touched upon the same issues in *The Search for Beauty in Islam*.[7]

Nevertheless, it is not the "expansion" of Islamic law that was problematic but rather the "imbalance" mentioned above. In fact, the "expansion" of Islamic law will prove helpful in guiding me to generate a theory of *Maqāṣid al-ʿAqīda* in this monograph, for not only did Muslim jurists develop a theory of legal objectives, known as *Maqāṣid al-Sharīʿa*, but they also developed auxiliary disciplines that contributed to the maturity of the field, most notably *Uṣūl al-Fiqh* (principles of Islamic legal theory) and *al-Qawāʿid al-Fiqhiyya* (legal maxims). And yet Islamic law (*Fiqh*) is regarded as the science of *furūʿ al-dīn* (matters complementary to the Islamic faith), as opposed to theology (I use "theology" in reference to *ʿAqīda*), which is regarded as the science of *uṣūl al-dīn* (matters primary to the Islamic faith).[8] Needless to say, this is not to condemn the development of law, but to say that far too little attention has been paid to developing parallel disciplines in Islamic theology. One may observe that the theological project in the Islamic tradition has largely become limited to definitions and deliberations about the nature and qualities of the transcendent God but has barely developed a systematic theory of objectives, let alone developing auxiliary disciplines.

Given the preceding and for the sake of the maturation of Islamic theology, this monograph aims to develop a genre of *Maqāṣid al-ʿAqīda* (objectives of Islamic theology). It not only attempts to trace and construct the "seeds" of *Maqāṣid al-ʿAqīda* in the Islamic theological tradition but also to draw inspirations from the full-fledged genre of *Maqāṣid al-Sharīʿa*. In doing so, the monograph grapples with the following questions: Why did such "seeds" not reach their theological fruition, as did *Maqāṣid al-Sharīʿa*? How do we guide the process of founding such an area? In what ways can the emerging *Maqāṣid al-ʿAqīda* benefit from the grown-up *Maqāṣid al-Sharīʿa*? What are the ramifications of having an underdeveloped theology? I do not know whether I shall answer those questions satisfactorily, but sometimes just raising questions opens a door for deeper and broader discussions.

Important Definitions and Clarifications

Maqāṣid al-Sharīʿa (singular: *maqṣad* or *maqṣūd*) commonly refers to the intents and objectives of the Lawgiver that the laws of Islamic *Sharīʿa* seek to achieve, preserve, and promote. Although the contributions of al-Ghazālī, ʿIzz al-Dīn ibn ʿAbd al-Salām (d. 1262),[9] and al-Shāṭibī (d. 1388)[10] are foundational to this genre, they did not attempt a definition of the term. Commenting on the absence of a definition, the contemporary scholar of *Maqāṣid* Aḥmad al-Raysūnī argued that it was, most probably, the linguistic clarity of *maqṣad/maqāṣid* that motivated those foundational contributors not to provide one.[11]

However, the contemporary Muḥammad al-Zuḥaylī attempted a precise definition, identifying *Maqāṣid al-Sharīʿa* as "the ultimate ends, objectives, consequences and meanings which the *Sharīʿa* has maintained and established through its laws, and consistently seeks to achieve, materialize and realize in all times and places."[12]

Two other definitions are worthy of mention and attention. While ʿAllāl al-Fāsī (d. 1964)[13] defined it as "the hidden meanings (*al-asrār*) and wisdom that the Lawgiver has observed in the legislation of all of the *Sharīʿa* dictums,"[14] Ibn ʿĀshūr (d. 1973)[15] defined it as "the deeper meanings (*maʿānī*) and inner wisdom (*ḥikam*) that the Lawgiver has observed in respect of all or most of the *Sharīʿah* decrees."[16] The difference between the two definitions raises the question of whether each and every legal precept of Islamic *Sharīʿa* has a wisdom behind it. According to al-Fāsī, "none" of the precepts of the *Sharīʿa* are without an objective, whereas Ibn ʿĀshūr maintained that "all or most" of the *Sharīʿa* dictums have their purposes.

In a similar vein, combining the word *maqāṣid* with the word *ʿaqīda* in this monograph will be employed in reference to the objectives and purposes that Islamic theology pursues and seeks to preserve and promote. Due to the absence of a discipline of *Maqāṣid al-ʿAqīda* as such in the Islamic tradition, one will look in vain to find an old definition of the term. However, reasoning with God,[17] deciphering the objectives of theological precepts, and asking if it is a necessary corollary of God's justice that He always must act according to the universal precepts of wisdom, are questions that preoccupied the minds of several Muslim theologians, notably Muʿtazilites[18] and Ashʿarites.[19] Wrestling with these questions, three salient test questions emerged: "First, did God create humankind for a reason (*ʿilla*)? Second, could God command people to accomplish the impossible (*mā lā yuṭāq*)? Finally, would God deliberately cause pain to innocent people without rewarding them in the end?"[20] While the Muʿtazilites affirmed the first question and negated the remaining two, the Ashʿarites did the opposite.

The Muʿtazilites argued that "since God created humanity for its own benefit as a way of showing His gracious benevolence (*tafaḍḍul*)," this can be taken as the reason behind mankind's creation. As for the remaining two questions, since God is Just, He "will not order people to carry impossible burdens, nor will he cause people to suffer in this life without compensating them in the life to come."[21] Those premises led them to the following conclusions: "1. Ends imply some kind of benefit. 2. God cannot possibly be in need of any benefit, and so no act of his could aim for this kind of benefit. 3. It is inconceivable that God should posit an act without an end in mind, for that act would be considered frivolous. 4. There cannot be anything frivolous in God's acts. 5. Therefore the benefit intended by God's acts is that of his creatures."[22] The Ashʿarite theologian Sayf al-Dīn al-Āmidī (d. 1233),[23] reflecting the standard Ashʿarite view, responded in the following manner: "1. Acts not directed to ends are only frivolous within our human frame of reference. 2. God's acts are governed by criteria other than ends, though we as humans cannot say what those criteria might be. 3. Further, the assertion that acts without intended ends are frivolous assumes that the intellect can discern what is intrinsically good (*ḥasan*) or bad (*qabīḥ*)."[24]

Despite the oppositional positions of the two schools, we will soon realize that the two positions tended to become more moderate with the likes of al-Ghazālī in classical Islam and Muḥammad ʿAbduh (d. 1905) in modern Islam. That is, those two theologians opened some space for more rational inquiry concerning the ends of certain divine actions, but in a very cautious language in order not to fall into the "theological trap" of Muʿtazilism, which is often perceived as unorthodox. Yet such singular attempts were not enough for the genre to actualize its full potential and reach its maturation, a fact that makes the present monograph a foundational work in the emerging genre of *Maqāṣid al-ʿAqīda*.

The Monograph's Epistemological Paradigm

This monograph challenges the common conception that while Christianity is more concerned with orthodoxy, Islam is more concerned with matters of orthopraxy.[25] It argues that the Islamic tradition started initially with both, orthodoxy and orthopraxy (embodied in theology, Sufism, and law). However, by al-Ghazālī's time, greater interest in Islamic law developed such that the Islamic tradition began to shift to a predominantly law-based tradition. Repeating al-Ghazālī's observation in his *Jawāhir,* so much work has been carried out on *Fiqh* that it has outstripped its needed measures.[26] On the contrary, Muslim scholars developed a sense of discouragement against theology in the minds of their students. For instance, al-Dhahabī (d. 1348),[27] in his *Bayān zaghal al-ʿilm* (Exposition of False Knowledge), urged "his readers to abstain from the study of theology and uses Ibn Taymiyya (d. 1328)[28] as a cautionary illustration of the potential of theological discussions to lead to acrimonious disputes and strife among Muslims."[29] This is not to say that theological inquiry did not develop in classical and postclassical Islam, but rather that it did not occupy a position similar to that of Islamic law. Therefore, the theological discussions involved were limited to definitions and deliberations about the nature and qualities of the transcendent God, without having a systematic theory of objectives, let alone developing distinct auxiliary disciplines.

George Makdisi noticed this shift, pointing out that law, not theology, has been "Islam's ideal religious science."[30] He observed that while classical Sunni madrasas taught jurisprudence, they did not teach theology, neither Ashʿarī nor otherwise, to the degree that some jurists-cum-theologians had to teach their theology privately at home after regular school time.[31] In his *Intent in Islamic Law: Motive and Meaning in Medieval Sunni Fiqh*, Paul Powers also observed this epistemic turning point, stating that "if intent matters greatly in Islamic law, Islamic law itself matters greatly to Islamic society. While theology, philosophy, mathematics, astronomy, medicine, and so forth all reached impressive heights of sophistication in the medieval Islamicate world, law, the undisputed queen of the sciences in medieval Islam, held a certain pride of place."[32] Or, as Marshall Hodgson calls it, the "Sharīʿah-mindedness" of Islam, on which he wrote:

> Every individual's life should be directly under the guidance of God's laws, and anything in society not clearly necessary to His service was to be frowned upon. Among both Sunnī and Shīʿī Muslims, a host of pious men and women who came to be called the "*ulāma*," the "learned," worked out what we may call the "Sharīʿah-minded" programme for private and public living centered on the Sharīʿah law. As might be expected, these "*ulāma*" scholars dominated Muslim public worship. They exercised a wide sway, but not exclusive control, in Muslim speculative and theological thought.[33]

Notwithstanding, Shahab Ahmed's *What Is Islam?* attempted to challenge this theory of the Sharīʿa-mindedness, contending that Islam is not the straightforward and scripture-based structure, as often perceived. He highlighted instead the massive expansion of the culture of mysticism and the different forms of popular piety as well as the Islamic folk culture.[34] Nevertheless, following the lead of Michel Foucault's concept of "episteme," which views religion primarily as a paradigm of linguistic discourse anchored upon a shared set of understandings about the foundation of knowledge,[35] I am convinced that the Sharīʿa-mindedness thesis is truer to the Islamic scholarly past.

Having said that, this monograph attempts to let Islamic theology have its share in the shaping of the Muslim mind alongside the *Sharīʿa*, so that the tradition may not become legalistic in nature. I believe that theology has the capacity to structure "the social, ethical, political, and spiritual aspects of a culture's ideas and meanings into a coherent whole. In that sense, theology has always studied what Michel Foucault called an episteme: the structure of knowledge that is the basis of an understanding about how reality works."[36] However, I do not aim to marginalize *Sharīʿa*, nor to replace it with theology, but rather to reintroduce Islamic theology to the center so that it may fulfill its potential and develop a more balanced religious discourse.

With that being said, the challenges that the Islamic tradition is facing today are groundbreaking. In his *Islamic Law, Epistemology and Modernity*, Ashk Dahlén observed that the entire contemporary Islamic tradition has to face a new epistemic and interpretative milieu, resulting from "a radical shift of categories of modern philosophy, science, culture and geography, the consequences of which Muslims in general have been unaware."[37] This shift involves a revolution in the very notion of "knowledge" per se, which is a very intrinsic notion to the Islamic tradition. Franz Rosenthal wrote, "There is no branch of Muslim intellectual life, of Muslim religious and political life, and of the daily life of the average Muslim that remained untouched by the all-pervasive attitude toward 'knowledge' as something of supreme value for Muslim being."[38]

To address this challenge, I appeal to Talal Asad's theory of the "discursive tradition." Asad defined a discursive tradition as a discourse which seeks to instruct practitioners about the correct form and purpose of a given practice, with a view to responding to the context in which it lives. Hence, it aims to connect conceptually a past and a future through a present to prevent any rupture from taking place.[39] With this in mind, the Islamic tradition is to be studied here not as a timeless tradition but rather as something of a work in progress that responds to the spirit of each age, contending that the Islamic tradition is not only built on change and reformation but also considers *tajdīd* (renewal) "a religious imperative." By this I refer to the Prophetic tradition that says, "At the beginning of every century God will send one who will renew its religion for this *Umma*."[40] As Daniel W. Brown observed, not only are the early Khārijite movement and the ʿAbbāsid uprising early examples of the dynamism of the tradition, but also the reformism of Ibn Taymiyya and, even further, the modern revolution in Iran and the emergence of Salafism as well as Islamic feminism are recent trends that look into tradition to justify change.[41]

The above discussion is one of the key reasons that Muḥammad ʿAbduh will occupy a significant place in this monograph. In my "Muḥammad ʿAbduh and the False Divorce between Tradition and Modernity,"[42] I argue that ʿAbduh probably never thought he was breaking from the tradition by being in conversation with Western modern epistemology. In fact, it is hard to establish that this very dichotomy between "modern" and "traditional" existed in the minds of either ʿAbduh or his interlocuters. Asad pointed out that the complexity in ʿAbduh's views illustrates the inadequacy of the type of binary thinking that places, as mutually exclusive, "orthodox Islam" in opposition to "ṣufī Islam," "rationality" to "traditionality," and so forth.[43] When large social changes transpire, Asad pointed out, the people in question are often uncertain about what exactly the kind of event it is they are handling, and unclear about the appropriate response.[44] Although it has been commonly thought that ʿAbduh's disagreement with other scholars was a sign of his departure from the tradition, Asad took ʿAbduh's disagreement as the very sign of his belonging to the tradition. By this he meant that traditional scholars for centuries have appealed to *ijtihād* (independent reasoning) when consensus (*ijmāʿ*) failed them, which is essentially what ʿAbduh practiced.[45] By appealing to *ijtihād*, I would go as far as to say, ʿAbduh was probably more loyal to the tradition than his adversaries.[46]

It is worthy of note too that while I draw heavily on traditional exegetical devices in this monograph, I also draw inspirations from reconstructivist schools in an attempt to bridge the gap between the current trends of "progressive-contextualist" Islam and the more "traditionalist-textualist" approaches.[47] In his *Reading the Qur'an in the Twenty-First Century*, Abdullah Saeed contended that the textualist-based approach to the Islamic tradition often either did not identify the ethico-moral values of the tradition or instead subjected them to the textual hermeneutics employed. As a corollary, the ethico-moral foundations of the Islamic tradition often disappear under those modes of readings.[48] Accepting Saeed's statement, this monograph aims to help heal this breach by considering the strengths of both sides: the exegetical devices of the past as well as the ethico-moral values picked up by more recent scholarship.

However, while Saeed believed that such ethico-moral values are subject to change, the values upon which I base this study are somewhat unchangeable, for they themselves are text-based. I take "texts" seriously inasmuch as I take "contexts," by drawing universal textual inspirations that may speak to changing contexts. I have more affinity with Ebrahim Moosa's approach of "critical traditionalism," as opposed to "dogmatic traditionalism," by not only "integrating" but also "interrogating" classical as well as modern scholarship. In the words of Moosa, "The critical work of any project seeking a paradigmatic change is to defamiliarize the canonical tradition, to interrogate it, literally to deconstruct it, in other words, to undertake close readings. But it must not imitate certain forms of postmodernism that only deconstruct, as if deconstruction in itself were an end."[49]

Similar to Moosa, who saw al-Ghazālī as an embodiment of this "critical traditionalism," al-Ghazālī will occupy a significant place in this monograph. Highlighting al-Ghazālī's critical interrogation of the tradition, Moosa wrote:

> The contemporary relevance of Ghazālī to Muslim thought lies precisely in his critical engagement with tradition, but more specifically in the way in which he modified, adjusted, recalibrated, amended, and supplemented the intellectual tradition. Unlike many of his contemporaries who either uncritically romanticized tradition or, in an apocalyptic spasm, took refuge in it, he took critical thought seriously. It was important for him, just as it is for us, to critically engage with the canonical tradition, a process that must culminate in radical questioning and defamiliarizing of the canonical tradition.[50]

In view of the preceding, this monograph will hopefully open up some promising lines of inquiry into this underdeveloped area of *Maqāṣid al-ʿAqīda*. If religionists, and more particularly Muslims, pay attention to its conclusions, they might be able to develop this genre with not only intellectually profound but also ethically significant implications. It is an invitation to scholars to start re-searching the classical annals of Islamic theology and some of the ways in which it can flourish.

It also provides new areas of convergence and divergence between Islam and other religions. To single out Islam's relation to Christianity as an example, owing to Christianity's assumed focus on theology and Islam's assumed focus on law, the parallels between the Christian and Islamic traditions have been largely imbalanced, lacking depth and invoking false friends. Hence, if Islamic theology is given a lease of life by such a study, it will hopefully open the door for more engaging and balanced discussions in interreligious relations.

Beyond the terrain of religious studies, the monograph may well contribute to the discourse of Islam in the public square and the domain of public policy, for the Islamic concept of public policy is closely linked to the question of *maqāṣid*. I believe that a more developed Muslim theology may shift the discussion from political and legal Islam to ethical Islam.

Key Arguments

Given the preceding discussion, this monograph argues that the development of Islamic theology (*Kalām/ʿAqīda*) was impeded by two key hindrances. First is the fact that Islamic theology for the most part had a defensive, rather than a positive, function. A quick examination of al-Ghazālī's and Ibn Khaldūn's (d. 1406)[51] definitions of *Kalām* may reveal this fact. The former argued that the aim of Islamic theology "was merely to preserve the creed of orthodoxy and to defend it against the deviations of heretics."[52] The latter defined it as the "science that involves arguing with logical proofs in defense of the articles of faith and refuting innovators who deviate in their dogmas from the early Muslims and Muslim orthodoxy."[53] Along the same lines wrote al-Farābī (d. 950)[54] in *Iḥṣāʾ al-ʿulūm* (Encyclopedia of the Sciences) and ʿAḍud al-dīn al-Ījī (d. 1355)[55] in *Kitāb al-mawāqif* (Book of Stations). This defensive role dominated the scene of Islamic theology such that the epistemic and positivist function of the field was largely sidelined.

Second is that *Kalām's* defensive function also meant that its epistemic paradigm was not primarily defined by its own theory of knowledge but rather by the paradigm of its immediate opponents, with a view to meeting the challenges of the moment. For instance, when Christian theologians appealed to Aristotelian logic in their debates with Muslim theologians, the latter were pressed to similarly appeal to it so that they could respond to the challenges at hand. Resultantly, Islamic theology's encounter with Greek logic and philosophy was inevitable. While this engagement with non-Islamic epistemes was not necessarily negative (in fact it was vital and revitalizing), it overshadowed the indigenous tools that might well have better suited the scriptural nature of the tradition. In fact, one may well argue that relying on such indigenous tools was one of the key reasons behind the epistemic maturity of Islamic law, as compared to Islamic theology. Had Muslim theologians developed a more native approach similar to that of the *fuqahāʾ*, the role of Islamic theology could have been more integral to the Islamic tradition. Accentuating this, Muḥammad Iqbāl (d. 1938)[56] argued that while Greek philosophy largely broadened the outlook of Muslim theologians, it obscured their vision of their own scriptural tradition. He wrote:

> This is what the earlier Muslim students of the Qur'an completely missed under the spell of classical speculation. They read the Qur'an in the light of Greek thought. It took them over two hundred years to perceive—though not quite clearly—that the spirit of the Qur'an was

> essentially anti-classical, and the result of this perception was a kind of intellectual revolt, the full significance of which has not been realized even up to the present day.[57]

In the light of this, this monograph attempts to develop the field of Islamic theology from "within," drawing inspiration from the indigenous methodologies of *Fiqh*, more particularly the area of *Maqāṣid al-Sharīʿa*. In doing so, the monograph does not *discredit* the engagement with non-Islamic philosophical and theological epistemes but rather *delays* such engagement until the discipline of Islamic theology is established from within, so that when it engages with non-Islamic epistemes, it can not only preserve its own character instead of adopting the tools and methods of other epistemes, but also enrich the different epistemes with which it comes into contact.

On a different note, having a more developed native theology may well provide more systematic answers to challenging questions facing contemporary Muslims. In this context, the monograph examines how the proposed *Maqāṣid al-ʿAqīda* can help address questions of theological exclusivism and *takfir* (excommunication).[58] Exclusivism and excommunication have often led the faithful to excommunicate fellow Muslims as well as non-Muslims even if the subject of the theological dispute is inessential. However, developing *Maqāṣid al-ʿAqīda* may well demonstrate that not every theological item in Islamic theology holds the same weight, which limits the space available for excommunication and exclusivism. For instance, while Q. 2:62 reduces the requirements of salvation to three—believing in God, the Last Day, and doing good deeds[59]— Q. 3:85 expands such requirements to include belief in "Islam," leaving the term "Islam" unqualified and disputed by exclusivists, inclusivists, and pluralists.[60] Exclusivists say that Islam is the *only* religious tradition, or even a certain interpretation of it that leads to truth and salvation, while other faiths are erroneous and their followers will be punished in hell;[61] inclusivists believe that Islam is the only religion that is *authentically* salvific, yet "sincere outsiders who could not have recognised it as such will be saved,"[62] and pluralists believe that "regardless of the circumstances, there are several religious traditions or interpretations that are equally effective salvifically."[63] With this spectrum of interpretations, questions of truth and salvation became thorny issues within the tradition and are still largely unresolved today.

Reconciling these various verses, classical Qurʾān commentators essentially resorted to one of two mechanisms: (1) subscribing to abrogation (*naskh*),[64] stating that, for instance, Q. 2:62 is abrogated by Q. 3:85, or (2) specifying the generality of Q. 2:62, saying, for instance, that the acknowledged Christians and Jews here are only those who adhered to these religions before the advent of Prophet Muḥammad, but when Muḥammad came, they followed his message.[65] However, the two ways involve various degrees of *arbitrariness* and *subjectivity*. By "arbitrariness" I refer to the usage of *naskh* when there is no *decisive* evidence that any of these verses was revealed before the other, let alone the weakness of *naskh* per se as an exegetical device, as shall be expounded later. And by "subjectivity" I refer to the imposition of the interpreter's outlook on the Qurʾān by deciding what was meant to be general and what was meant to be particular.

Given the above, the monograph argues that developing a genre of *Maqāṣid al-ʿAqīda* may well help reconcile these seemingly antithetical interpretations in a non-arbitrary way by domesticating and appropriating the threefold taxonomy *al-ḍarūriyyāt* (primaries), *al-ḥājiyyāt* (complementaries), and *al-taḥsīniyyāt* (supplementaries), even though this threefold typology was primarily introduced by jurists to the service of *Maqāṣid al-Sharīʿa*. That is to say, what ambiguates these verses are the assumed equality of weight between each. However, I contend, if this taxonomy is applied, these verses may well be reconciled without needing to resort either to the arbitrary usage of abrogation or to the subjective employment of specification (*takhṣīṣ*), as shall be expounded in the fourth chapter of this monograph.

Structure of the Monograph

This monograph consists of five chapters. The first chapter operates on the assumption that although *Maqāṣid al-ʿAqīda* does not stand as a distinct subject in the Islamic tradition, it has, to varying degrees, been in the minds of some key theologians, most notably al-Ghazālī and ʿAbduh. Given al-Ghazālī's cardinality to this monograph, chapter 1 divides into the pre-Ghazālian preliminary discussion of *Maqāṣid al-ʿAqīda*, embodied in the contributions of al-Ḥakīm al-Tirmidhī (d. 869),[66] Ibn Bābawayh al-Qummī (d. 991),[67] and Abū al-Ḥasan al-ʿĀmirī (d. 992),[68] followed by some post-Ghazālian interventions, personified in the writings of the following six figures: Muḥammad al-Zāhid al-Bukhārī (d. 1151),[69] Fakhr al-Dīn al-Rāzī (d. 1210),[70] ʿIzz al-Dīn ibn ʿAbd al-Salām, Ibn Taymiyya, Shāh Walīullāh al-Dehlawī (d. 1762),[71] and Rashīd Riḍā (d. 1935).[72] Then the chapter singles out ʿAbduh's contribution due to its distinctness, pointing out that this selection is neither exhaustive nor exclusive but rather illustrative of the nature of such preliminary deliberations on *Maqāṣid al-ʿAqīda*. It then ends with a section explaining that although these theologians proffered some preliminary engagement with "questions" of *Maqāṣid al-ʿAqīda*, none of them consolidated a "methodological framework" to systematize the derivation of *Maqāṣid al-ʿAqīda*. Therefore, this section chiefly deals with the key reasons that may have contributed to the underdevelopment of *Maqāṣid al-ʿAqīda*.

The second chapter moves to questions of "form," discussing the "sources" and "methods" upon which *Maqāṣid al-ʿAqīda* can rely, with a view to delineating and diagnosing the process of deriving *Maqāṣid al-ʿAqīda* from the Qurʾān and *ḥadīth*. Drawing inspirations primarily from al-Ghazālī, the chapter offers some samples of how this derivation may operate and the exegetical and theological challenges that may face the derivation process.

The third chapter moves from questions of "form" to questions of "content," wrestling with the question of what the objectives of *Maqāṣid al-ʿAqīda* might be. This chapter is comprised of two sections. The first begins by "interrogating" the classical "theory" of *Maqāṣid al-Sharīʿa* and critiques it for its *ḥudūd*-centeredness (*ḥudūd* is often translated as "codes of penalties") and its reducing of the function of *Maqāṣid* to mere "preservation," as compared to functions of "acquisition" and "promotion." The second section aims to "generate" the ultimate objective of Islamic theology, that is, the pursuit, preservation, and promotion of Truth. In doing so, the chapter offers a lengthy discussion on the nature of Islamic Truth, contending that the theological truth that Islam aims to pursue, preserve, and promote is not necessarily "fully" present but is "provisionally" and "partially" so. Therefore, Islam urges the faithful to seek this truth wherever it may appear. Consequently, theology is viewed here as a "handmaiden" to the Ultimate Truth, not a "superintendent" to it. I do so by drawing on the Kantian distinction between the "phenomenon" (the way we see things) and the "noumenon" (the-thing-in-itself).[73]

The fourth chapter moves from "interrogating" *Maqāṣid al-Sharīʿa* to "integrating" some of its key "exegetical tools" toward the development of *Maqāṣid al-ʿAqīda*. By "exegetical tools" I primarily refer to the threefold taxonomy of *al-ḍarūriyyāt* (primaries), *al-ḥājiyyāt* (complementaries), and *al-taḥsīniyyāt* (supplementaries). The chapter begins by explaining its extendibility and usability in the emerging genre of *Maqāṣid al-ʿAqīda*, grappling with some of the challenges that may question or impede this extendibility. Having carefully domesticated this taxonomy in theology, the rest of the chapter puts the taxonomy into theological practice, using it to measure the weight of three essential notions in Islamic theology: *al-firqa al-nājiya* (the saved denomination), the weight of deeds as compared to faith, and the role/importance of Prophet Muḥammad in Islamic theology. For the achievability of this task, I confine my treatment to the Ashʿarite school, as it has been the most dominant school in Islamic theology.[74]

The final chapter touches upon some of the ramifications of lacking a *maqāṣidī* approach to Islamic theology in modern and contemporary Islam. This chapter uses a case study of the Sunni-Shiite-Wahhabi conflict as an embodiment of a theology that is wandering in an uncharted territory. By this I refer to the lack of a compass to the different theological schools of Islam in this era. The chapter begins by dispelling the claim that Ibn Ḥanbal (d. 855)[75] and Ibn Taymiyya may have contributed to worsening the Sunni-Shiite relations and will show that it is rather the Wahhabi non-*maqāṣidī* approach that tended to feed such narratives of hate. The chapter then goes on to show how a *maqāṣidī*-oriented approach to Islamic theology, embodied in al-Ghazālī's canon of interpretation, ʿAbduh's Theology of Unity, and Maḥmūd Shaltūt (d. 1963),[76] initiatives, may be used to help bridge the widening gap between these different schools.

The monograph ends with a summary of the aims that it set out to achieve and the conclusions that it hopefully met, emphasizing that this monograph is nothing but a door-opener to this subject and that there are trajectories in this fertile area to be explored further. Based on this study, the conclusion offers some recommendations for future research endeavors and puts forward some theological implications if this research is taken seriously.

Important Caveats

Before moving to the nitty-gritty of this subject, two caveats are in order. The first has to do with my periodization. I use early Ashʿarism in reference to the first two centuries of the school from the time of its eponymous founder, al-Ashʿarī (d. 935), until al-Ghazālī's time (d. 1111), when the school assumed its maturity. Mediaeval Ashʿarism is used to indicate the time from al-Ghazālī till the eve of modernity in the nineteenth century, more particularly, up until the emergence of ʿAbduh's theological discourse. Modern Ashʿarism is employed in reference to ʿAbduh's school as a branch of modern Ashʿarism and its encounter with other Ashʿarite strands. It is vital to note, however, that this periodization is slightly arbitrary, for I follow the lead of G. M. Trevelyan (d. 1962), who wrote, "Unlike *dates*, *periods* are not facts. They are retrospective conceptions that we form about past events, useful to focus discussion, but very often leading historical thought astray."[77] Second, due to the novelty of this approach, the conclusions reached by the end of this monograph are essentially "tentative" and "suggestive." Regardless of the validity of such conclusions, if the monograph succeeds in directing attention to this area and demonstrates its intellectual potentiality, I believe it will have successfully accomplished its aim.

I

Historical Roots of Maqāṣid al-ʿAqīda

DESPITE THE ABSENCE of a genre that is called *Maqāṣid al-ʿAqīda* as such in the Islamic tradition, one may argue that its roots were loosely dispersed in the writings of some key Muslim theologians, most notably al-Ghazālī and ʿAbduh. While this chapter will chiefly focus on those two figures, it will briefly highlight the contributions of three pre-Ghazālian theologians (al-Ḥakīm al-Tirmidhī, Ibn Bābawayh al-Qummī, and Abū al-Ḥasan al-ʿĀmirī), and six post-Ghazālians (Muḥammad al-Zāhid al-Bukhārī, Fakhr al-Dīn al-Rāzī, ʿIzz al-Dīn Ibn ʿAbd al-Salām, Ibn Taymiyya, Shāh Walīullāh al-Dehlawī, and Rashīd Riḍā). Nonetheless, it should be noted that this treatment is not exhaustive but primarily representative of the potential roots of *Maqāṣid al-ʿAqīda* in the Islamic tradition.

Although enough has been said on why al-Ghazālī and ʿAbduh will be constantly consulted in this monograph, I add here two other reasons. First, I aim to challenge the view that presents al-Ghazālī as an "unadventurous theologian" who "counselled the restraining of the common run of Muslims from theology because of its danger to Islamic faith and practice through the sophistical uses to which it is prone."[1] Those who view al-Ghazālī as such tend to quote his likening of theology to "a dangerous medicine that should be prescribed only in the direst cases and by the most skilled physicians,"[2] highlighting that al-Ghazālī assigned merely an apologetic function to Islamic theology, embodied in protecting the Muslim community from internal false doctrines (*bidʿas*), as well as from external ones, such as those from Christian and Jewish polemicists.[3] In contrast to this view, this monograph attempts to introduce a positivist function to theology through a holistic reading of al-Ghazālī's genre, represented in its creation of a relation between the faithful and his Lord through theological inquiry. As for ʿAbduh, he is central to this monograph for one other key reason. That is, while al-Ghazālī

The Higher Objectives of Islamic Theology. Mohammed Gamal Abdelnour, Oxford University Press.
 DOI: 10.1093/oso/9780197648636.003.0001

was perhaps the first to breach the Ashʿarite reluctance toward demystifying *Maqāṣid al-ʿAqīda*, it was only with ʿAbduh that this shift breached into a gateway and developed beyond the Ghazālian contours, attempting in his *Risālat al-tawḥīd* to design a systematic and practical theology speaking to the spirit of the age and being responsive to modern challenges. Hence, both thinkers cannot then go unnoticed in our coverage. I shall now delve into the pre-Ghazālian discussion of *Maqāṣid al-ʿAqīda*.

Maqāṣid al-ʿAqīda *before al-Ghazālī*

Tracing the seeds of *Maqāṣid al-ʿAqīda*, al-Ḥakīm al-Tirmidhī seems to have been the first to demystify some of the objectives of Islamic theology in a somewhat systematic manner. Not to be confused with the renowned *ḥadīth* collector Abū ʿĪsā al-Tirmidhī (d. 892), al-Ḥakīm al-Tirmidhī was a prominent Sufi figure. With his spiritual-philosophical insights, he is commonly perceived as a forerunner of the likes of Ibn ʿArabī (d. 1240).[4] Although *Ṣirāṭ al-awliyāʾ* (Path of the Saints) is his most popular work, what is of relevance to us here is his *Ithbāt al-ʿilal* (The Demonstration of Objectives), where he included the idea of "pursuing objectives" in the title of the book. Even though in it he primarily focuses on the objectives of Islamic law, he touches upon some aspects of significance to the objectives of Islamic theology. However, due to the novelty of his approach, this book, according to the historian Shams al-Dīn al-Dhahabī (d. 1274), was one of the reasons behind al-Tirmidhī's exile from his place of birth,[5] for al-Tirmidhī was swimming against the current by arguing that not only do "all" of God's proscriptions and prescriptions have objectives lying behind them, but also that comprehending those proscriptions and prescriptions lies within the capacity of the human mind.[6]

Al-Tirmidhī contended that worshiping God alone, which is a theological imperative, is the foundation of other legal objectives consolidated later by al-Ghazālī and al-Shāṭibī, emphasizing that when people acknowledge God's Oneness, the protection of their souls, dignities, and progenies is granted a priori.[7] He proceeded to say that verbalizing one's acknowledgment of God's Oneness is a necessity for one's legal rights to be protected. The result of verbalizing one's belief in God's Oneness is not only the protection of one's blood, progeny, and property in this world (*dunyā*) but also one's salvation in the Hereafter (*ākhira*). Thus, he took the verbalization of faith, which is a theological question, as his starting point to the five famous objectives of the *Sharīʿa*. Namely, the preservation of human well-being: religion, life, intellect, lineage, and property. [8]

The place of the Divine Names is also central to al-Tirmidhī's understanding of *Maqāṣid al-ʿAqīda.* For instance, he took the manifestation of Divine Justice and Mercy as the prime reason behind the happenings of the Day of Judgment. For instance, he contended that the Day of Judgment is made "lengthy" for God's Justice to become conspicuous to the people so that they may see for themselves the way God judges with ultimate justice.[9] More distantly, he held that deeds are important, plus faith, as they show that Divine Justice and Mercy are not granted randomly or arbitrarily. If God were to place certain people in hell and others in paradise according to their faith alone, people would be in a state of bewilderment about the criterion and objectivity of God's judgment. Hence, when people's deeds are weighed in front of their eyes, Divine Justice and Mercy become evident and transparent.[10]

In his *al-Ḥajj wa asrāruhu* (Pilgrimage and Its Secrets), al-Tirmidhī illustrated the centrality of theology in his theory of legal objectives, ascribing the signification of the *Ḥajj* to its symbolism of one's submission to God and its embodiment of the worshiper's desiring none but Him alone.[11]

What is more is that Islamic theology for al-Tirmidhī seems intertwined with Islamic law. For example, while he held that the *Sharīʿa* provided the "way" to reach God, he believed that theology provided the truth about God Himself. Walking seven times back and forth between the two hills of *al-Ṣafā wa'l-Marwa* in the Muslim pilgrimage is a symbolic expression of one's need of both *Sharīʿa* (represented in law) and *ḥaqīqa* (represented in theology).[12] Hence, he may well be taken as a preconfiguration of Ibn ʿArabi's binary of *ḥaqīqa* (truth) and *Sharīʿa* (exoteric way).

While al-Tirmidhī primarily represented a more rationalistic approach to *Maqāṣid al-ʿAqīda,* Ibn Bābawayh comes from a Shiite traditionist background. In Shiite Islam, he was arguably the most eminent of traditionists and a key jurist of the school of Qom. His *Kitāb al-tawḥīd* (Book of Divine Unity) represented an attempt to illustrate the compatibility of the *imāmate* traditions with God's Unity and Justice.[13] Of more relevance to *Maqāṣid al-ʿAqīda* is his *ʿIlal al-Sharīʿa* (Objectives of the Divine Law). Although the book is essentially dedicated to Islamic law, he touched upon the objectives of some creedal beliefs, reflecting the intertwinement of Islamic law and Islamic theology. In doing so, he quoted a tradition from al-Ḥusayn ibn ʿAlī (d. 680), which stated, "Truly God the Almighty has not created His servants except to know Him, so that when they know Him, they would worship Him."[14] He proceeded to quote another tradition in which Jaʿfar al-Ṣādiq (d. 765) was asked, "Why did God create the World?" His answer was "God did not create it in vain nor was it left alone, He rather created it to make His Omnipotence manifest, and to charge people with obedience so that they may be worthy of His pleasure; He did not create them to bring a benefit to Him nor to draw harm off Him, but rather created them for their own benefit and to deliver them to Eternal Blessing."[15]

Ibn Bābawayh then related a discussion by al-Faḍl ibn Shādhān (d. 873), who grappled with the question of the reason behind God's necessitation of verbalizing one's acknowledgment of God's existence, offering the same response that al-Tirmidhī offered. That is, if one's acknowledgment of God was not publicly verbalized, for what other reason could one's blood, property, dignity, progeny be protected?[16]

The above discussion indicates that the five objectives of the *Sharīʿa* started as a theological endeavor and were based on a theological paradigm. The fact that two such proponents of *Maqāṣid al-ʿAqīda,* i.e., al-Tirmidhī and Ibn Bābawayh, even though they belonged to different theological backgrounds, agreed that the protection of the objectives of *Sharīʿa* goes back to theological objectives, indicates the cardinality of theology to the genre of *Maqāṣid* as a whole.

Ibn Bābawayh then attended to the wisdom behind the Qurʾān's description of God as being dissimilar to any other being (*laysa kamithlihi shay'*: nothing is like Him), arguing that one of the reasons behind this divine attribute is that if God were not to be dissimilar to other beings, it could conceivably be argued that He is not Everlasting, nor is He Just. Eliminating His Eternality and Justice can easily result in distrusting His threats as well as His promises, and also in the ruin of people's lives on Earth.[17] Elsewhere, he was asked, "Why did God veil Himself from people?" He replied, quoting ʿAlī ibn al-Ḥusayn, "People, by nature, are ignorant. Had God revealed Himself to them, they would be too familiar with Him. Hence, they would neither duly glorify Him nor would they revere Him, just as one would glorify the Kaʿaba upon seeing it for the first time. However, when one gets accustomed to seeing it, the feeling of awe goes away with familiarity."[18]

Ibn Bābawayh also grappled with the reason behind having the *imāms* besides the Qurʾān as sources of authority in Shiism, mentioning that the reason is simply that the Qurʾān does not speak for itself but rather needs enlightened men to guide people to its authentic interpretation. Otherwise, the Qurʾān is open to debate in terms of what its verses signify. Thus, there is a need for a category of people who are perceived as infallible.[19] He proceeded, throughout the book, to discuss the wisdom behind the other acts of worship, such as prayer, almsgiving, and fasting.

In Abū al-Ḥasan al-ʿĀmirī, we see a more philosophically oriented discussion of *Maqāṣid al-ʿAqīda*. The philosophical underpinning of al-ʿĀmirī's approach owes much to his studies under the Muʿtazilite polymath Abū Zayd al-Balkhī (d. 934)[20] and his discussions with as al-Tawḥīdī (d. 1023)[21] and Ibn Miskawayh (d. 1030)[22] when he moved to the cities of Ray and Baghdad, respectively. One common theme across his writings is his main concern to offer a rational defense of Islam against a type of philosophy that considered itself of superior value to knowledge gained from revelation, clearly fitting within al-Kindī's (d. 873)[23] philosophical school, which tried to reconcile philosophy with revelation by illustrating that real philosophy could not run counter to the revealed truths of Islam. Together with al-Kindī, he stood against the philosophical tradition of the likes of al-Farābī (d. 950), contending that revelation must be superior to philosophy, as revelation was indispensable for the perfection of the human intellect. Although this school showed appreciation for Greek philosophy, it took it to task for its lack of the light of prophecy.[24]

Although he never mentioned the term *maqāṣid* in his magnum opus, *al-Iʿlām bi-manāqib al-islām* (Exposition on the Merits of Islam), al-Āmirī somewhat laid down the preliminary foundations of a systematic theory of *Maqāṣid al-ʿAqīda*. He came at his conclusions by studying, next to Islam, five world religions—Christianity, Judaism, Zoroastrianism, Magianism, and Manichaeism—attempting a rational justification for the theological, moral, and ritual superiority of Islam. He identified four dimensions that exist in commonality in those faith traditions—theological, ritual, social, and legal—with a view to answering the question of what makes Islam superior to those faith traditions and therefore makes it more worthy of adoption.[25] He probably needed to grapple with such questions because he lived in the fourth century of Islam, which witnessed a phenomenon of religious skepticism, wherein the superiority of Islamic truth needed to appeal to reason more than ever before, especially after the influx of Greek philosophy. Describing this time, Paul L. Heck wrote:

> At the heart of skepticism in classical Islam, then, were doubts about visible Islam, the religio-moral norms of Islamic law: customs and practices related to ritual, personal, and interpersonal ethics and etiquette, as well as commercial and other transactions and a whole host of other norms shaping society. Religion here is very much understood as communal ethics, which in the case of Islam meant obedience to the revealed law. And yet, decisive meta-communal criteria for determining

> that the ways specific to Islam were superior to those of other nations seemed to be lacking, making it a real concern for defenders of Islam to account for the reality of religio-moral pluralism without either dismissing the transcendent justification of the Islamic way of life as articulated through the revealed law (*Sharīʿa*) or disregarding universal moral principles that the human intellect, regardless of cultural specificity, is able to affirm.[26]

Responding to the challenges of his day, al-ʿĀmirī offered a point-by-point demonstration of the particularity and superiority of Islam over these faith traditions, arguing that what distinguishes Islam from those faiths is its pursuit of *balance* between several extremes. He described Islam as "the mean between the extremes of other religions, thus making it the logically sound system by which to attain the common good."[27] Beginning with Islam's theological system, he pointed out that Islam's emphasis on the monotheistic nature of God comes as a balance between "Jewish anthropomorphism, Christian trinity, Zoroastrian duality, and polytheist idolatry."[28] Confirming this balanced nature of Islamic theology, he quoted Q. 3:64: "Say: People of the Book! Come to a *common word* between us and you, that we worship none but God, and that we associate not aught with Him, and do not some of us take others as Lords, apart from God. And if they turn their backs, say: 'Bear witness that we are Muslims.' "[29]

Similarly, the Islamic conception of prophecy is also balanced. That is, neither does it exaggerate the prophets' status to make them deities, as Christians did with Jesus, said al-ʿĀmirī, nor does it defile them, as Jews did with many of their prophets. Islam respects prophets as God's chosen humans who are selected to deliver His message, though they are not themselves deities. He then quoted Q. 2:136: "Say: We believe in God and that which is revealed unto us and that which was revealed unto Abraham, and Ishmael, and Isaac, and Jacob, and the tribes, and that which Moses and Jesus received, and that which the Prophets received from their Lord. We make no distinction between any of them, and unto Him we have surrendered."[30]

Furthermore, he argued that the Islamic revelation, i.e., the Qurʾān, surpasses the other Divine Books in form and content, illustrating that although Islam respects all Divine Books, it recognizes the specialty of the Qurʾān. The Qurʾān, argued al-ʿĀmirī, apart from its wonderous content, "is the most eloquent of all heavenly books, while other scriptures are merely collections of human wisdom."[31]

The same applies to Islamic angelology and eschatology. Angels are more discreetly and prudently conceived in Islam than in the other faith traditions. Islam's theory of angelology lies in between the Jewish underestimation of angels and the Zoroastrian-polytheist divinization of angels. As for Islam's philosophy of eschatology, it neither believes in metempsychosis/transmigration of souls, nor does it believe in the eternal annihilation of human bodies. It believes that every soul will bear its own labor and that the body will be resurrected by God's Will.[32]

Methodologically speaking, the discreetness and prudence of Islamic theology have a bearing on Islam's appeal, not only to scripture in comprehending theological formulations but also to Islam's correspondence with reason.[33] Reason and scripture go hand in hand in Islam. Hence, Islam is peerless, al-ʿĀmirī contended, in the amount of emphasis it places on reasoning to be in line with Scripture.[34]

What we may gather from this discussion is that the key objective of Islamic theology in al-ʿĀmirī's thought is the achievement of the quality of "balance" between radical conceptions of theological matters. Even though he did not theorize for the idea of *Maqāṣid al-ʿAqīda* as such, the comparisons and conclusions he drew may well serve as a basis for this emerging genre. Having reached this point, we are now in a good position to delve into the Ghazālian corpus.

Maqāṣid al-ʿAqīda *with Al-Ghazālī*

Al-Ghazālī was born around 1056 in today's northeastern Iran, studied in various cities in his pursuit of knowledge, and finally settled in Nishapur. In Nishapur, he was trained at the hands of the celebrated *Imām al-Ḥaramayn* al-Juwaynī (d. 1085).[35] He swiftly worked his way through the madrasa system to occupy a chair in 1091 at the legendary Niẓāmiyya College in Baghdad. Around 1095, al-Ghazālī went through a spiritual crisis on account of which he left the glamorous life and prestigious career he led in Baghdad to wonder and wander in the Muslim world, secluding himself from the life that filled him with arrogance, pride, and attachment to worldly pleasures. With this crisis of faith, al-Ghazālī came to realize that he was walking a path of damnation; hence, he reassessed his intentions and set out on his life-changing journey. After around ten years spent mostly in the cities of Damascus, Jerusalem, Mecca, and Medina, he decided to go back to the academy to eventually become a lecturer at the Niẓāmiyya College in Nishapur. After retiring, he completed the circle of his life when he moved to Tābarān, the very town in which he was born.[36]

Al-Ghazālī's contribution to *Maqāṣid al-Sharīʿa* is beyond doubt,[37] but close to no attention has been given to his contribution to *Maqāṣid al-ʿAqīda*. While I came across no studies in English scholarship that are dedicated to this aspect of his thought, only one study in Arabic carried the title *Maqāṣid al-ʿAqīda ʿinda al-imām al-Ghazālī* (Theological Objectives according to the Master al-Ghazālī) by a contemporary Moroccan scholar with the name of Muḥammad ʿAbdu, who thoroughly read al-Ghazālī's corpus with *Maqāṣid al-ʿAqīda* being his key analytical tool.[38] However, the study does not develop *Maqāṣid al-ʿAqīda* as a distinct discipline on its own merits.

Al-Ghazālī's contribution to the realm of *Maqāṣid al-ʿAqīda* is unique. The word *maqāṣid* in the context of theology occurs in al-Ghazālī's *Jawāhir al-Qur'ān*. In it, he showed that the knowledge of God and the Last Day are the noblest of Islamic sciences, for this is the knowledge of *al-maqṣid*. The nobility of this science, said al-Ghazālī, goes back to the fact that all other forms of knowledge are pursued for its sake, while this science is sought for its own sake and not that of anything else (*fa'inna sā'ir al-ʿulūm turādu lahu wamin ajlihi, wahuwa lā yurādu li-ghayrihi*). In other words, other forms of knowledge are a means to this science, while this science is not a means to anything else, but an end in itself.[39] Apart from this occurrence, *maqāṣid*, in its theological sense, does not occur elsewhere in his corpus; instead he engaged with it under the term *asrār al-dīn* (secrets of the faith) throughout his oeuvre. In his *al-Mustaṣfā min ʿilm al-ʿuṣūl* (The Essentials of Islamic Legal Theory), he wrote, "I have penned many treatises on the branches and roots of *Fiqh*, then I devoted myself to knowing the path to the Hereafter, and to deciphering the hidden secrets [*asrār*] of the *dīn* about which I authored lengthy treatises, such as *Iḥyā' ʿulūm al-dīn* [The Revival of Religious Sciences], short ones such as *Jawāhir al-Qur'ān*, and medium-sized ones such as *Kimiyā' al-saʿāda* [The Alchemy of Happiness]."[40]

Unpacking the above, al-Ghazālī, as he did with *Fiqh*, divided the study of theology into two major sections: roots and branches (*uṣūl wa furūʿ*). While the "branches" of theology are dealt with in his *al-Iqtiṣād fī al-iʿtiqād* (Moderation in Creed) and *al-Risāla al-qudsiyya* (The Jerusalem Treatise), the "roots" of theology can be traced in his *Iḥyā'* and *al-Maqṣad al-asnā fī sharḥ asmā' Allāh al-ḥusnā* (The Best Means to Explaining the Divine Names).

Appealing to Q. 21:23, which states, "He is not questioned about what He does, but they [humans] will be questioned," pre-Ghazālian Ashʿarites were of the view that humans are in no position to ask questions about what God intends or aims for, as opposed to the Muʿtazilite theologians who saw legitimacy in such questions, as has been illustrated at the outset of the monograph. Nevertheless, al-Ghazālī introduced some sort of a median position between Ashʿarism and Muʿtazilism on this, asserting in his *al-Mustaẓhirī* (The Exotericist) that the Islamic revelation comes with particular and general objectives behind every specific and general precept.[41] Furthermore, in his *Shifāʾ al-ʿalīl* (Remedy for the Sick), he opined that Islamic theology and law are meant to preserve the interests of worshipers in the Here as well as in the Hereafter.[42] He went further to say that the interests of the world are not sought for their own sake but for the sake of driving people toward the ultimate fulfillment of being with God in the Hereafter.[43]

In his *al-Maqṣad al-asnā,* he began with what spurred him to pen a book on the secrets of the names of God, relating that someone asked him to explain the meanings and significations of the Divine Names. Expressing his apprehension of delving into such a massive ocean, he wrote, "[The questioner's] questions were incessant, and made me take one step forward and another backward, hesitating between heeding his inquiry and so satisfying the duty of brotherliness, or declining his request by following the way of caution and deciding not to venture into danger, for human powers fall far short of attaining this goal."[44]

The statement above embodies the standard apprehension of Ashʿarite theologians about attempting to decipher the secrets of Divinity. Al-Ghazālī further explained that there are two reasons that may discourage a wise theologian from plunging into such a stormy sea. First, this is not a legal question where one may take the risk and be excused if one errs, but rather a theological matter that demands "certitude" and where error is not easily tolerated. In al-Ghazālī's words, "How could human powers follow the way of investigation and scrutiny regarding the divine attributes? Can the eyes of bats tolerate the light of the sun?"[45] Additionally, Scripture contains only implicit, not explicit, indications of this knowledge, hence it is the most difficult to pursue.[46] Second, delving into this subject is swimming against the tide, which is the Sunni's common rejection of pursuing theological objectives. Hence, "weaning people away from their habits and familiar beliefs is difficult. . . . [W]hoever mixes with people is right to be cautious."[47] Yet he eventually defeated this fear, remembering that "it is difficult for one who has seen the truth to pretend not to have seen it."[48]

Al-Ghazālī's rethinking such a fundamental Ashʿarite position, in tandem with some other methodical Ashʿarite premises,[49] caused some scholars to question his allegiance to Ashʿarism. In fact, Richard Frank argued that al-Ghazālī wrote his *Fayṣal al-tafriqa* (The Decisive Criterion) as a refutation to those who accused him of unbelief due to his deviation from early Ashʿarite teachings in his *Iḥyā'* and elsewhere. Frank opined:

> *Iḥyā* was followed by *Maqāṣid* and *Mishkāh,* in both of which the formal teaching of traditional Ashʿarite *Kalām* is rejected outright and the central elements, psychological, metaphysical and cosmological of al-Ghazālī's higher theology presented plainly and without circumlocution. The traditional form and content of *Qudsiyya* and its placement at the beginning of *'Iḥyā* could hardly have been expected to assure al-Ghazālī's readers of his orthodoxy and there ensued a strong reaction on the part of some against his theological teaching because of its departure from the traditional theology of the schools. This is made clear in the opening of *Fayṣal* (pp. 5ff.), where al-Ghazālī speaks of "a party of those who are envious of one of our books which treats of the essential truths concerning religious duties and practices and who believe that there are things in it which are contrary to the teachings of the earlier fellows of the school and the professors of theology and that to deviate from the teaching of al-Ashʿarī even by so much as a span is unbelief." [50]

Having established the preceding points, it is now time to move to the crux of al-Ghazālī's *maqāṣidī*-oriented explanations of Islamic theology. But before we proceed, it is worthy of mention that I call al-Ghazālī's following insights "*maqāṣidī*-oriented," as opposed to being *maqāṣidī*-based, due to the fact that the subject of *Maqāṣid al-ʿAqīda* was not fully developed by al-Ghazālī's time. Therefore, it would be anachronistic to cast the title *Maqāṣid al-ʿAqīda* on his insights without being conscious of this distinction.

Maqāṣidī-Oriented Explanations of the Divine Names and Attributes

Al-Ghazālī contended that the objectives of knowing the Divine Names go far beyond mere knowledge; it is primarily for the faithful to have a share of those names and recognize that their perfection and happiness lay in being molded by the moral implications of the divine qualities of God. However, he realized that not many scholars, let alone common people, are qualified to grasp the reality and implications of the Divine Names and Attributes. He put it this way:

> You should know that whoever has no part in the meanings of the names of God—great and glorious—except that he hears the words and understand the linguistic meaning of their explication and their determination, and except that he believe with his heart in the reality of their meanings in God Most High—such a one has an ill-fated lot and a lowly rank, and ought not boast of what he has achieved. For hearing the words requires only the soundness of the sense of hearing, through which sounds are perceived, and this is a level in which beasts share. As for understanding their determination in language, all one needs is a knowledge of Arabic and this level is shared by those adept in language and even by those Bedouin who are ignorant of it. As for faith affirming their meanings of God—may He be praised and exalted—without any revelatory vision, all one needs is to understand the meaning of the words and to have faith in them, and this level is shared by the common people, even by young boys. For once one has understood the teaching, if these meanings were presented to him, he would receive them and memorise them, believe them in his heart and persist in them. These are the levels of most scholars, to say nothing of those who are not scholars. In relation to those who do not share with them in those three levels, these should not be denied credit, yet they are clearly deficient with respect to the acme of perfection. For "the merits of the [merely] pious are demerits in those who have drawn near to God."[51]

Having disqualified certain types of laymen and scholars from comprehending and sharing in the moral implications of the Divine Names, al-Ghazālī pointed out that those who have drawn near to God share in the moral implications of the Divine Names in a threefold manner. The first is knowledge of the meanings of those Names "by way of witnessing and unveiling, so that their essential realities are clarified for them by a proof which does not permit any error."[52] Although this degree is the lowest in this threefold hierarchy, there is a world of difference between the faith of such a believer who is at this degree and that of a person who inherited their faith from their parents or teachers through mere blind acceptance and uncritical imitation.[53]

Ascending to the second degree of sharing in those meanings, al-Ghazālī clarified that this degree absorbs what has been disclosed in the previous degree, coupled with great appreciation for the bounties of God in granting one such absorption. This appreciation leads to a state of desperation and aspiration to partake of the qualities of God in every possible manner, so that one may draw closer to the Reality of God. With the possession of such qualities, such believers reach a state that is comparable to the closeness of the angels to God—in terms of quality, not place. However, two reasons may deprive a seeker of God from reaching such a lofty degree: first, being ignorant and uncertain that the Divine quality at hand is one of the qualities of perfection; second, if the seeker's heart is preoccupied with anything other than God. Thus, emptying the heart of worldly passions and lowly desires is a prerequisite step for reaching this stage. He likens those who reach this level to the "angels."[54]

Moving to the third and highest degree signifies moving beyond the "angelic" stage to the "godly," whereby the seeker of God exerts every possible effort to acquire whatever is possible of those perfect qualities of God, to emulate them, and to adorn the soul with their beauty. With this, one gets close to God and becomes a companion of the close angels of God. Acquiring qualities similar to the angels' results in being in proximity to God similar to theirs.[55] So, if the second degree makes the believer *malā'ikiyyan* (angel-like), the third makes them *rabbāniyyan* (god-like).

Al-Ghazālī used some examples to clarify how molding the character on God's example can be conceptualized and materialized. He examined each name of the Divine Names in a way that explains what each name means on God's side and what its imitation means on the believer's side. For example, God's name *al-Mutakabbir* (the Prideful One), on the side of God, means that God considers everything unworthy of consideration compared to Himself. This is in line with the tradition that says, "Pride is my cloak and greatness is My robe, and he who competes with Me in respect of either of them I shall cast into Hell-fire."[56] God sees majesty exclusively in regard to Himself and looks at others as a king would look at his subjects. As for the believer's share in that attribute of God, it lies in their renunciation of the world, liberating themselves from all that would hinder their heart from seeking God and disdaining everything but Him. So the believer's aspiration should not go beyond God. However, al-Ghazālī clarified that there is another type of renunciation which does not go under this category, which is the renunciation of the common believer who worships God in "a contractual manner," so to speak, purchasing the good of the Hereafter by abandoning that of the Here. Such a type of renunciation is good in terms of advancing one's own purchasing and bargaining with God, yet it remains lowly compared to the stage in point, for the stage in point seeks God for God's sake and not for the sake of any other gains, i.e., Paradise.[57] Therefore, this degree encompasses those who renounce the passions of the world as well as the passions of the Hereafter, be it sex, food, Paradise, or whatever people long for.[58] In his *Iḥyā'*, he argued that the result of adopting such an attribute in the manner described here is that one becomes "king-like" in the Here before the Hereafter. Explaining the nature of this king-like state, al-Ghazālī gave a parable of a king who asked a saint, "Have you got any need that I can fulfil for you?" The saint replied, "How can I seek the fulfilment of my need from you when my sovereignty is vaster than yours." The king asked, "How is that?" The saint replied, "He who is your master is my slave." The king asked further, "How is that?" The saint replied, "You are the slave of greed, anger, passions, and appetite, but I have mastery over them all. So, they are my slaves."[59]

God's names *al-Raḥmān* (the Merciful) and *al-Raḥīm* (the Compassionate) are also worthy of coverage. Al-Ghazālī contended that the believer's participation in the divine name "the Merciful" should be in accordance with the state of the one with whom the believer deals. If it is a heedless worshiper, mercy would then lie in weaning them from the path of heedlessness by guiding them toward wakefulness, through gentle exhortation and kind counseling. As for showing mercy toward the disobedient, it lies in looking at them with eyes of compassion but not eyes of contempt, sparing no effort to eliminate such disobedience by all possible means, all out of mercy to the disobedient lest they be exposed to God's wrath and then be unworthy of being in proximity to God.[60]

If the believer's participation in the name *al-Raḥmān* lies in fulfilling the "spiritual needs" of fellow humans, their participation in the name *al-Raḥīm* lies in fulfilling their "physical needs." It lies in not turning away from the destitute without helping them to the best of the believer's ability, nor turning away from the poor in one's vicinity without exerting one's optimum efforts to rid them of their need. If one cannot help monetarily, help can come through one's good reputation (*jāh*) or by interceding on their behalf with another person. If one cannot help, neither with wealth nor with good reputation, then one should help with prayer or even by expressing grief on account of their need, out of sympathy and love toward them, as if the seeker of God were thereby sharing in their hardship and need.[61]

Maqāṣidī-Oriented Explanations of the Divine Essence

Upon discussing the exoneration of God from location and space, al-Ghazālī answered his interlocuter by raising the discussion to the level of *maqāṣid*. The questioner asked, "[I]f God is not specified as being neither above nor underneath, what is the point of raising the face and hands to the heavens when invoking God? And what is to be inferred from what Prophet Muḥammad said to the slave woman whom he willed to manumit but wanted first to be certain of her faith, and hence asked her: where is God? Her response was a gesture towards the sky, and he commented that she was a believer?"[62] Answering the first question, al-Ghazālī contended that this is like someone saying "[I]f God is not located in the shrine of the Kaʿaba, then why does it matter if we visit this shrine in pilgrimage? Moreover, if God is not on earth, then why do we humble our faces by touching the earth when we prostrate in prayer?"[63] Extracting the objective, al-Ghazālī argued that the wisdom behind this is not that God is literally in the Kaʿaba nor that He is in the heavens, but rather because such notions bring to the heart of the believer a sense of surrendering to God and greater awareness of God's presence. Otherwise, all directions are the same with God.[64] It is the heart that God looks to, and the limbs of the body are there to put the heart in its proper posture to flourish spiritually. This is the way in which God has created the heart, namely, to be influenced by actions of the body. Similarly, He created the limbs of the body to be influenced by the convictions of the heart. The same can be said about the second question. That is, reverence in the limbs of the body comes in the form of upward gestures, which suggest the elevated status of the revered person. According to the ordinary usage of conversational language, it is customary to express the elevated status of a person by saying of him that he is in the seventh sky, metaphorically indicating the high stature of such a person.[65] Al-Ghazālī then lamented the understanding of those who miss these secrets of acts of worship. It is worth quoting him at length:

> See, then, with what subtlety religion has known how to guide hearts and bodies to the respect and reverence that are due to God most high. [See] also how ignorant a person is shown to be who sees only superficially the members of the body and, negligently, does not bother to delve more deeply into the mysteries of the heart. Such an ignorant person supposes that the most important thing in all of this is what is indicated by the organs of the body in their gestures and attitudes

> without noticing that, on the contrary, the first and principal thing is to know the sentiment of respect within the heart, a sentiment that, in having respect for [God], indicates high esteem, not a high place in space, and that the organs of the body fill no role here other than simple subjects and servants of the heart, serving it in that task of showing to [God] the respect that is his due—but only to the degree that such is possible—that is, through gestures or indications in the direction of certain points.
>
> This is the subtle mystery that abides in raising our faces to the heavens when we want to show respect and reverence to God most high. And prayer cannot but be a plea or petition for any one of the divine mercies or benevolences. The keep of those blessings are the heavens, and the guardians charged with distributing them are the angels whose fixed abode is the kingdom of the heavens. That is why God most high says "And in the heaven is your providence and that which ye are promised." Now, instinct moves us spontaneously to turn the face in the direction of the closet in which is kept the food that we desire. The subjects that hope to receive something from the rulers, when they know that the gifts will be apportioned, gather at the door of the treasury and their faces along with their hearts are inclined to the place where the treasure is found, even though they do not believe that the king is personally present at the place of the treasure. This is the same thing that turns the faces of religious people in the direction of heaven by instinct and by the revealed law. Clearly the common people simply believe that the Lord whom they worship is in fact in the sky, and this belief is also one of the causes that moves them to raise their faces in prayer. The Most High is Lord of all lords. I affirm that those who deviate [from His truth] greatly err.[66]

Al-Ghazālī appeals to another tradition to point out that exonerating God is one of the objectives of Islamic theology, i.e., the tradition of God's Descent every night to the lowest heaven to answer the prayers of devoted believers. So, when one hears the tradition about the Descent of God every night, it is one's duty to know that the word *nuzūl* (descent) is a homonym that is used at times literally and at other times metaphorically. While the literal indicates a movement from up to down, the metaphorical does not require any movement, similar to when God says in the Qurʾān, "and He sent down to you of cattle eight pairs" (Q. 39:6), yet no one has seen calves or cows descending from above. Hence, "sending them down" doubtlessly has a meaning similar to what al-Shāfiʿī (d. 820)[67] indicated when he said, "I went into Egypt and they did not understand me [due to the complexity of his language], so I descended, then I descended, then I descended."[68] Obviously, al-Shāfiʿī did not intend the literal meaning of the word "descend," which implies movement. Hence, the believer needs to know that "descend" on the side of God here is not to be understood literally, since God is not a material object. If one cannot understand the metaphor here, then one's duty is to know that if one is incapable of understanding how the calf can descend from above, one is even more incapable of understanding how God could descend.[69] Given that the tradition of the Descent is meant to convey a subtle message about God to encourage believers to stand up for night prayers, al-Ghazālī lamented that many people are misled by the above irrelevant whims and delusions, missing the very point of the tradition.[70] Reiterating the creedal objective of such traditions and indicating how scholars, let alone the populace, are heedless of such objectives, al-Ghazālī wrote:

> Thus observe how the revelation treats with care the hearts and organs of mankind in driving them to glorify God (Exalted is He), and how ignorant is the one whose perception is dim, who is aware only of the surface acts of the external organs and bodies. He is heedless of the secrets of the hearts in their glorifying God without the need to specify any direction. He thinks that the truth of the matter lies in that to which the external organs point. And he does not know that the primary seat for glorification is the heart that it glorifies by believing in the loftiness of His rank, and not of His place, and that the external organs are, in this task, servants and followers, serving the heart by participating in the glorification to the extent that is possible for them; and what is possible for the external organs is only their pointing in certain directions.[71]

Al-Ghazālī illustrated in his *Fayṣal* that when the objective of exonerating God from unsuitable humanly conceptions is ignored, the door to the practice of *takfīr* (excommunication) is wide open. Every sect declares those who hold different views from its own to be disbelievers and to be guilty of deeming Prophet Muḥammad a liar in what he told about God, even though the aim of all sects is to understand God in a manner far above anthropomorphism. None of them would disagree with this objective. And yet, when it comes to such questions, the Ḥanbalite, for instance, labels the Ashʿarite an Unbeliever, claiming that the latter "deems the Prophet to be a liar in his attribution of aboveness (*al-fawq*) and (a literal) mounting of the Throne (*al-istiwā' ʿalā 'l-ʿarsh*) to God. The Ashʿarite brands the Ḥanbalite an Unbeliever, claiming the latter to be anthropomorphist (*mushabbih*) who deems the Prophet to be a liar when he says (about God), 'Nothing is anything like Him.'"[72] On the other hand, the Ashʿarite lumps the Muʿtazilite in with disbelievers, on the basis that the Muʿtazilite deems the Prophet to be a liar when he informs us of the Beatific Vision of God in the Hereafter. Conversely, the Muʿtazilite flags the Ashʿarite a disbeliever on the basis that his belief in the divine attributes implies a belief in a multiplicity of eternals besides God and a denial of the truth that Prophet Muḥammad taught about the Divine Unity.[73]

Maqāṣidī-Oriented Explanations of the Divine Actions

Having touched upon some of the ethical and theological implications of God's essence, His Attributes, and Names, what remains is His actions. In al-Ghazālī's section on *tafakkur* (pondering) in his *Iḥyā'*, he argued that speculating about the objectives of God's actions is safer than speculating about His Essence and His Attributes, reiterating the tradition that encourages believers to think deeply about the creation of God, but not His Essence or His Attributes, as no human intellect is fully capable of comprehending His being in its reality. The tradition says, "Reflect deeply upon the creation of God and do not reflect upon God. Verily, you will never grasp His true measure."

Al-Ghazālī took understanding God's actions as a key to having better understanding of the Divine Attributes. Upon his explanation of the Divine Name "the Just," he wrote:

> One cannot know one who is just without knowing his justice, and one cannot know his justice without knowing his action. So whoever wants to understand this attribute must comprehend the actions of God most high from the kingdoms of the heavens to the ends of the earth, to the point where one does not notice any fault in the creation of the infinitely good One, and turns again and sees no rifts in it, yet turns one more time only to have his sight become weak and dulled; for the beauty of the divine presence has overwhelmed him and bewildered him with its harmony and its regularity: for such a man, something of the meaning of His justice—the Most High and Holy One—clings to his understanding.

> He created the categories of existing things, the physical and the spiritual, the perfect and imperfect among them; and He gave to each thing its created existence, in which He is generous, and also ordered them in a placement suitable to them, in which He is just. Among the large bodies of the universe are the earth, water, air, the heavens and the stars, and He created them and ordered them, placing the earth lowest of all, putting water above it and air above the water and the heavens above the air. And if this arrangement were to be reversed, the order would be untenable.[74]

Al-Ghazālī examined the actions of God in four places of his corpus: *Kitāb al-ṣabr wa'l shukr* (Book of Patience and Gratitude), *Kitāb al-tafakkur* (Book of Pondering) in his *Iḥyā*, *Jawāhir*, as well as *al-Ḥikma fi makhlūqāti'l-Allāh* (Wisdom in God's Creation). In *Kitāb al-ṣabr wa'l shukr*, he contended that there is wisdom behind the creation of everything and that God's wisdom behind His actions is infinite. Nevertheless, wisdom is of two types: open and hidden. Open wisdom can be obtained through the pursuit of knowledge and pondering upon God's creation. For instance, God's wisdom in creating the sun is for the people to distinguish day from night and to know that daytime is for pursuing provisions and nighttime is for seeking rest. God created eyes for us to see and not to hear, ears to hear and not to see, hands to catch and not to walk, feet to walk and not to catch, noses to smell and not to hear. Each part has been assigned a special function. If a faithful person does not use a part for which it has been created, he becomes unthankful to God for this particular part. For example, he who wrongly beats another with his fist becomes unthankful for the gift of hands, as hands have been made for distracting harms and attracting benefits but not for destroying a thing or assaulting an innocent. Originally, man was given all these blessings to remember God. However, this remembrance is not possible without a body, and the body needs food; getting food is not possible without earth, water, and air; earth requires sun. So all these have been created to serve the body, and the body is meant to be a vehicle for the remembrance of God.[75]

Open wisdom leads to hidden wisdom. An example of hidden wisdom is how the body relates to the soul. The body is meant to act as an outer cover to the soul. However, people cannot have access to the reality of the soul, for it is a spiritual being and intellect cannot get to its secrets. About this soul, God said in Q. 17:85, "They ask you about the soul. Say, the Soul is part of my Lord's domain. You have only been given a little knowledge."[76]

Maqāṣidī-Oriented Explanations of the Divine Predestination

One day Prophet Muḥammad came out to his Companions when they were arguing about Predestination. He was agitated and said, "Have you been commanded to do this, or were you created for this purpose? You are using one part of the Qur'ān against another part, and this is what led to the doom of the nations who came before you."[77] Having cited this tradition, al-Ghazālī did not wrestle with the reality of *Qadar* (predestination), believing that God meant its essence to be mysterious. However, he did not hesitate to offer some guidelines as to the benefits of believing in Predestination.

He began by stating that being content with Predestination is beneficial in the Here as well as in the Hereafter. Concerning the Here, the benefit lies in being unworried and unstressed about one's affairs, given that everything has already been decreed. As for the Hereafter, one earns God's pleasure and reward based on one's state of content with God's decrees while in the Here. On the contrary, being discontented is harmful in both the Here and the Hereafter. Regarding the Here, discontent keeps one occupied with self-direction and self-management. As for the Hereafter, it invokes God's wrath.[78] Upon explaining the benefits of believing in God's Name *al-Ḥakam* (the Arbitrator), he wrote:

> The religious profit to be gained from beholding this attribute of God most high is to know that the matter is settled and not to be appealed. For the pen is already dry, [having written] what exists. The causes are already applied to their effects, and their being impelled towards their effects in their proper and appointed times is a necessary inevitability. Whatever enters into existence enters into it by necessity. For it is necessary that it exist: if it is not necessary in itself, it will be necessary by the eternal decree which is irresistible. So man learns that what is decreed exists, and that anxiety is superfluous. As a result, he will act well in seeking his livelihood, with a tranquil spirit, a calm soul, and a heart free from disruption.[79]

Maqāṣidī-Oriented Explanations of the Existence of Evil

Al-Ghazālī discussed the *maqāṣid* of the existence of evil on earth in his *al-Maqṣad al-asnā*. Upon discussing the divine name "the Merciful," he imagined a questioner who asks: How is it that the attribute of mercy be ascribed to God when He sees people afflicted, yet does nothing to remove their affliction?

How can He allow it to happen in the first place? Al-Ghazālī opened the discussion by setting a couple of premises. First, God, the Merciful, certainly intends good for people. Second, there is no pure evil, as such, in existence except that it underlies some good within it that, if it were to be removed, the underlined good would be invalidated, and eventually the result would be an evil that is worse than the evil contained in the good. For example, although the amputation of a hand is a clear evil, within it lies the well-being of the entire body, which is more important than maintaining a corrupt hand. Thus, if the amputation is avoided here, the entire body would be jeopardized, which is certainly a worse evil. Hence, cutting off a hand for the maintenance of the whole body is clearly good in the guise of evil. Al-Ghazālī then cited the tradition that says, "My [i.e., God's] mercy precedes My anger," to indicate that good is accomplished essentially in the actions of God and evil happens accidentally. So the existence of evil does not run counter to the Divine Mercy.[80] He gave another example, where he said:

> A small child's mother may be tender towards him and so keep him from undergoing cupping [a traditional therapeutic type of medicinal treatment], while the wise father makes him do it by force. An ignorant person thinks that the compassionate one is the mother rather than the father, while the intelligent understand that the father's hurting him by cupping reflects the perfection of his mercy and love as well as the completeness of his compassion; whereas the mother was his enemy in the guise of a friend, since a little suffering, when it is the cause of great joy, is not evil but good.[81]

Having said that, if a particular evil happens to you without your seeing any good contained in it, or should you think it feasible that a particular good be accomplished without its being contained in evil, you should question the soundness of your own discretion in both trains of thought. As for the first scenario, know that minds are not up to comprehending good and evil as God intends them. One here is like the ignorant person who thinks that execution, rightly deserved, is an unmitigated evil, but disregards the common good contained for the entire community in such an execution. As for the latter scenario, one should question one's understanding that it was possible for this good to be accomplished without its being embedded in that evil. That is, the possibility or impossibility of everything possible or impossible is unintelligible to most people; things are not normally as simple as they appear. God's good and evil are beyond our partial conceptions of good and evil. Instead of questioning God's mercy, one needs to question one's own reasoning.[82]

Maqāṣidī-Oriented Explanations of the Function of the Qurʾān

At the outset of *Jawāhir al-Qurʾān*, al-Ghazālī asked reciters of the Qurʾān to sail to the midst of the fathomless ocean of the meanings of the Qurʾān in search of its jewels. He then proceeded to guide reciters to the manner in which the journey should go.[83] Martin Wittingham observed that much of the theorizing in *Jawāhir* is associated with al-Ghazālī's hierarchical classification of Qurʾānic verses, illustrating that al-Ghazālī identified ten types of verses, corresponding to those subjects in the Qurʾān: "The divine essence, divine attributes, divine works, the life to come, the straight path, the purification and beautification [of the soul], the conditions of the saints, the conditions of God's enemies, [His] arguments with the infidels, and [finally] the bounds of legal judgements."[84]

Al-Ghazālī made it clear that the whole objective of the Qurʾān is to clarify to people what God wants from them. In *Iljām al-ʿawām ʿan ilm al-kalām* (Restraining the Masses from the Science of Philosophical Theology), he suggested that people should come to know the attributes of God not by the arguments of polemical or apologetic theologians, as they tend to create confusion in the hearts and minds of the masses, but rather by the clear and simple Qurʾānic proofs, which are intelligible to the mind and comforting to the heart. For example, regarding the demonstration of the Oneness of God, it suffices to look at Q. 21:22, which says, "If there had been a number of gods in them (Heaven and Earth), they both would be ruined," and that the coming together of a number of leaders is cause for vandalism to the affairs of leadership, as mentioned in Q. 23:91: "God has not taken any son, nor has there ever been with Him any deity. [Had there been], then each deity would have taken what it created, and some of them would have sought to overcome the others. Exalted is God above what they describe."[85]

As for the truthfulness of Prophet Muḥammad, it suffices to think of Q. 17:88: "Say: If men and Jinn were to all come together in order to produce the like of this Qurʾān, they would not bring forth the like of it even if some of them would have aided others in doing so." And Q. 2:23, which states, "And if you are in doubt about what We have sent down upon Our Servant [Muḥammad], then produce a *sūra* (chapter) the like thereof and call upon your witnesses other than God, if you should be truthful." As for the Last Day, it is sufficient for one to look at Q. 36:78–79: "And he presents for Us an example and forgets his [own] creation. He says: Who will give life to bones while they are disintegrated? Say: He will give them life who produced them the first time; and He is, of all creation, Knowing." Also, Q. 75.36–40: "Does man think that he will be left *suda* [neglected without being accountable]? Was he not a *nuṭfa* (mixed male and female discharge of semen) poured forth? Then he became an *ʿalaqa* (a clot); then [God] shaped and fashioned (him) in due proportion, and made him in two sexes, male and female. Is not He Able to give life to the dead?"

Al-Ghazālī pointed out that the proofs of the Qurʾān are like food that every person can take and benefit from, whereas the proofs of polemical theologians are like medicine in that only certain individuals may benefit from them but they will be harmful to others. It is like water that quenches the thirst of the infant child who is nursing as well as the strong adult, whereas other proofs are like the food that benefits a strong man at times but may make him ill at others, and infants find no benefit in them at all.[86] Hence, the masses should be dissuaded from philosophical theology and rely on Qurʾānic norms of reasoning.

From the above discussion, what sets the Qurʾān apart from other sources of reasoning is that it suits people with various intellectual capabilities; a philosopher would benefit from it, and an uneducated person would also benefit. Hence, al-Ghazālī likened the Qurʾānic discourse to "water" and the theologians' approach to "medicine." While everyone will surely benefit from "water" and it has no harm, medicine is needed only under certain conditions and for certain types of people. The Qurʾān has been designed in such a manner to do the job of *bayān* (clarification). Note here that the great architect of legal *maqāsid*, al-Shāṭibī, argued along the same lines that the major objective of the Qurʾān is "clarification."[87]

Al-Ghazālī then pushed the discussion further: "[I]f the Qurʾānic approach is so effective in clarification, why did God not use words that are not open to different interpretations, thereby leaving no room for discord?" Al-Ghazālī's answer is that this is the nature of the Arabic language, and God has spoken to the people in the language they can understand. Additionally, there are no words in the Arabic language that explicitly indicate those intended meanings without being open to different interpretations. Hence, God has provided us, in addition to the Qurʾān, with the light of prophecy, so as to set those vague expressions in context, apart from the light of reason and reflection. And yet the fact remains that words of such nature are not the norm in the Qurʾān but rather the exception. So, having the Qurʾān open, in exceptional places, for different interpretations is a necessity that is unavoidable due to the nature of the Arabic language.[88]

Finally, al-Ghazālī asked another question on behalf of this imaginative debater: "[W]hy did God not unveil the ambiguity about His essence, and simply say, for instance: 'He exists,' 'He is not a divisible or indivisible material object,' 'He is neither inside the world nor outside of it,' 'not connected and not unattached,' and so forth."[89] Al-Ghazālī's response is that, if the reality of God was expressed in such a manner it may well have been rejected by those who rush to say that this is simply impossible, or they would have fallen into the trap of extreme exoneration that ends up with denial of the divine attributes (*taʿṭīl*). The undisputable reality is that God wants mercy for people. Hence, He addresses them in a language they can comprehend so that they can also bear its implications and come closer to Him.[90]

Maqāṣid al-ʿAqīda *after al-Ghazālī*

While post-Ghazālian scholars such as Muḥammad al-Zāhid al-Bukhārī, Fakhr al-Dīn al-Rāzī, ʿIzz al-Dīn ibn ʿAbd al-Salām, Ibn Taymiyya, and Shāh Walīullāh al-Dehlawī, and modern ones such as Rashīd Riḍā may also seem relevant to this emerging field, their contributions are not as solid as those of al-Ghazālī and ʿAbduh, for their contributions remain either incidental or not strictly theologically oriented . An example of an incidental treatment of the subject is al-Zāhid al-Bukhārī's *Maḥāsin al-Islām* (The Merits of Islam). Although he began the book with some interesting *maqāṣidī* insights, his primary focus is on *Maqāṣid al-Sharīʿa* and not *Maqāṣid al-ʿAqīda*. Reiterating the ideas of al-Ḥakīm al-Tirmidhī and Ibn Bābawayh al-Qummī, he argued that the objective of publicly verbalizing the testimony of faith, which is a theological article, is for *Maqāṣid al-Sharīʿa* to be established and respected, i.e., when one pronounces the faith testimony publicly, one's blood, property, and so forth are protected, as these objectives are predicated on this theological condition.[91] However, he did not offer any extensive discussions beyond that.

As for al-Rāzī, even though he agreed that God prescribes "laws" in the interest of humans, he gave extremely vehement arguments against the idea of attempting to comprehend similar "theological" endeavors.[92] In his *al-Maḥṣūl fī ʿilm uṣūl al-fiqh* (Harvest of the Science of Legal Theory), he provided an extensive dialectical discussion discouraging scholars from pursuing what can be termed *Maqāṣid al-ʿAqīda*. Reflecting the standard Ashʿarite position, he was reluctant to attribute any motivating cause, such as consideration for human interests, behind the divine theological commandments. He said that, for instance, with the existence of disbelief and disobedience on earth, one cannot claim that God does what is in the interest of humans. God's very giving humans the freedom to choose belief or disbelief is in and of itself destructive, for if God wants what is in the best interest of humans, He would not have allowed a human to choose disbelief. And if we say disbelief is the choice of man, not God, then we can no longer say that God is the creator of everything on earth, which runs counter to our belief in God's omnipotence. Al-Rāzī proceeded to say that if the human is able to choose belief, it also means he is able to choose to disbelieve. If he chooses disbelief over belief, it must have happened due to a predestined decree imposed by God. Hence, we will end with the same conclusion: God does not do what is in the best interest of humans. On the other hand, al-Rāzī argued, how can we say that God observes human interests when He has burdened humans with more than they can bear in terms of calamities and afflictions, etc.? If this is established, then we cannot claim that God considers humans' interests when He acts.[93]

Navigating through his *al-Tafsīr kabīr* (The Large Commentary), al-Rāzī made this point even clearer.[94] For instance, in his commentary on Q. 2:6, "Indeed, those who disbelieve—it is all the same for them whether you warn them or do not warn them—they will not believe," he contended that if God says that such disbelievers will never believe, it means that belief for them is impossible and that God wanted them to be disbelievers. If this is the case, how can it be said that God considers human interest?[95] Similarly, Q. 110:3 mentions that the Prophet's uncle, Abū Lahab (d. 624), who rejected Muḥammad's message, "will burn in a Fire of flame," and yet God still demands of Abū Lahab that he believes in His Prophet while He knows that it is impossible for him to do so.[96] Here, too, al-Rāzī commented, it cannot be said that God considers human interests.[97]

Similar to al-Zāhid al-Bukhārī's incidental treatment of the subject, ʿIzz al-Dīn ibn ʿAbd al-Salām, in *Maqāṣid al-ʿbādāt* (Objectives of Worship), commenced this brief book with what might be taken as a theological objective, highlighting that all acts of worship are meant to assist in drawing the faithful closer to God. However, he continued to offer discussions that are of more relevance to *Maqāṣid al-Sharīʿa*, such as the objectives of prayer, followed by a discussion on the objectives of fasting, and ending the book with a discussion on the objectives of pilgrimage. As stated earlier, although he did not offer any serious theological discussions in relation to *Maqāṣid al-ʿAqīda* as we perceive it here, his argument that all acts of worship revolve around the objective of drawing closer to the Almighty might serve as a theological objective.[98]

As for Ibn Taymiyya, even though he had some critical interventions on the realm of *maqāṣid*, he neither claimed to be a theologian, as such, nor did he pursue theological discourse for its own merit. That is, his theological inquiry was for what he deemed "to be the articulation and defence of authentic Islamic doctrine."[99] Nonetheless, it is worthy of mention that he subtly critiqued the classical theory of *Maqāṣid al-Sharīʿa* on account of its "essentialism" and for its exclusion of key theological questions. He wrote, "[Jurists] have abandoned clear objectives of many internal [theological articles] and external *ʿibādāt* (acts of worship) of Islam, including knowing God, His Angels, His Books, His Messengers, the states of the heart such as the love of God, revering Him, devoting one's faith to Him, placing one's trust in Him, and other than these of the interests of this world and the Hereafter."[100] He also argued that they have neglected "justice" as a primary Islamic objective. In his *al-Jawāb al-ṣaḥīḥ li-man baddala dīn al-Masīḥ* (The Correct Reply to Those Who Altered Christ's Religion), he asked: how can "justice" be neglected when disbelief (*kufr*) is considered in Islam a form of injustice? By this he referred to Q. 31:13, which says, "Verily! Joining others in worship with God is a great injustice."[101]

Shāh Walīullāh al-Dehlawī's contribution in his *Ḥujjat Allāh al-bāligha* (The Conclusive Proof of God) offered another incidental treatment of the subject, where he provided some intriguing insights into *Maqāṣid al-ʿAqīda*, most notably, his discussions of the theological implications of faith in God and Predestination. For instance, he argued that God must be known to people so that they may attain the perfection which is possible for them by molding their characters after His model.[102] Commenting on the tradition that says "God's right upon His servants is that they worship none but Him," he contended that such rights, in reality, do not benefit God in any way for He is beyond needs, but they are the rights of a person's soul over itself in order for it to reach its perfection. Then he advised believers not to stop at the externalities, but to dig deeper into the realities of theology.[103] Under the section "Honoring the Emblems of God," he discussed the objectives of God's revelation of the Qurʾān in the form of a "book," averring that human subjects get accustomed to hearing the proclamations of their king, and their reverence for their king was connected with their reverence for such proclamations. Hence, God revealed the Qurʾān in this manner, so that people may relate to it and, through this relation, they may accept its guidance. If such was not the case, they would find it almost impossible to connect to something they do not recite and transmit as a manifesto of guidance. He offered similar insights in reference to the idea of prophecy, the Kaʿaba, and prayer.[104]

As for Riḍā, although he offered more extensive discussions on the genre of *maqāṣid* in general, his treatment remains primarily law-based. Indeed, his emphasis on the theory of *maṣlaḥa* (public interest) may attest to this fact.[105] However, his contribution to the area of *maqāṣid al-Qurʾān* (objectives of the Qurʾān) cannot go unnoticed. In his *al-Waḥy al-Muḥammadī* (The Muḥammadan Revelation), he not only provided some rational and historical proofs that the Qurʾān is of divine origin, but also offered some original insights into what might be termed *maqāṣid al-Qurʾān*, exhibiting a critical analysis and a comprehensive treatment of the ten key objectives of the Qurʾān. These objectives are (1) illustrating the essential pillars of faith; (2) establishing prophethood and issues related to it, such as the performance of miracles; (3) refining the human mind and liberating it; (4) reforming morality and ethics; (5) elaborating the general privileges of Islam in its theological, legal, and ethical dimensions; (6) elucidating the general principles of the Islamic theory and practice of politics; (7) reforming economic practices and providing guidelines; (8) formulating Islam's philosophy of war; (9) granting women their human, religious, and civil rights; (10) the elimination of slavery and showcasing ways of doing so.[106]

Having reached this point, we are now in a better position to move to the second most important figure to this genre after al-Ghazālī, i.e., ʿAbduh, and assess his contribution to the subject. Although the discussion offered here will not be as detailed as the one on al-Ghazālī, it is more extensive than the discussions on the post-Ghazālīan figures briefly treated above.

Muḥammad ʿAbduh's Contributions to Maqāṣid al-ʿAqīda

ʿAbduh was an Egyptian jurist, religious scholar, and theologian. He was schooled in Al-Azhar,[107] where he studied the classical curriculum and earned the title of *ḥāfiz* after he had memorized the Qurʾān by heart at the age of twelve. Having mastered traditional studies, he graduated from Al-Azhar in 1878 as a qualified Azharite teacher. Beyond the boundaries of Al-Azhar, he spearheaded the creation of a religious-intellectual society in Egypt that worked toward eliminating public religious illiteracy, and he initiated proposals to reform the structure and content of education in Egypt, including Al-Azhar. ʿAbduh witnessed a lot of turmoil in his life and underwent exile, but he used his exile as a means to expand his influence and spread his reforms. He met with many European thinkers and influential leaders of the Muslim world. In 1899, he was appointed Egypt's grand mufti, holding this position until he died in Alexandria on 11 July 1905.[108]

Although the trinity of Jamāl al-Dīn al-Afghānī (1838–1897), ʿAbduh, and Riḍā is normally studied together due to their intellectual affinity, this section will singularly focus on ʿAbduh's conception of *Maqāṣid al-ʿAqīda*, for it was he who came to be a more systematic theologian than the former and more intellectually consistent than the latter. By this I mean that al-Afghānī was not a theologian as such, but primarily an intellectual activist with a dense interest in religion, and Riḍā, though a man of scholarship, did not produce a theological work as such, and also shifted from ʿAbduh's school toward Wahhabi Salafism after the latter's death.[109] However, it cannot be denied that both al-Afghānī and Riḍā had some theological insights dispersed here and there, and these must have influenced ʿAbduh's theological thought. In fact, it can conceivably be argued that ʿAbduh's magnum opus, *Risālat al-tawḥīd* (Theology of Unity), is an embodiment of al-Afghānī's political aspirations translated into theological terminology.

In *Risālat al-tawḥīd*, ʿAbduh showed that disregarding a *maqāṣidī* approach to Islamic theology was a primary reason for Islamic theology's failure to do its job efficiently, likening theological debates, present and past, to the situation of two groups of brothers who have been divided even though they were heading to a shared goal. Encountering each other in the night, unable to recognize each other in the darkness, each group fought for what the other had. These heated battles resulted in the loss of most of the men before reaching their destination. When morning came, with its clarity, those who remained alive recognized one another. Had they known they were fighting their brothers, they instead would have supported one another in reaching their shared goal without losing or excluding anyone.[110] By this parable, ʿAbduh referred particularly to the theological contention on whether or not God's actions are bound to consider the public good. One theological school, the Muʿtazilites, pushed the issue to the extreme, putting God under "obligation" to consider the public good. Another theological school, the Ashʿarites, pushed it to the other extreme, denying all motives in God's actions. Unpersuaded by either view, ʿAbduh declared that both agree the divine actions are always based on "wisdom." It is then up to us to take what they agree about and tie their miscellaneous threads back to one common truth. That is, the actions of an intelligent being are never aimless. If this is so in relation to humans, how much more with the Creator of the human mind itself, especially when the universe is full of examples of His wisdom? However, God remains under no "obligation," as such.[111]

ʿAbduh argued that belief in God's Unity and molding the Muslim community by its example is one of the key objectives of Islamic theology, contending that the whole science of Islamic theology is titled as such after its most central theme, that is, *tawḥīd* (unity).[112] Not only is *tawḥīd* an important theological concept; it is also one cause of the well-being of the Muslim community. Narrating the story of Joseph, the Qur'ān has Joseph say in Q. 12:39, "Are numerous lords better than God, the One, the Supreme?" What ʿAbduh inferred from this verse is that there is a linkage between the Unity of God and the well-being of humans. A multiplicity of gods distracts humans, not only spiritually but also in their worldly interests; that is, each group becomes fanatically competitive about what it aims for, and such a state of fanatical competitiveness aborts their attempts at success and vandalizes their endeavors for progress. A common faith in one single God brings these warring sects into a single unity under one authority and one undisputed judge, i.e., God. Consequently, the community will be formed cohesively with the bond of brotherhood that essentially ensures its well-being.[113] Additionally, ʿAbduh saw in the preservation of Divine and human Unity the preservation of the five higher objectives of Islamic law.[114] However, it should be noted that ʿAbduh used the term *waẓīfa* (function) more frequently than *maqṣad* to identify the objective of various theological precepts of Islamic theology,[115] asserting that the *waẓīfa* of Islam is to guide the masses to the Oneness of God in His essence, Oneness in His acts, and Oneness in His transcendental attributes.

Recognizing the Oneness of God carries within it the freedom of humans from being enslaved to other than God—the freedom of the heart, as compared to the freedom of the body. ʿAbduh wrote:

> Islam uprooted paganism . . . and all souls were likewise liberated from the evil forces belonging with their delusions and found release from the divisions that raged about objects of worship. Thus the whole level of humanity was lifted: human values responded to the new sense of human dignity implicit in worshipping none but the one creator of heaven and earth, the master of all men. Men everywhere could now say with Abraham—indeed were duty bound to say: "I turned my face to Him who created the heavens and the earth, as a true worshipper (*ḥanīf*): I am not one of those who take other gods for God and profess as the Prophet was commanded. My prayer, my devotion, my life

> and my death are God's, the Lord of the worlds. He has none like unto Him. So am I commanded. I am the first of the Muslims" (Surah 6.163). So, man came blessedly to see himself free and honourable: his will was freed from the bonds that tied him to the will of others, whether of fellow men supposedly also an offshoot of the Divine, or of rulers and masters, or against fictitious entities to which imagination attributed powers of will, such as tombs and stones, trees and stars and the like. So, man's initiative was released from the captivity to mediators, intercessors, divines, initiates, and all who claimed to be masters of hidden cults and pretended to authority over the relations men have with God through their works. These "mediators" set themselves up as disposers of salvation with the power of damnation and bliss. In sum, man's spirit found freedom from the slavery of deceivers and charlatans.[116]

Islam's theology of Unity liberated not only the hearts of the people but also their minds. It freed their minds from the blind imitation of traditionalism; they became no longer enslaved to their forefathers, but rather gave themselves to the one God who gifted them with "minds," with which they can judge for themselves. Islam's theology of Unity broke the power of traditionalism over humankind's intellect and erased its deep-seated impact on the mind when it prohibited *taqlīd* (uncritical imitation) in theology.[117]

For this unification and liberation to take place, ʿAbduh appealed to two traditional exegetical devices. First was the principle of *maṣlaha* (commonly translated as "public interest"). Although the principle did exist in the *Fiqh* literature, ʿAbduh gave it a more general meaning than it previously had. It had traditionally been no more than an exegetical tool in which the jurist should assume that God's objective in making His revelation was to promote human well-being, and, consequently, he should select that interpretation which best led to this objective. ʿAbduh, however, widened the scope of *maṣlaha* and deepened its impact by making it a rule for "deducing specific laws from general principles of social morality."[118] Second was the principle of *talfiq* (amalgamation or piecing together), which refers to the idea that a scholar may select that interpretation of revelation, whether or not it came from his own school, which best suited the circumstances and achieved the higher goal.[119] Although this principle had been endorsed by some classical authorities, ʿAbduh used it in a more consistent manner, suggesting a systematic comparison of all legal and theological opinions of precedent scholars with a view to assembling a "synthesis" which would amalgamate the good aspects of all.[120] Therefore, he used *maṣlaha* and *talfiq* as means toward bridging the long-standing conflicts between schools of theology and law, as means toward the unity of all Muslims.

While al-Ghazālī's *maqāṣidī*-oriented approach primarily aimed at healing the breach between Muslim sects at an intrafaith level, ʿAbduh's *maqāṣidī*-oriented approach extended its usage to an interfaith level in a bid to bridge the gap between the three monotheistic religions: Judaism, Christianity, and Islam. He argued that when Islam came, humanity was disconnected by religious sectarianism, where believers were quarrelling, excommunicating one another, assuming that in so doing they were defending God and fighting for His cause. Islam reproached all that and asserted that the religion of God is one across all ages. God said in Q. 3:64, "Say, O people of the Book, come, hear one word which will bring us into concord. We will worship none but God and not take other gods instead of Him, and that none of us will set up other lords in His place. If they refuse, say: 'Bear witness that we are surrendered (*muslimūn*).'"[121] God's Unity is then the essential meaning that unites the three monotheistic faiths when discord permeates the world of religion. This Divine Unity, properly understood, should put an end to wrangling and stubborn contention.[122]

It is worthy of note that ʿAbduh did not deny that there are different forms of worship in the monotheistic religions. What he denounced was that these forms have become the basis of discord, even though they were meant to be a sign of God's mercy, to guide each people according to His knowledge of what is best for them at any given time.[123] Islam came to put limits to the exclusivists and separationists. Hence, it permitted the Muslim to marry with the People of the Book, take part at their table, and it taught that, at times of discord, they should always be high-minded.[124] ʿAbduh averred that Islam alerts people to the fact that religion should not be a means for separatism but rather a means for socialism. Hence, Islam erased all racial discrimination between nations. This view of Islam sharply contrasts with the exclusivist claims of those who assume a privileged religious status with God and denied it to others.[125]

Practicing what he preached, ʿAbduh, in his exile in Beirut in the 1880s, presided over the *Jamʿiyyat al-taʾlīf wa al-taqrīb* (Society of Reconciliation and Ecumenism), which was a diverse society, having Christian, Jewish, and Muslim members from different walks of life, aimed at furthering harmony between the three monotheistic religions.[126] Apparently, the Society worked on creating a global correspondence network instead of separate meetings.[127] According to Riḍā, the Society also aimed at teaching Europeans about true

Islam and its merits, depicting Islam as the natural continuation and evolution of Christianity and Judaism. Confirming those theological imperatives, in his epistle to Isaac Taylor,[128] ʿAbduh wrote:

> I was in venerable Jerusalem to visit the holy places which the people of the Three Religions unitedly exalt. The visitor notices in these [places] that it is as if there is one family tree (*dawḥa*), that is, the true religion (*al-dīn al-ḥaqq*), from which numerous twigs branch out. [I]ts unity in type and character and the singularity of its origin are not impaired by the visitor's observations of the variety of [the tree's] leaves or the splitting of its branches. . . . [T]he visitor decides, furthermore, on the similarity of the [tree's] fruit, identical in colour and flavour[. I]t has been concentrated in the Islamic religion, which draws from all [of the tree's] roots and its stems. . . . [T]hus, [the Islamic religion] is its epitome (*fadhlaka*), and the destination (*ghāya*) where its course ended.[129]

Finally, having examined the loosely dispersed roots of *Maqāṣid al-ʿAqīda* through the lens of the aforementioned pre-Ghazālīan and post-Ghazālīan theologians, I contend that, with the exception of al-Ghazālī's and ʿAbduh's contributions, the subject was not sufficiently developed but remained largely rudimentary and treated in passing. The logical question that arises from this coverage then is: What hampered the maturity and development of a full-fledged discipline of *Maqāṣid al-ʿAqīda*? This is the question we shall attempt to address in the following section.

Explaining the Underdevelopment of Maqāṣid al-ʿAqīda

Six reasons are offered here to explain the underdevelopment of *Maqāṣid al-ʿAqīda*. ***First***, while the principles of *qiyās*[130] (deductive analogy) and *taʿlīl* (verification of considered objectives) were welcomed in mainstream schools of Islamic law, this was not the case for Islamic theology. Assuming that *taʿlīl* limits God's omnipotence and sovereignty, traditional Ashʿarism taught that such theological objectives are inaccessible to humans. Confirming this, the chief architect of *Maqāṣid al-Sharīʿa*, al-Shāṭibī, stated that the interests pertaining to the Islamic creed cannot be known except through revelation and that speculative reasoning has no place in the context of theology.[131]

Although the Muʿtazilites did not differentiate between theology and law in this regard, assuming that *taʿlīl* was not only acceptable but also commendable in theology,[132] they too did not develop a systematic theory of *Maqāṣid al-ʿAqīda*. Two key reasons may explain this. First, they were largely reactionary to the immediate theological questions of the day, which seem to have clouded their formation of a more positivist and more systematic theology. Also, as Josef van Ess illustrated in *The Flowering of Muslim Theology*, their theology was largely shaped in conversation with Greek philosophy.[133] As a corollary, their engagement with the Qurʾān and its theological objectives was minimal. In the words of Muḥammad Iqbal (d. 1938), "[A] careful study of the Qurʾan and the various schools of scholastic theology that arose under the inspiration of Greek thought disclose the remarkable fact that while Greek philosophy very much broadened the outlook of Muslim thinkers, it, on the whole, obscured their vision of the Qurʾan."[134]

However, it should be noted that neither did the Ashʿarites deny that humans were created with intelligence and an ability to reason with God, nor did the Muʿtazilites deny the authority of revelation. Rather, it was a disagreement on what the "starting point" is. While the starting point for the Ashʿarites was "revelation," the starting point for the Muʿtazilites was "reasoning." Hence, the primary question at the heart of this discussion was not whether or not God has wisdom behind his theological commandments but rather who has the authority to get to the wisdom lying behind revelation. Furthermore, *taʿlīl* involved another theological complexity; that is, it had two attributes of the Divine in play: Divine Omnipotence and Divine Wisdom. While Ashʿarites highlighted Divine Omnipotence, Muʿtazilites highlighted Divine Wisdom. To the Muʿtazilites, since God is Just and Wise, He cannot order what is antithetical to reason or act in a way that runs counter to the well-being of humans. Consequently, humans are invited to ponder not only the purposes of Islamic law but also those of Islamic theology. Conversely, since the Ashʿarites asserted and started from God's Omnipotence, they believed that God, although all Wise and all Just, can act beyond our own boundaries of reason; what gives goodness to the good and defines the evilness of the evil is known through revelation alone. The centrality of those two attributes to both parties is exemplified in the following debate between the founder of Ashʿarism, Abū al-Ḥasan al-Ashʿarī (d. c. 936), and his Muʿtazilite teacher, Abū ʿAlī al-Jubbāʾī (d. 915):

AL-ASHʿARĪ: O shaykh, what do you say regarding the fate of three people [in the Hereafter]: a believer, an unbeliever, and a child?

AL-JUBBĀʾĪ: The believer is among the [honored] classes; the unbeliever is among the doomed; and the child is among those who escape [perdition].

AL-ASHʿARĪ: If the child should desire to ascend to the ranks of the honoured, would this be possible?

AL-JUBBĀʾĪ: No. It would be said to him, "The believer simply earned this rank through his obedience, the likes of which you do not have to your credit."

AL-ASHʿARĪ: If the child should respond, "This is not my fault. Had You allowed me to live longer, I would have put forth the same obedience as the [adult] believer."

AL-JUBBĀʾĪ: God would respond, "I knew that had I given you [additional] life, you would have disobeyed Me, for which you would have been punished. So, I observed your best interest and caused you to die before reaching the age of majority [at which time you would have become responsible for obeying Me according to the religious law]."

AL-ASHʿARĪ: What if the [adult] unbeliever should then protest: "O Lord, You knew my fate just as You knew his. Why did You not observe my best interest as You observed his?"

At this, Al-Jubbāʾī is said to have fallen silent.[135]

This dialogue represented a defining moment in the Ashʿarite theological background. It pointed out that the Ashʿarites vigorously rejected the Muʿtazilite argument, which implied that God is bound by principles that lie outside of His self-determined commands. Conversely, they argued that God is not only free and empowered to do as He pleases, but also that nothing that God does can be judged evil or wrong, irrespective of its content as well as its bearings on His creation.[136]

Second is the existence of traditions, particularly in *ḥadīth*, that discourage reflection about the Divine essence of God. An example of a *ḥadīth* was quoted earlier: "Reflect deeply upon the creation of God and do not reflect upon God. Verily, you will never grasp His true measure." Such traditions imply that pursuing *Maqāṣid al-ʿAqīda* is potentially risky for the faithful. In fact, we have seen how al-Ghazālī cited the above *ḥadīth* to show the theological hazard underlying such attempts.[137]

Third is confusing *maqṣad* (objective) with *ʿilla* (underlying cause) and *maṣlaḥa* (interest/benefit). To start with *ʿilla*, Sunni theologians always emphasized that God acts without underlying causes; to ascribe causes and motives to God is to ascribe "needs" to Him. While humans may have underlying motives, as they are, by definition, needy and imperfect, God, on the contrary, is perfect. He is in no need of doing things driven by any such causes. Whatever He wills, He immediately says "Be" and it "becomes." Hence, they denied any causes or motives behind God's actions. However, this overemphasis on the denial of *ʿilla* from God's perspective entailed decreased emphasis on another, no less important attribute of God: *ḥikma* (wisdom). God is *al-Ḥakīm* or the "All-Wise." Hence, He does not do things aimlessly or pointlessly. However, it was with theologians such as al-Ghazālī that this distinction began to be made clear, though not without challenges. As for *maṣlaha,* Sunni theologians thought it is inappropriate to attribute it to God, as the word itself signifies temporality and utilitarianism, whereas God is far above such interests.[138] With such lack of clarity, it is hard to imagine a systematic theory of *Maqāṣid al-ʿAqīda* developing.

Fourth is the lack of transdenominational theological maxims. To appreciate the value of such maxims in the development of a theory of *maqāṣid* one can simply look at the realm of Islamic law, wherein legal maxims (*al-Qawāʿid al-Fiqhiyya*) helped considerably in building a higher legal theory of *maqāṣid* largely accepted by the four Sunni schools—Hanafī, Mālikī, Shāfiʿī, and Ḥanbalī. Conversely, Islamic theology failed to develop such maxims, for how could it do so when theological notions such as *al-firqa al-nājiya* (the saved group) occupied a prominent position within Islamic theology? That is to say, such notions, by definition, stimulate theological exclusivism, denoting that each group holds the one and only truth that is leading to the valid path of salvation, taking its proof from the *ḥadīth* that reads "There will befall my nation what befell the children of Israel. The children of Israel divided into seventy-two religious' groups and my community will divide into seventy-three religious' groups, one more than they. All of them are in hellfire except one religious' group."[139] The reason I consider that the notion of "the saved group" contributed to the hampering of *Maqāṣid al-ʿAqīda* is that *maqāṣid* is, by definition, inclusivist, while this notion is naturally exclusivist.[140] Therefore, they can barely meet. Although theologians like al-Ghazālī critiqued it, it still occupied a significant position in Islamic theology. In fact, the Wahhabi movement extensively employs it, accentuating that "he who grasps this seventy-three tradition, grasps the essence of Islam."[141]

This is not to say that there were no attempts at deriving such maxims at all, but that they were insufficient to build a systematic theory of *Maqāṣid al-ʿAqīda*. Otherwise, the Ashʿarite Tāj al-Dīn al-Subkī (d. 1370)[142] attempted to derive some theological maxims in his *al-Ashbāh wa'l-naẓā'ir* (The Likes and the Analogous). However, the five maxims he derived remain largely denomination-specific. Take, for instance, the maxim "[W]hat gives goodness and evilness to a certain thing is revelation." Moved by his Ashʿarite allegiance, he had to follow it with a qualification: "as opposed to the Muʿtazilites."[143] Ibn al-Wazīr (d. 1373),[144] in his *al-ʿAwāṣim wa al-qawāṣim* (The Protectors and Destroyers), as well as his *Īthār al-ḥaqq ʿalā al-khalq* (Putting Truth before People), offered some attempts to coin theological maxims.[145] However, these too remained denomination-specific to traditionist theology. Consequently, they did not advance the discipline significantly.

I consider Ḥassan al-Shāfiʿī's[146] *Muqaddima ta'sīsiya l-ʿilm al-qawāʿid al-iʿtiqādiyya* (Foundational Prolegomena to the Science of Theological Maxims) to be a serious contribution to the field. This is for two reasons. Although he considers himself an Ashʿarite, he methodically frees himself from any theological denominationalism throughout this brief but profound treatise. Additionally, he attempted to coin some original theological maxims. For instance, *al-ta'wīl* (interpretation) is authentic only when three conditions are met: it conforms to the norms of the Arabic language, it gathers together all pertinent texts that relate to one theme, and the interpreter himself is qualified to handle *ta'wīl*. The three conditions are unanimously accepted by Muslim theologians, classical and modern.[147]

Fifth is the nature of the Islamic theological episteme. While Islamic legal theory left a space for *probability* which tolerated a multiplicity of truths in the realm of law, this was not the case for Islamic theology. By "probability" I refer, for instance, to Imām al-Shāfiʿī's celebrated statement: "My opinion is right, and may yet be proven wrong; while the opinion of my opponent is wrong but may yet be proven right."[148] On the contrary, there was no space for such *probability* in classical Islamic theology. Recalling al-Ghazālī's vacillation about delving into *Maqāṣid al-ʿAqīda*, he stated that theology calls for "certitude," and error in it is not normally tolerated, unlike law, where one may take the risk of speculation and be excused if erring.[149]

Sixth is the epistemic separation between theology and Sufism. That is, the common presumption that theology addresses the mind and Sufism addresses the heart largely weakened the contribution that Sufism could provide to the higher questions of Islamic theology. Although there definitely was Sufi engagement with scholastic theology, that engagement remained in the periphery of theology. This separation has significantly contributed to the dryness of Islamic theology and the ambiguity of its vision. Had the major questions addressed by Sufi theologians, including the nature of God, experiential knowledge (*maʿrifa*), theodicy, prophecy, soteriology, and eschatology, been given their due consideration by scholastic theologians, it could have had a significant impact on the development of *Maqāṣid al-ʿAqīda*. In fact, one could ascribe the uniqueness of al-Ghazālī's contribution to *Maqāṣid al-ʿAqīda* to the hybridity in his thought between theology and Sufism.[150] Realizing this dichotomy and marginalization of Sufism in theological circles, Paul L. Heck wrote that "it is common to think about theology in Islam simply as *kalām* (dialectic theology) whereby the representatives of Islam's various sects defend their creedal definitions. However, Sufism demands reflection that goes beyond apologetics to what could be called systematic theology, religious reflection on 'the whole,' i.e. God and existence."[151] Ayman Shihadeh's collection of articles by established scholars of theology in his *Sufism and Theology* is an important attempt toward relinking the two subjects.[152] Clarifying the contribution this collection of articles makes, Heck wrote the following:

> This collection of articles very helpfully illustrates how Ṣūfism is actually part and parcel of the theological spectrum of Islam, and that at a time when, in contrast to earlier Orientalist assumptions, we now better understand how integrally related it is to Sharīʿa as well. This collection, then, is part of the current endeavour to relocate Ṣūfism at the heart of Islam. This, of course, is not to overlook Ṣūfism's familiarity with religious as well as political controversy. Indeed, the various contributions, which illustrate the topic in question with examples from the twelfth to the twentieth century, speak to the accusations that the defenders of Ṣūfism have always faced. But they also show that despite the perennial anti-Ṣūfism, Ṣūfism was never something that could be dismissed, not only because it provides a deeply spiritual experience for believers, but also because it addresses questions of a specifically theological character. It therefore has appeal to the Muslim mind no less than the Muslim heart.[153]

This brings me to the end of this chapter, whereby I set out to achieve two aims: first, to examine the contributions of some pre-Ghazālian and post-Ghazālian theologians to the genre of *Maqāṣid al-ʿAqīda*, singling out al-Ghazālī's and ʿAbduh's contributions, due to the distinctness of their interventions; second, to explain the reasons that may have led to the underdevelopment of a systematic theory of *Maqāṣid al-ʿAqīda*. In doing so, I gathered six reasons: (1) the rejection of *taʿlīl* in orthodox theology, (2) confusing *maqṣad* (objective) with *ʿilla* (underlying cause) and *maṣlaḥa* (interest/benefit), (3) having traditions that seem to discourage reflection on God and His essence, (4) lacking transdenominational maxims, (5) lacking epistemic probability in theology, (6) separating Sufism from theology. Having reached this point, we are now in a better position to move to the constructive aspect of the monograph, which will occupy us throughout the remaining four chapters.

2

Sources and Methods of Maqāṣid al-ʿAqīda

THE PREVIOUS CHAPTER pointed out that there are some roots to *Maqāṣid al-ʿAqīda* in the Islamic theological tradition, but those roots were neither sufficiently nor efficiently developed. Some of the potential causes of underdevelopment were also investigated in the chapter. This chapter initiates the process of constructing a systematic theory of *Maqāṣid al-ʿAqīda*, beginning with the ultimate source of Islamic epistemology, i.e., the Qur'ān, followed by the Sunna. We will attempt to explore not only the tools those two sources employ to identify *Maqāṣid al-ʿAqīda* but also some of the complexities involved in dealing with those two sources.

The Qur'ān and Maqāṣid al-ʿAqīda

The Qur'ān is the logical starting point for such a project, for it is often demonstrative of the wisdom behind its commandments and recommendations. In his *Iʿlām al-muwaqqiʿīn ʿan Rabb al-ʿĀlamīn* (Pronouncement for Those Who Sign on Behalf of the Lord of the Worlds), Ibn al-Qayyim (d. 1350)[1] observed that the Qur'ān is replete with many tools that indicate and identify *maqāṣid*, either explicitly or implicitly, and in various modes of expression, identifying the rationale, purpose, benefits, and ends of its legal rulings.[2] Kamali put it even clearer when he pointed out that the Qur'ān is "a goal-oriented book." Examining some of its verses, he contended that this goal-orientedness holds true for verses that focus on civil transactions (*muʿāmalāt*) as well as those that focus on devotional matters (*ʿibādāt*). For example, in depicting the ritual of ablution to perform prayer, the Qur'ān

The Higher Objectives of Islamic Theology. Mohammed Gamal Abdelnour, Oxford University Press.
 DOI: 10.1093/oso/9780197648636.003.0002

states the following: "God does not intend to inflict hardship on you. He intends cleanliness for you and to accomplish His favor upon you." So the verse does not stop at clarifying the ritual, but it also mentions the rationale behind it and explains God's intention. Furthermore, the Qur'ān declares that the aim of *jihād* is to allow "those have been wronged," as Q. 22:39 states, to remove injustice and establish justice. Therefore, the Qur'ān asserts that the key goal of *jihād* is to combat injustice. Hence, the Qur'ānic prescriptions and proscriptions are not simply confined to "dos" and "don'ts." Instead, they often provide justifications and objectives. This exemplifies that the Qur'ān's primary concern is with values, most notably "justice and benefit, mercy and compassion, uprightness and *taqwā*, promotion of good and prevention of evil, fostering goodwill and love among the members of the family, helping the poor and the needy, cooperation in good work, and so forth."[3]

Given the preceding, my contribution here lies in extending the above principles to the theological realm, arguing that the Qur'ān is goal-oriented not only in legal rulings but also in theological matters, and that theology is not simply confined to patterns of "believe this" and "do not believe that." In fact, I argue that *taʿlīl* is central to the theological narrative of the Qur'ān. In the following, I contend that *taʿlīl* appears in the Qur'ān in three primary forms: conjunctional prepositions, nominal sentences, and verbal sentences. Although the following survey is not exhaustive of all *taʿlīl* indicators across the Qur'ān, the examples highlighted are representatives of how the Qur'ān uses such indicators in reference to *Maqāṣid al-ʿAqīda*.

A. *Li'allā* (لِئَلَّا*: so that)*

An example of this particle is Q. 4.165: "[We send] messengers as bringers of good tidings and warners ***so that*** mankind will have no argument against God after the messengers." In this verse, the Qur'ān assigns two functions for the sending of prophets, as bearers of glad tidings and as warners of punishment, indicating that God does so for a purpose, that is, so that mankind might have no argument against God or allege that they did not receive any guidance or warning.

Aḥmad ibn ʿAjība (d. 1224),[5] the great Sufi master and Qur'ān commentator, in his *al-Baḥr al-madīd fī tafsīr al-Qur'ān al-majīd* (Oceanic Exegesis of the Glorious Qur'ān) is one of the few Qur'ān commentators who may well have understood this verse in reference to *Maqāṣid al-ʿAqīda*, quoting a *ḥadīth* supporting his understanding. The *ḥadīth* states, "There is none who is more anxious to accept the apologies of the people than God Himself and it is because of this that He has revealed the Book and sent the Messengers."[4] Although al-Rāzī, in his *al-Tafsir al-kabīr*, which is also known by the title *Mafātīḥ al-ghayb* (Keys of the Unseen), went along the lines of Ibn ʿAjība's interpretation, he quickly remembered his theological allegiance, i.e., Ashʿarism, and theological opponents, i.e., the Muʿtazilites. So he remarked that Muʿtazilites should not take this verse as support for their claim that God "must" have a reason behind every decree of His. In response to their reliance on this verse, he said the word *ḥujja* (apology/argument) should not be taken "literally" and that what is meant here is: we send messengers for the people so that they may not think that they have a *real* apology or argument.[6]

As for the Muʿtazilites theologians, they took this verse at face value, which is in harmony with their theological paradigm that is in harmony with reasoning with God. In his *al-Kashshāf* (The Revealer), al-Zamakhsharī (d. 1144),[7] the great Muʿtazilite exegete, understood the word *ḥujja* "literally" and argued that people could have an argument against God if He did not send messengers.[8]

B. Exceptive and Restrictive Particles, such as illā (إلا: except)

Given that the Qur'ān is replete with many verses in which such particles are used, it may suffice here to mention one example, i.e., Q. 17:107: "and We have not sent you, [O Muḥammad], ***except as*** a mercy to the worlds." The Qur'ān here employs the particle *illā*, preceded by negation, to indicate that the sole objective of Muḥammad's prophethood, which is a theological imperative, was nothing but as a mercy for humankind. Ibn ʿAjība contended that the Prophet is a form of mercy not only because he is a cause for happiness and enlightenment in the Here as well as in the Hereafter but also because the prescriptions and proscriptions of the religion that he came with serve one in attaining and maintaining mercy.[9] Ibn Jarīr al-Ṭabarī (d. 923)[10] mentioned that the Prophet is a mercy for believers, but also for the whole world—even though some other commentators restrict his mercy to believers only. Some others contend that he is a mercy to disbelievers in the sense that his adversaries were spared from going through the same types of destruction suffered by the adversaries of previous prophets.[11] Be that as it may, the point here is that the Qur'ān explicitly confirms a "prime cause" behind Muḥammad's prophethood.

C. *Lām al-taʿlīl* (لام التعليل*: in order that)*

An example of this particle is Q. 11:7: "It is He who created the heavens and the earth in six days—and His Throne had been upon water—***in order that*** He might test you as to which of you is best in deed." This verse clearly mentions that people are tried in this life "in order for" God to make manifest who among them is most virtuous in action. Hence, the trials that one encounters in life are not in vain. In fact, "when met with the correct response, they can only help strengthen one's spirituality, improve one's character, and increase one's love for God and trust in Him. From this perspective, trials are a Blessing and a Mercy from God."[12] To indicate this wisdom, the Qur'ān uses the *subjunctive* preposition *lām al-taʿlīl,* which signifies a sense of "rationalization."

While al-Zamakhsharī used this verse to highlight God's recognition of having wisdom behind His actions on earth and that He does so in the interest of humans,[13] al-Rāzī objected. Similar to the case above, although he recognized that this verse may lend support to such a rationalistic interpretation, he quickly remembered his theological paradigm, concluding that the *lām* here is not *lām al-taʿlīl* (the *subjunctive* preposition) but rather *lām al-amr* (the *jussive* mood, meaning "should" or "let"). According to his interpretation, the meaning would be "let you be tried," not that God necessarily considers the interests of humans.[14]

D. *Lʿalla* (لعل *: so that)*

The three Qur'ānic verses, Q. 6:151–153, which detail the Ten Commandments as accentuated in the three monotheistic traditions are good examples of the usage of the particle ***lʿalla*** in a causative manner. These three verses repeat the word ***lʿalla*** three times to signify the rationale of those Commandments. It is worth quoting the verses at length here:

> Say, "Come, I will recite what your Lord has prohibited to you. Do not ascribe anything as a partner to Him, and to parents, good treatment, and do not kill your children out of poverty; We will provide for you and them. And do not approach immoralities—what is apparent of them and what is concealed. And do not kill the soul which God has made sacred, except by right. This has He instructed you ***so that*** you may use reason. And do not approach the orphan's property except in a way that is best until he reaches maturity. And give full measure and weight in justice. We do not charge any soul except [with that within]

> its capacity. And when you testify, be just, even if [it concerns] a near relative. And the covenant of God fulfill. This has He instructed you ***so that*** you may remember. And, this is My path, which is straight, so follow it; and do not follow [other] ways, for you will be separated from His way. This has He instructed you ***so that*** you may become righteous.

E. Ḥattā of causation (حتى التعليلية : so that)

An example of the usage of this preposition for the function of causation is Q. 41:53, which says, "We will show them Our signs in the horizons and within themselves ***so that*** it becomes clear to them that it is the truth." The verse explains that the aim of God's displaying of His signs in the universe and in ourselves is to reveal the truth so that humans may be guided.

While Qur'ān commentators disagreed on what is decisively meant by this verse, they agreed that it shows some of the objectives of God's revelation of His signs. Al-Rāzī in his *al-Tafsīr al-kabīr* illustrated that many interpret "Our signs in the horizons" in relation to the conquering of the lands surrounding Makkah, and those signs "within themselves" as an indication of the conquest of Makkah itself. Others understood "signs in the horizons" to be in reference to celestial bodies, as well as the created design referred to across the Qur'ān, and those "within themselves" to indicate the many phases of human life, including conception, gestation, maturation, and demise, as referred to throughout the Qur'ān.[15] What is of close relevance to our discussion here is the antecedent of the pronoun "it" (*hu*) in "it is the truth." Some commentators say it is a reference to the Qur'ān, others say it is a reference to Islam, and various others say it is a reference to everything which Prophet Muḥammad called people to.[16] Irrespective of these various views, commentators are in agreement that there is a wisdom/objective behind God's exposure of His signs. To express this, the verse uses the preposition *ḥattā*.

H. Verbal Sentences (الجمل الفعلية)

Q. 7:172–173 clearly use this tool:

> And [mention] when your Lord took from the children of Adam—from their loins—their descendants and made them testify of themselves, [saying to them], "Am I not your Lord?" They said, "Yes, we have testified." [This]—***lest*** you should say on the day of Resurrection,

"Indeed, we were of this unaware." Or [*lest*] you say, "It was only that our fathers associated partners with God before, and we were but descendants after them. Then would You destroy us for what the falsifiers have done?"

Unpacking those verses, in multiple places the Qur'ān mentions the Covenants that took place between God and the believers, most notably with Abraham, the Israelites, the Christians, and the People of the Book collectively. However, the Covenant mentioned here is a universal one. To many commentators, this verse is connected with the Qur'ānic concept of the *fiṭra*, the primordial nature upon which humans were created, "indicating that the innate recognition of God's Oneness constitutes the essence of being human. Even though human beings do not remember the pretemporal covenant, their testimony to God's Lordship is understood to have left an indelible imprint upon their souls and to have established moral responsibility for them."[17]

What is of special relevance to us here is that the verse concludes by explaining that the aim of this questioning and testifying is so that humans could not come on the Day of Judgment alleging to have been unaware of God's Deity or their duty to worship Him. The linguistic tool used here to signify causation is the verbal sentence in its entirety. However, one may ask: How can one be responsible for a testimony that one cannot remember having committed to? Hence, some exegetes contended that it is for this human incapability to remember the Covenant that messengers were sent as "reminders" to humans of what they already knew internally but have only forgotten. Hence, "those who deny and reject the prophetic messages sent to them are described as *kuffār*, a word most commonly translated 'disbelievers,' but whose etymological meaning signifies the 'covering over' of something, which in the religious sense refers to covering over the innate awareness of the truth of God's Lordship and Oneness that they bear within themselves."[18]

Neither āl-Zamakhsharī nor āl-Rāzī offered any purpose-driven explanations to these verses, but Ibn ʿAjība did offer such insights, using a language of purposefulness. He stated that God did not do all this for no purpose, but rather for hating that humans would say on the Day of Judgment that they were heedless of such a Covenant.[19]

J. Nominal Sentences (الجمل الإسمية)

Perhaps Q. 2:213 would serve as an evident example of such sentences. It states, "Mankind was [of] one religion; then God sent the Prophets as bringers of good tidings and warners and sent down with them the Scripture in truth to judge between the people concerning that in which they differed." This verse refers to the period between Adam and Noah. While some exegetes argued that people were "unified in disbelief," which was then rectified by Noah and then Abraham, others went for the opposite, arguing that people were in a state of unity in submission (*islām*) to God whereby all humans followed one religion. More distantly, other exegetes ascribe this oneness to the person of Adam, meaning that humanity began as one individual who is Adam, but then they multiplied. Even more distantly, "others understand one community as an allusion to the pretemporal covenant all human beings made with God, described in 7:172."[20] Be that as it may, the relevance of this verse to us is its expressing that the objective of sending prophets is to reform the behavior of humans and correct their wrongdoings.

With this representative presentation, I hope that I have successfully demonstrated that the Qur'ān uses a language of reasoning in reference to theological questions and that it does not abstain from ascribing "purposefulness" to God, despite the theological subtleties involved. In what follows, I aim to showcase how the Sunna does a similar job with *Maqāṣid al-ʿAqīda.*

The Sunna and Maqāṣid al-ʿAqida

First of all, should the Sunna be binding to the emerging genre of *Maqāṣid al-ʿAqīda*? Some qualifications and clarifications need to be made before we answer this question. Prophet Muḥammad is unquestionably the most well acquainted with the secrets of this religion. Hence, the knowledge that comes through him is, in principle, indispensable to any Islamic discourse, for what he conveys, especially of the metaphysical world (*ʿālam al-ghayb*), cannot be divulged by experimentation in the way a physician, for example, comes to know things. Nor are such things comprehensible through rational endeavors. Indeed, as al-Ghazālī wrote, "rational beings in their entirety all acknowledge that the mind cannot find a way to what comes after death [until it dies] and cannot direct [others] to the way sins harm and how good acts benefit [after death]; especially not in any detailed and all-encompassing fashion in the way that the Divinely revealed laws have."[21] In fact, this knowledge of the Prophet led a group of scholars to argue that the Prophet did not die until God disclosed to him knowledge of all the created world, whether in the Here or in the Hereafter.[22]

Despite these references to the epistemic authority of Prophet Muḥammad, a significant degree of caution must be exercised here, for, in reality, it is not the authority of the Prophet that is at stake, but rather that of the Sunna, which constitutes the locus of what we know about what he taught. Therefore, the key question becomes primarily one of "authenticity" and not one of "authority." Having realized the speculative (*ẓannī*) nature of the Sunna, mainstream Sunni theologians did not consider reports of the Sunna to be authoritative and binding in theological articles, as theology was thought to be demanding "certitude," which is lacking in the vast majority of the Sunna tradition, for they engender "speculative" rather than "certain" knowledge of past events.[23]

Sunna becomes even more problematic when a *ḥadīth* is stripped of its context and the prophetic input in it is mixed with that of the narrator, which is often the case. Abou El Fadl called this problem the problem of "multiple authorship" and "authorial enterprise." By these concepts he referred to the process of determining the extent to which the Prophet had really said what is ascribed to him, contending that when assessing such reports, it needs to be borne in mind that these reports are an outcome of not simply what the Prophet said but rather what a number of Companions have seen or heard, recollected, selected, and transmitted as attributable to the Prophet; hence *ḥadīths* have multiple authorship.[24] All these elements influence both the authenticity of *ḥadīth* as well as its authority. Therefore, he argued, "each tradition attributed to the Prophet is the end-product of an authorial enterprise."[25]

Will these perplexities deter us from taking the Sunna seriously in this theological enterprise? The short answer: no. However, three key qualifications will be applied. First, I depart from the classical theory which reads the Qurʾān in the light of the Sunna,[26] to take the view that reads and understands the Sunna in the light of the Qurʾān. This is for an obvious reason, i.e., the Qurʾān's incomparable authenticity. Second, instead of reading the Sunna atomistically and individualistically by deducing rulings from each *ḥadīth* on its own merit, I read it holistically and thematically to infer general conclusions, by gathering together all pertinent reports relating to one theme. This method is somewhat similar to what al-Shāṭibī introduced to *Maqāṣid al-Sharīʿa*, i.e., inductive reasoning (*istiqrāʾ*), as a method for identifying the higher objectives of Islamic law. This holistic approach is premised on the idea that an authentic understanding of the Sunna is achieved only if all the relevant *ḥadīths* dealing with a given concept "are analysed and subsequently synthesized into a larger framework of its interpretation by means of a corroborative induction."[27] In doing so, we may overcome the *ẓannī* nature of the Sunna, for while individual *ḥadīths* may not engender certainty on their own ground, when read together their epistemic value may move from probability to certainty, for a decisive conclusion may be drawn from a plurality of indecisive (*ẓannī*) traditions. For instance, as al-Shāṭibī pointed out, nowhere in the Qur'ān does it say that the *Sharīʿa* is there for the benefit of people. However, if all the relevant verses are gathered together, they end up inferring this decisive conclusion.[28]

The third qualification is to examine the context (*siyāq*) of each *ḥadīth*, where possible, so that we may know what the Prophet had really intended. Al-Ghazālī provided us with an example of how knowing the "context" may help us read the Sunna in a *maqāṣidī*-oriented manner. The Prophet is reported to have said once to his wives, "[O]ne who has the longest hands amongst you would meet me most immediately [after death]." The narrator of this tradition, his wife ʿĀ'isha, then said, "[T]he wives of the Prophet began to measure their hands as to whose hand was the longest and it was the hand of Zaynab that was the longest amongst them, because she used to work with her hand and spend (that income) on charity." Having heard the tradition, some of the wives of the Prophet took the word "longest" literally, and hence they started to measure and compare each other's hand sizes, until it was made clear to them that what he meant is "openhandedness through giving," not the physical size of the human body part. The Prophet uttered this tradition in a context in which it was understood that the objective is "openhandedness," but when the expression was stripped of its context, some of the wives were misled. It could not be said that the Prophet uttered an unqualified or a loose statement, as his statement was directed at those in attendance within a discussion about generosity/charity and those attending understood it rightly. However, transmitters often narrate "a text" without reporting its "context," either because the context was not transmittable or they deemed it unnecessary, thinking that anyone who would hear it would understand it as they themselves did, without realizing that they themselves may have understood it only because they themselves knew the context.[29]

With these principles in mind, this monograph operates on the premise that the Sunna should not be excluded from this genre, but rather be employed with the qualifying tools of *istiqrā'* and *siyāq* so that we may trace and deduce *Maqāṣid al-ʿAqīda* from its canonical collections and therefore verify the surety of those *maqāṣid* by following closely the consistency of our premises and conclusions.

Maqāṣid al-ʿAqīda *between Exotericism and Esotericism*

If all that has been said in the previous section is conceded, then one key challenge needs to be addressed before we move to the theorization of *Maqāṣid al-ʿAqīda*. That is, scriptural texts often lend themselves to different interpretations, ranging between esotericism and exotericism. Coming from a textualist orthodox perspective, the natural question that arises is: How do we know if we are not falling into any of these extremes in our pursuit of *Maqāṣid al-ʿAqīda*? Here I appeal to al-Ghazālī's genre, for what he has to offer is paramount.

Al-Ghazālī asked whether the explicit text implies implicit purposes that should be sought after. In his *Qawāʿd al-ʿaqāʾid* (The Foundations of the Articles of Faith), he thoroughly examined this question. In response to those who deny that there are internal purposes to the externalities of the texts, he argued that the division of truth into hidden and obvious is indisputable. It is only denied by the ignorant who do not go beyond uncritical imitation of their teachers or their forefathers.[30] To support his position, he quoted Q. 29:42, which states, "These similitudes do We set forth to men: and none understands them except those who know." Then he mentioned that the Prophet also said, "If you only knew what I know, you would laugh little and cry much." If the lack of able recipients, al-Ghazālī said, was not the reason, why then did the Prophet not explain such mysteries to his attendees? Commenting on Q. 65:12, "It is God who has created seven heavens and as many earths; the Command comes down among them," al-Ghazālī quoted Ibn ʿAbbās's (d. 687)[31] statement, "[W]ere I to offer its interpretation, you would stone me," and in another narration, "[Y]ou would have said: he is an unbeliever." Al-Ghazālī also quoted the following tradition: "Verily there is to the Qurʾān an external meaning and an internal meaning." The Prophet is reported to have said, "We, prophets, were ordered to communicate with people according to their own abilities of understanding."[32] All these references are highlighted by al-Ghazālī to make the case that we should go beyond the external meanings of texts.

Having established the twofold division of internal and external aspects of religious truth, al-Ghazālī pointed out that the internal meaning is of five types. ***First*** is when the reality of something is in and of itself subtle and goes beyond the comprehension of the masses. This type includes discussions about some of the attributes of God and the reality of the soul (*rūḥ*). The Prophet did not go beyond stating the obvious meanings of certain Divine attributes, such as Knowledge and Power, due to the fact that people also have certain qualities which they know as knowledge and power. Consequently, they would understand the Divine attributes of Knowledge and Power only by way of analogy in relation to themselves. To give an example, the pleasure of sexual intercourse is ungraspable for a child, except in relation to an experienced pleasure, such as that of eating, which is a pleasure that they can comprehend but is actually far different from sexual pleasure. And yet the difference between Divine Knowledge and Power and human knowledge and power is vaster even than the difference between the pleasures of sex and eating. One understands things in relation to oneself or one's internal and external experiences. Alluding to this type, the Prophet said, "I shall not praise You [Lord] as You praised Yourself," admitting his inability to grasp the essence of the majesty of God. For the same reason, it is rightly said, "No one has truly known God except God Himself." Concluding this discussion, al-Ghazālī mentioned that perhaps the Prophet meant this type of esoteric knowledge when he said, "Verily God has seventy veils of light. If He would remove them, the majesty of His face would consume everyone whose eyes might happen to behold His glory."[33]

Second are things which are themselves intelligible for the masses, yet mentioning them is dangerous to most listeners—though they are not so for the Prophets and godly persons. An example of this is the secret of Predestination. Indeed, certain types of truths may be damaging to some people, just as the light of the sun is damaging to the eyes of bats. For instance, many have mistakenly understood the fact that nothing happens on earth expect by God's Will, including unbelief, adultery, and sin, as a divine approval of evil itself.[34] Another example of this type is that God did not divulge the Judgment's appointed time, out of consideration for people's welfare and well-being. If the appointed time was to be divulged, either the intervening period would be too distant, resulting in people's heedlessness and laxity, or it would be too close, which may result in people's fearful obsession with it, leading to the negligence of the cultivation of Earth. So revealing its appointed time in both ways would lead to the destruction of lives in the Here and would hinder chances of salvation in the Hereafter.[35]

Third is when the reality of something is neither unintelligible nor damaging, but it is expressed metaphorically so that its impact on the listener may go deeper. Of this type are the words of the Prophet when he said, "Is he who raises his head from prostration before the *imām* not afraid that God will transform his head into that of a donkey?" Nevertheless, this never did occur in a literal sense, but rather metaphorically, since the head of the donkey is just a parable; it is mentioned not for its form but for its characteristic of foolishness. Thus, whoever would raise his head from prostration before the *imām*, his head would become like that of a donkey only in terms of foolishness. In another instance, God expresses His Power in a metaphorical sense when He says in Q. 16:42, "Our words to a thing when We will it is but to say, 'Be,' and it is." The signification of this verse is not feasible, for if the word

"Be" was addressed to the thing before it came into existence, it would simply be an "impossibility since the non-existent does not understand this address and, therefore, cannot obey."[36] And if it was addressed to the thing after it has come into existence, it would be superfluous, since the thing is already in existence and does not need to be brought into existence. However, since this allegory is more impactful upon the hearts in purveying the idea of Divine Power, it was preferred.[37]

Fourth is when man comprehends the reality of something in a general way and then, after further examination and experience, he comprehends its particulars such that it becomes a part of him. That is, he moves from a superficial knowledge about something to a deeper level. An example is a man who sees someone in the night and then sees him nearby in the day. While he certainly realizes differences between the first and second picture, the latter picture is not opposed to the former but rather complementary to it.[38]

Before we move to the fifth type, it is worth stating that although people may differ in their comprehension of these four types, none of them suggests an esoteric meaning which is not in harmony with the exoteric meaning. Rather, the exoteric and the esoteric meanings complement one another, just as the pith is completed by the husk and preserved by it. Hence, the key axiom is that not every esoteric interpretation is acceptable arbitrarily; it need not negate the exoteric meanings of the scripture. Otherwise, it becomes an invalid interpretation.[39] This axiom is so significant in our derivation of *maqāṣid.*

Fifth is when words are used completely metaphorically. While the unenlightened takes them literally, the enlightened will comprehend the secret behind such words. An example of this type is Q. 41:11: "Then turned He to the heaven when it was smoke, and said unto it and unto the earth: Come both of you, willingly or loth. They said: We come, willingly." The unenlightened would think the Heaven and the Earth have an ability to communicate with God, whereas the enlightened would surely take it metaphorically as symbolizing submission to God's Will.[40]

In this fifth category, al-Ghazālī pointed out, the overlap between the esoteric interpretation and the exoteric reaches its zenith, whereby they may go beyond the point of reconciliation. Hence, people are either, in this respect, radicals or moderates. Radicals are of two extremes. Some radicals have gone so far in the metaphorical interpretation that they have removed completely, or mostly, the exoteric meanings of scripture. For example, philosophers explain away all soteriological representations metaphorically, arguing that such texts symbolize only mental and spiritual pain or gain, refusing the bodily resurrection but accepting only the immortality of the soul. On the other side of the spectrum, other radicals went so far in their literal interpretation to deny the metaphorical interpretation of the word "Be" in Q. 16:42, claiming "that these words were words of actual speech with enunciated letters and sounds brought into existence by God every moment He creates a thing."[41] In the middle lay the moderates, who allowed metaphorical interpretation in everything related to the Divine attributes but have taken things relating to the Hereafter literally; these are the Ashʿarites. Their train of thought is often subtle and obscure, yet they are guided by revelation and reason together. To them, the esoteric and exoteric facets of truth may well be in harmony with one another, and no inherent dichotomy needs to be there.[42]

In his *Mishkāt al-anwār* (The Niche of Lights), al-Ghazālī recognized that his readers may understand from this approach that he was giving license to overlooking the exoteric text of the Qur'ān to more esoteric interpretations of it. Hence, he warned his readers not to misunderstand this subtlety. He wrote, "Do not assume from this specimen of symbolism and its method that you have any license from me to ignore the outward and visible form, or to believe that it has been annulled." Then he gave an example of a possible misreading of this subtlety, using the example mentioned in the Qur'ān, of God asking Moses to remove his shoes before encountering Him on Mount Sinai. Al-Ghazālī did not deny that Moses was literally asked to remove his shoes, but he added to this interpretation a metaphorical one, asserting that what Moses understood from the divine command "Remove your shoes" was to get rid of the Two Worlds, and hence he obeyed the divine command literally by removing his sandals, and spiritually by removing himself from the Two Worlds. "Here you just have this cross-relation between the two, the crossing over from one to the other, from outward word to inward idea."[43]

Hence, the difference between al-Ghazālī and the Bāṭinites[44] becomes clear. He contended that the exclusion of the literal interpretation is the way of the Bāṭinites, "who, looked, utterly one-sidedly, at one world—the Unseen—and were grossly ignorant of the balance that exists between it and the Seen."[45] However, by negating the Bāṭinites, al-Ghazālī did not place himself in agreement with the literalist readers of the scripture (*Ḥashawīyya*) who do not read any inward meaning underneath the surface of the letter of the text, even if such inward meaning were to serve the purpose of the text. He critiqued both ways; whoever abstracts and isolates the outward from the whole is a literalist, and whoever abstracts the inward is a Bāṭinite. What al-Ghazālī argued for is a path that combines both, the inward as well as the outward, in a conciliatory manner in conformity with the tradition that says "The Qur'ān has an outward and an inward."[46]

When those subtleties are not dealt with carefully, we are doomed to misunderstand the scripture. An example of this misunderstanding is a man who hears the tradition "The angels of God enter not a house wherein is a dog or a picture" and yet keeps a dog at home, believing that the outward meaning is not intended here, assuming that what was meant by the Prophet is to turn the dog of anger out of the house of the Heart, because anger prevents the knowledge that comes from the angelic light. This is a one-sided understanding of the tradition that annuls the outward meaning of the Prophetic text, al- Ghazālī wrote. The right interpretation is to take the Prophetic order at its face value, but to also dig deeper to discover the inward meaning. That is to say, that which makes a dog a dog is not just its physical and visible shape but also its underlying traits of ferocity, ravenousness, and anger. Hence, if a house must be kept clear of dogs in their physical form, then it is in even more need of being cleared of the qualities of dogs.

However, it takes a wise person, said al-Ghazālī, to combine the inward and outward interpretations of the text and keep them both in line.[47] Being conscious of the intricacies involved in the process of keeping a balance between those dimensions, al-Ghazālī offered his readers a rule of thumb that will be useful to the genre of *Maqāṣid al-ʿAqīda*. The rule is that "every inward that nullifies the outward is invalid" (*kullu bāṭinin khālafa al-ẓāhir fa-huwa bāṭil*); they must go hand in hand.[48]

Therefore, what is to be taken from this discussion in relation to *Maqāṣid al-ʿAqīda* is the critical need to dig deeper into the secrets of the scriptural texts, for literal interpretations would not reveal much of the *maqāṣid* of the Qurʾān and Sunna. However, falling into purely esoteric interpretations is another extreme that needs to be avoided. One can only hope that this monograph will meet those standards set by al-Ghazālī. To achieve this, this monograph tries to synthesize two modes of knowledge: textual-hermeneutic knowledge (*bayānī*) and demonstrative knowledge (*burhānī*). The *bayānī* mode refers to transmitive knowledge in which authority is given to the scriptural text (*naṣṣ*), whereas the *burhānī* mode refers to knowledge gained by syllogistic and logical reasoning, using premises that are "undoubted" to result in "undoubted" conclusions. Having said that, I recognize that *burhānī* methods are "surely" helpful when applied to empirical subjects, but this "surety" is questionable when applied to nonempirical subjects such as theology.[49] Nevertheless, I am motivated to take this risk, primarily moved by the fact that theologians who managed to synthesize those two modes of knowledge, al-Ghazālī being a case in point, besides intuitive knowledge (*ʿirfānī*), seem to have revolutionized the Islamic tradition and revitalized its sources, when they used inference (*istidlāl*), deduction (*istinbāṭ*), and induction (*istiqrāʾ*) as methods to systematically draw rulings and precepts from this scriptural tradition.

Finally, having examined the sources to be consulted, the methods to be used, and the complexities that need to always be borne in mind, we are now well positioned to move to the next chapter, which is the meat of this monograph, namely, the actual theorization for *Maqāṣid al-ʿAqīda*.

3

From Maqāṣid al-Sharīʿa *to* Maqāṣid al-ʿAqīda

IN THE CONTEXT of *Maqāṣid al-Sharīʿa,* early consensus on the numeration of the objectives of Islamic law started with al-Juwaynī (d. 1085) and al-Ghazālī, who set them at five types of preservation: first, the preservation of *al-nafs* (life), via *ḥadd al-qiṣāṣ* (penalty of retaliation); second, the preservation of *al-dīn* (religion), via *ḥadd al-ridda* (penalty for apostasy); third, the preservation of *al-nasl* (family or lineage), via *ḥadd al-zinā* (penalty for illicit sexual intercourse); fourth, the preservation of *al-māl* (property or wealth), via *ḥadd al-sariqa* (penalty for robbery); fifth, the preservation of *al-ʿaql* (mind), via *ḥadd shurb al-khamr* (penalty for drinking alcohol). Al-Qarāfī (d. 1285) later added the *maqṣad* of the preservation of *al-ʿirḍ* or *karāma* (honor) based on the existence of a penalty against slander or bearing false witness, which is *ḥadd al-qadhf* (penalty for the false accusation of adultery).[1]

"Interrogating" the Classical "Theory" of Maqāṣid al-Sharīʿa

A number of observations on this fivefold theory is in order. First, one may notice that this fivefold typology have emerged as a positive corollary to the *ḥudūd* (penalties). To put it more basically, given that the Qur'ān and Sunna prescribe certain physical punishments to be meted out at the misconduct of humans, there was a pressing need to explain those penalties. This fivefold scheme of preservation offered itself as a compelling tool of explanation. Therefore, one may reasonably say that this scheme is primarily *ḥudūd*-based, which is a problematic base per se, for *ḥudūd* are culturally specific and contextually dependent.

The Higher Objectives of Islamic Theology. Mohammed Gamal Abdelnour, Oxford University Press.
 DOI: 10.1093/oso/9780197648636.003.0003

Second, there seems to be some inconsistency in this *ḥudūd*-based scheme itself. Lumping together the preservation of *ʿaql*, *dīn*, and *nafs*, which are internal and nonmaterial entities, with the preservation of *māl* and *nasl*, which are external and material entities, does not seem linear or logical. Intuitively, one would have expected the classification to either consistently predicate *maqāṣid* on nonmaterial entities, such as *nafs*, or consistently predicate them on objectified possessions, such as *māl*. However, this inconsistency is understandable (but not necessarily justifiable) when we observe that this scheme is primarily an outcome of measuring *maqāṣid* against *ḥudūd*.

Third, taking *ḥudūd* as the starting point of *Maqāṣid al-Sharīʿa* leads to another type of inconsistency. That is, according to Q. 2:255[2] and Q. 10:99,[3] Islam ensures freedom of faith and assures that God has no interest in a faith that comes through compulsion, yet, according to this fivefold scheme, once one accepts Islam as a religion, this right is abandoned due to the penalty of apostasy.[4] So, one is left with a conflict of rights and penalties in this framework.

Fourth, this scheme seems to have "reduced" Islam to a code of law when it subdued theology (i.e., the perseveration of faith) to Islamic law by considering its preservation as one of its objectives, even though theology is commonly regarded as the science of *uṣūl al-dīn* (matters primary to the Islamic faith),[5] as opposed to law, which is often viewed as the science of *furūʿ al-dīn* (matters complementary to the Islamic faith). Therefore, it is the *uṣūl* that should have capacity to preserve the *furūʿ*, and not the other way around.

Fifth, not only did this fivefold scheme reduce Islam to a code of law, but it also involved an intellectual jump from the genus (Islam) to one of its particulars (*Sharīʿa*), underestimating the roles that theology and Sufism may have to play in the shaping of the Muslim theory of *maqāṣid*. As stated at the outset of this monograph, Islam's higher objective is not only the pursuit and achievement of Justice (the function of Islamic law) but also the pursuit and achievement of Truth (the function of Islamic theology) and Beauty (the function of Sufism), all in line with the well-known *ḥadīth* of Angel Gabriel (*ḥadīth Jibrīl*), to which we shall turn shortly. Therefore, *Sharīʿa* (Islamic law) is only a subcategory of Islam. This intellectual jump indicates a need to develop a theory (or theories) of *Maqāṣid al-ʿAqīda* and *Maqāṣid al-Taṣawuf* and also, and more importantly, a theory (or theories) of *Maqāṣid al-Islām*, which is the genus under which theology, law, and Sufism operate.

Sixth, this classical conceptualization of *Maqāṣid al-Sharīʿa* may well have resulted in giving *Maqāṣid al-Sharīʿa* a function of mere "explanation" (i.e., explaining the *ḥudūd*), as opposed to having a function of "information," whereby it could "inform" the fatwa-making process. However, historically, this function of "information" did not exist as such, for *Maqāṣid al-Sharīʿa* remained on the periphery of the legal tradition, essentially becoming an area of "abstraction," as opposed to "action," largely alienated from the minds of most jurists when forming their fatwas. It was only in modern Islam when *Maqāṣid al-Sharīʿa* was brought to the fore.

Seventh, the classical theory is more "conservative" than "acquisitive." Namely, it largely reduced the role of *Maqāṣid al-Sharīʿa* to the function of "preservation" (*ḥifẓ*), underrating the function of "acquisition" (*ṭalab*). While the *faqīh* (Muslim jurist) in the former is concerned with "persevering" the higher objectives of the tradition, in the latter he is additionally concerned with "pursuing" the means that may capture those higher objectives and the instruments that may "promote" them.

Finally, and more germane to our subject, centralizing *ḥudūd* may have contributed to the underdevelopment of *Maqāṣid al-ʿAqīda*, for the weakest of all *ḥudūd* in terms of authenticity and the most controversial in terms of authority is the penalty of apostasy, which is the one and only theology-related penalty in this scheme. Had the genre of *Maqāṣid al-Sharīʿa* taken a value-based system instead of a *ḥudūd*-based system, I argue, different objectives may have been developed. Realizing this lacuna, Adis Duderija wrote the following:

> When engaging in the process of developing Qur'anic hermeneutics and Islamic legal theory (*usūl ul-fiqh*) and, generations upon generations of Islamic legal theorists (*usuliyyūn*), jurists (*fuqahāʾ*) and exegetes (*mufassirūn*) have primarily concerned themselves with the questions of what the Qur'an has to say on a particular issue or theme but not what the Qur'an tacitly assumes to be normative as understood by its direct audience and as evident in the Qur'an's content. They did not fully recognize the interpretational implications of the Qur'anic pre-suppositions present in its discourse, especially in relation to developing a Qur'anic hermeneutic and Islamic legal theory whose most powerful hermeneutical tool would entail ethico-religious values and purposive (qasd) based–approach [*sic*] to interpretation of the Qur'an and Sunna and the purposive nature of Islamic law and its philosophy.[6]

It should be noted that I am not unique in my critiques of the classical theory. ʿAllāl al-Fāsī in his *Maqāṣid al-Sharīʿa al-islāmiyya wa makārimuhā* (The Objectives of *al-Sharīʿa* and Its Merits) recognized a number of issues with the classical *ḥudūd*-based theory of *maqāṣid* and therefore attempted to develop the idea that the governing and defining value behind this *ḥudūd*-based scheme is the pursuit and achievement of "justice."[7] The same applies to Mohamed S. El-Awa in *The Objective of Justice in the Noble Qur'ān*. Similarly, al-Raysūnī wrote the treatise *Maqāṣid al-maqāṣid* (The Objectives of the Objectives) in an attempt to develop an underlying value-based structure to the genre of *Maqāṣid al-Sharīʿa*.[8] That is to say that not a few contemporary scholars have felt the need to look for "ethical values" behind the Islamic legal system. Therefore, they argued that "justice" is the byproduct of the legislation and application of *ḥudūd*. Put differently, "*maqāṣid* exist to promote justice."[9]

In the light of the above critiques, the proposed alternative here not only attempts to base the Islamic tradition on a system of ethical values, but it also aims to give the genre of *maqāṣid* two other functions in addition to the function of "preservation." Those two functions are "acquisition" and "promotion," whereby "acquisition" precedes the function of "preservation," and "promotion" succeeds it. Hence, *maqāṣid* will not only be viewed as "preservers" of Truth, Justice, and Beauty but also as "acquirers" and "promoters" of such values. In doing so, the function of the *maqāṣid* would also move from mere "explanation" of *ḥudūd* and its likes to having an active "participation" in the formation and promotion of the underlying values of the tradition. This "active participation" would also ensure that *maqāṣid* would not be seen as "static entities" but rather as "dynamic" ones that speak to the actual realities of Muslims and help them materialize the higher objectives of their tradition in their respective social and cultural realities. This is partly why I believe in the concept of "provisional truth," as shall be explained later in the book.

"Generating" the Higher Objective(s) of Islamic Theology

In light of the above critique, what I am offering here is the widening of the scope of *maqāṣid* to include the genres of theology and Sufism and the basing of this genre not on "penalties" but rather on "moralities." To recall the argument with which I began this book, I contend that there are three transcendental values that Islam came to pursue, preserve, and promote: Truth (*al-Ḥaqq*), Justice (*al-ʿAdl*), and Beauty (*al-Jamāl*). These three values correspond to three aspects from the Islamic fields of interest: theology, law, and Sufism. I argue that while Islamic law's major objective is the pursuit, preservation, and promotion of Justice and Sufism's major objective is the pursuit, preservation, and promotion of Beauty, Islamic theology's major objective is the pursuit, preservation, and promotion of Truth.

These three values are extracted from the well-known *ḥadīth* of Gabriel (*ḥadīth Jibrīl*). The narrative of this *ḥadīth* contains three constituents that embody the best summary of the core of Islam: first, *islām* (submission), with its five pillars (faith testimony, prayer, charity, fasting, pilgrimage); second, *īmān* (faith), with its six articles (faith in God, His angels, His books, His messengers, the Last Day, and Predestination); third, *iḥsān* (excellence), which is simply exercising that which is beautiful and excellent. This *ḥadīth* exists, with some variation in words, in both *Ṣaḥīḥ al-Bukhārī* and *Ṣaḥīḥ Muslim*, the soundest books of *ḥadīth* in the Sunni tradition and is described by al-Nawawī as the pillar (*aṣl*) of Islam.[10] The Companion ʿUmar ibn al-Khaṭṭāb (d. 644) narrated that while a group of the Companions were sitting with the Prophet, a man came up to them whose clothes were extremely white and whose hair was extremely black, upon whom signs of traveling could not be seen, and none of them knew who he was. He sat down knee to knee with the Prophet and said:

> "[T]ell me about *islām*." The Prophet said: "Islam is that you witness that there is no god but God and that Muḥammad is the Messenger of God, and you establish the prayer, and you give the *zakāh* (charity), and you fast [on] Ramadan, and you perform the *ḥajj* (pilgrimage) to the House (*Kaʿaba*) if you are able." He replied, "You have told the truth," and we were amazed at him asking the Prophet and [then] telling him that he told the truth. He then said, "Tell me about *īmān*." He said, "That you believe in God, His angels, His books, His messengers, and the Last Day, and that you believe in Predestination, the good of it and the bad of it." He said, "You have told the truth." He said, "Tell me about *iḥsān*." He said, "That you worship God as if you see Him, for if you do not see Him then, truly, He sees you." He said, "Tell me about the Hour." He said, "The one asked about it knows no more than the one asking." He said, "Then tell me about its signs." He said, "That the female slave should give birth to her mistress, and you see poor, naked, barefoot shepherds of sheep and goats competing in making tall buildings." He went away, and I remained some time. Then the Prophet asked, "ʿUmar, do you know who the questioner was?" I said, "God and His Messenger know best." He said, "He was Jibrīl who came to you to teach you your *dīn* (religion)."[11]

With this *ḥadīth* in mind, I deduce the above three key values: Truth (*al-Ḥaqq*), Justice (*al-ʿAdl*), and Beauty (*al-Jamāl*). Truth is contained in theology, Justice is contained in law, and Beauty is contained in Sufism. The combination of the three leads to "goodness" (*al- Ṣalāḥ*), as stated in Q. 16:97: "Whoever *does* good, whether male or female, while he is a *believer*—We will surely cause him to live a *good* life, and We will surely give them their reward according to the best of what they used to do." Consequently, I contend that Islamic theology's overriding objective is the pursuit, perseveration, and promotion of Truth (*al-Ḥaqq*).

One might ask, however, why *al-Ḥaqq* and not *falāḥ* (success) or *najāh* (salvation) or any other outcome-based theory? I would say that *falāḥ* and *najāh* and any other outcome-based theory may well serve as a valid objective, not to Islamic theology per se but rather to Islam, the genus, which is a separate genre in itself that has also been overshadowed by the overemphasis on *Maqāṣid al-Sharīʿa*, as I clarified earlier. As for my choice of *al-Ḥaqq* as the overriding objective of Islamic theology, I relied upon four principles identified by Ibn ʿĀshūr, who is arguably the most significant contributor to the *Maqāṣid al-Sharīʿa* in the twentieth century. These four principles are certitude (*thubūt*), evidence (*ẓuhūr*), consistency (*inḍibāṭ*), and regularity (*iṭṭirād*). First, he argued that a *maqṣad* is *certain* when it engenders decisive knowledge or high probability bordering on certainty. Second, a *maqṣad* is *evident* when it is so obvious that scholars would neither dispute its meaning nor, most of them, confuse it with anything else. Third, a *maqṣad* is *consistent* when its interpretation is decisive and has precise limits to it that it does not exceed or fail to meet. Fourth, a *maqṣad* is *regular* when its interpretation does not change according to circumstances of place, people, or age.[12] An example is the preservation of lineal identity (*ḥifz al-nasab*), which is the purpose of the *Sharīʿa* in instituting marriage; it is evident, certain, consistent, and regular that it cannot be confused with the preservation of lineal identity through, for instance, love relationships (*mukhādana*), whereby a female prostitute would attribute her child to a specific man among those who have had sexual intercourse with her.[13]

While Ibn ʿĀshūr applied those principles to "legal" texts, I extend them to "theological" texts too. The rationale behind the applicability of those principles to theology is that these are not "law-based" or "law-specific" principles, but rather text-based principles. If they successfully apply to law-specific texts, there is nothing that may hamper their applicability to theology-specific texts. Hence, these universal principles can arguably be used to test any text-based tradition.

Using inference, deduction, and induction as methods to systematically apply the principles of *certitude*, *evidence*, *consistency*, and *regularity* to theology-specific texts, I found that the pursuit, preservation, and promotion of *al-Ḥaqq* meets each of those principles. In what follows I explain how the place of *al-Ḥaqq* in the Islamic tradition is *certain*, *evident*, *consistent*, and *regular*.

According to the *Arabic Dictionary of Qur'anic Usage*, *al-Ḥaqq* has the following meanings: (1) recognized share, as in Q. 70:24, which says, "And those within whose wealth is a recognized share for the petitioner and the deprived"; (2) justification, as in Q. 3:112, which states, "[T]hey killed the prophets without justification"; (3) due/duty, as in Q. 6:141, which states, "Eat of [each of] its fruit[s] when it yields and give its due [*zakāh*] on the day of its harvest"; (4) correct argument/just claim, as in Q. 24:49, which says, "But if the just claim is theirs, they come to him submissively"; (5) liability, as in Q. 2:282, "[L]et the one who has the liability [debtor] dictate"; (6) an attribute of God when it comes with the definite article, as in Q. 22:6, "That is because God is the Truth"; (8) true, as in Q. 3:62, "This is the true account"; (9) real, as in Q. 51:23, "By the Lord of the Heavens and earth, it is real."[14]

Despite the multiplicity of the meanings of *al-Ḥaqq*, the common denominator in these meanings is "truth," as in Q. 2:42, which says, "And do not mix the truth with falsehood or conceal the truth while you know [it]." This "truth" has many manifestations in the Islamic tradition, extending to the behavior of individuals, to the intellect, to knowledge, to truthful speech.[15] Even more, it extends to God, as one of His Divine Names, indicating that God is the Ultimate Reality and the Absolute Truth, and there is no iota of doubt in His being the One and only deity who is worthy of worship. Q. 31:30 clearly states that "God is the Truth, and that what they call upon other than Him is falsehood." In his *al-Maqṣad al-asnā*, al-Ghazālī contended that the truest assertion in Islamic theology is the believer's statement: There is no true god but God.[16]

Q. 7:43 asserts that the believers on the Day of Judgment will say, "Certainly, the messengers of our Lord had come with the 'truth.'" Furthermore, Q. 8:7 states, "But God intended to establish the Truth by His words." More distantly, Q. 9:33 accentuates, "It is He who has sent His Messenger with guidance and the 'religion of truth' to manifest it over all religion." Even more distantly, in Q. 10:35 Prophet Muḥammad is asked to invite the disbelievers to choose their deities according to the question of who guides one to the "ultimate Truth." The verse literally says, "Say, 'Are there of your partners any who guides to the truth?' Say, 'God guides to the truth. So, is He who guides to the truth more worthy to be followed or he who guides not unless he is guided? Then what is [wrong] with you—how do you judge?' "

Q. 17:105 summarizes the mission of the Qur'ān in "coming with the truth." The verse says, "And with the truth We have sent the Qur'ān down, and with the truth it has descended." Q. 23:71 states, "If the Truth had followed their lowly desires, the heavens and the earth and whoever is in them would have been ruined." God is not only true in Himself but also the source of all truths. His actions are true, His words are true, and the Religion He chose for people is the religion of truth. His actions are true in the sense that they are in harmony with wisdom and uprightness. His Books are mines of truth conveyed to humans at the hands of His truthful messengers. Q. 8:7 relates that God intends to establish the truth on earth and that His aid and honor are stretched to the ones who seek the truth and act upon it. Q. 26:88–89 asserts that on the Day of Judgment nothing will benefit people, neither wealth nor children, "save for him who comes to God with a sound heart." Qur'ān commentators say that a sound heart is a heart that knows God, that He is real, that the Hereafter is also a reality.[17]

The *certitude*, *evidence*, *consistency*, and *regularity* of *al-Ḥaqq* are also evident in the Sunna. On the authority of the Companion ʿAbdullāh Ibn ʿAbbās, al-Bukhārī narrated that whenever the Prophet offered the late-night prayer, he would say, "O God! . . . You are the Truth, and Your Promise is the Truth, and Your Speech is the Truth, and meeting You is the Truth, and Paradise is the Truth and Hell (Fire) is the Truth and all the Prophets are the Truth, and the Hour is the Truth."[18]

While *Maqāṣid al-Sharīʿa* gives special importance to the preservation of the mind (*al-ʿaql*) by prohibiting alcohol, *Maqāṣid al-ʿAqīda* gives equal importance to the perseveration of the heart (*al-qalb*), by virtue of its being . . . the locus of Truth. In fact, the Qur'ān often ascribes the function of reasoning and understanding to the heart rather than the mind, where it says in Q. 7:179, "We have indeed created for Hell many among jinn and men: *they have hearts with which they understand not*." Hence, according to this verse, the heart is the seat of understanding, intelligence, and knowledge. In Q. 41:5, the disbelievers say to the Prophet, "Our hearts," not minds, "are under coverings from that to which you call us, and in our ears is a deafness, and between us and you there is a veil."[19] Additionally, the Prophet is reported to have said, "In the body there is a lump of flesh: when it is healthy, the whole body is healthy, and when it is rotten, the whole body is rotten. Yea, it is the heart."[20] According to the Qur'ān, the heart (*qalb*) "is the organ associated not only with sentiment, but also with consciousness, knowledge, and faith."[21] Al-Ghazālī described in the most poetic manner the centrality of the heart as the locus of truth. It is worth quoting him at length on this:

> The honour and excellence of man, in which he surpasses all other sorts of creatures, is his aptitude for knowing God, praise be to Him. This knowledge is man's beauty and perfection and glory in the present world, and his provision and store for the world to come. He is prepared for this knowledge only through his heart, and not by means of any of his members. For it is the heart that knows God, and works for God, and strives toward God, and draws near to Him, and reveals that which is in the presence of God. The members of the body, on the other hand, are merely followers, servants and instruments that the heart uses and employs as the king uses his slave, as the shepherd makes use of his flock, or as the craftsman uses his tool.
>
> For it is the heart that is accepted by God when it is free from all save Him, but veiled from God when it becomes wholly occupied with anything other than him. It is the heart upon which claims are made, with which conversations are carried on, and with which remonstrance is made, and which is punished. It rejoices in nearness to God and prospers if kept true, and is undone and miserable if debased and corrupted. It is that which in reality is obedient to God, the Exalted, and the acts of devotion that are manifest in the members of the body are but its light. It is that also which is disobedient and rebellious against God, the Exalted, and the acts of turpitude that course through the members are but its effects. By its darkness and its light there appear the good and evil qualities of its external appearance, since "every vessel drips that which it contains." The heart is that which, if a man knows it, he knows himself, and if he knows himself, he knows his Lord. It is that which, if a man knows it not, he knows not himself, and if he knows not himself, he knows not his Lord. He who knows not his own heart is still more ignorant of everything else, since the majority of mankind know not their own hearts and their own selves, for intervention has been made between them and their own selves. For God intervenes between a man and his heart (8:24). His intervention consists in preventing man from observing it [i.e., his heart], and watching over it, and becoming acquainted with its qualities, and perceiving how it is turned between two of the fingers of the Merciful and how at one time it lusts for the lowest of the low and is brought down to the plane of the demons; and at another time, it

> mounts up to the highest of the high, and advances to the world of the angels who are drawn near to God (*al-malālika al-muqarrabūn*). He who knows not his heart, to watch over it and be mindful of it, and to observe what shines on it and in it of the treasures of the world of spirits (*al-malaktūt*), he is one of those of whom God, the Exalted, has said, those who forget God; and He made them to forget their own souls. Such are the rebellious transgressors! (59:19). Thus, the knowledge of the heart and of the real nature of its qualities is the root of religion and the foundation of the mystic traveler's way.[22]

Furthermore, the locus of the divine revelation to Prophet Muḥammad is his heart, according to Q. 26:193–194: "The Trustworthy Spirit [Gabriel] has brought it down Upon your heart, [O Muḥammad]—that you may be of the Warners." Moreover, no one benefits from this revelation except those who heed it with their hearts in accordance with Q. 50:37, which says, "Indeed in that is a reminder for whoever has a heart or who listens while he is present."

The antithesis of the preservation of the heart is the pursuit of one's own lowly desires limitlessly and excessively. This point occupied al-Shāṭibī's *al-Muwāfaqāt*. In his words, "The aim of the *Sharīʿa* is to bring the subject (*al-mukallaf*) out of the urges of his own desideratum to free him from his own whims so that he may be the worshipper of God by his own choice."[23] God considered the pursuit of lowly desires as the antithesis of truth, Q. 38:26 explicitly says: "[We said]: O David, indeed We have made you a successor upon the earth, so judge between the people in truth and do not follow [your own] desire, as it will lead you astray from the way of God." More distantly, Q. 79:41–42 confirms, "But as for he who feared the position of his Lord and prevented the self from [unlawful] inclination, then indeed, Paradise will be [his] destination." With this, said al-Shāṭibī, God has summarized it all: either following revelation or following one's own desires. Al-Shāṭibī then said, "Reflect upon this; in each place in which God has mentioned desire, He has considered it blameworthy and has also rebuked those who pursue it. . . . All this makes it clear that the intention of the Lawgiver is to take the subject out of the pursuit of his own desires and to bring him under the realm of worship of the Master."[24]

Moving from scriptural proofs to historical and customary attestations, al-Shāṭibī wrote, "It has been known through experiences and regularities that the interests of this world and the next cannot be secured through an uncontrolled pursuit of desire, and by corresponding to personal fancies, because they necessarily lead to chaos, mutual fighting and hence destruction, which run counter to these interests." Then he said, "Praise be to God then, who revealed in His Book, in Q. 23:71, 'But if the truth had followed their inclinations, the heavens and the earth and whoever is in them would have been ruined.'"[25]

Having said that, the question that remains to be asked, however, is: What is the nature of the "truth" that Islamic theology came to pursue, preserve, and promote? How does Islamic theology view itself in comparison to other truth-claims? Does it see itself as the only path to truth? Or does it recognize any validity to non-Islamic theologies/truths? These are the questions that will occupy us in the following pages.

The Nature of the Islamic Truth

The Threefold Typology—Exclusivism, Inclusivism, and Pluralism—emerged in the 1980s to consolidate discussions on those questions, which evolved to form a subject on its own, called "Theology of Religions."[26] Using this Typology in his survey of the Islamic views on truth, Rifat Atay argued that Exclusivism has been the most dominant view in the Islamic theological tradition; it is a view that is held by approximately 95 percent of Muslims, scholars and the masses alike. To show this, he focused primarily on the Māturīdī tradition, exemplified in the works of its eponymous founder, Abū Manṣūr al-Māturīdī (d. 944).[27] In *A Comparative History of Catholic and Aš ʿarī Theologies of Truth and Salvation*, I showed how Exclusivism has also been the most prevalent view in classical Ashʿarism, which, if coupled with Māturīdism, constitutes what has loosely been known as Sunni Islam. In her *Christian and Islamic Theology of Religions*, Esra A. Dag confirmed those conclusions, writing:

> In spite of the Qurʾanic affirmation of non-Islamic traditions' certain values, early scholars developed a supersessionist theory which assumed that other religions were superseded by Islam. The doctrine of abrogation in Islamic studies has been discussed in the literature of Islamic jurisprudence (*uṣūl al-fiqh*). . . . The classic, medieval and contemporary forms of exclusivism have been shaped in the light of supersessionist theory. Thus, the positive affirmation of non-Islamic traditions in the Qurʾan has been regarded as abrogated. In other words, the Qurʾanic verses which value the Christian and Jewish traditions have been considered to be part of this abrogation process.[28]

Despite the dominance of the Exclusivist position, a Pluralist trend emerged in the modern Muslim tradition, following the lead of Ibn ʿArabī (d. 1240) and his followers.[29] For instance, Mohammed Arkoun (d. 2010) critiqued this Exclusivism, holding that the tools of legitimization of classical Islamic theology do not possess any "epistemological relevance for us today," as their findings are badly damaged by the "biases imposed by the ruling class and its intellectual servants."[30] He therefore distinguished three levels of divine revelation. First is the absolute level, which is unknowable by humankind, even though the prophets revealed some fragments of the word of God. Second are the prophetic manifestations of the word of God, such as those of the Israelite prophets, Jesus and Muḥammad, from a period when revelation was orally transmitted and preserved through memorization. The third level is the textual objectification of God's word in the Torah, the New Testament, and the Qur'ān.[31] Therefore, to him Pluralism is inevitable. Also, Farid Esack, who, in his *Qur'an, Liberation and Religious Pluralism* endorsed an ethical form of pluralism, believing that truth plurality is the will of God and that the Qur'ān accepts religious others, their spirituality and their salvation.[32] Furthermore, in *The Other in the Light of the One: The Universality of the Qur'an and Interfaith Dialogue*, Reza Shah-Kazemi attempted to go beyond the threefold typology of Exclusivism, Inclusivism, and Pluralism, with a theory of "universalism," in which he posited that each religion manifests a different response to the same reality.[33]

Having said this, I am now in a better position to express my voice on the question of theological truth in Islam. However, before I do so, some insights on the Kantian distinction between the "phenomenon" (the way we see things) and the "noumenon" (the-thing-in-itself) are in order.[34] This distinction has often been made, especially by John Hick,[35] as a key axiom supporting the Pluralist narrative, due to the deep epistemological divide that it created between the knowable and unknowable, the thinkable and unthinkable.[36] Therefore, it is no wonder that it has often given a larger platform to the Pluralist theory. Having said that, although I do not subscribe to theological Pluralism, this Kantian distinction is foundational to my understanding of the Islamic truth, for I take a "methodological," not a "theological," inspiration from it. I see the vitality of this Kantian distinction in challenging the sense of "theological absolutism" prevalent in various theological traditions, including Islamic theology, and that it was this dogmatic absolutism that Kant was fighting against, not theology in the first place.

Furthermore, the Kantian distinction demands another positive method that I find helpful in my understanding of the Islamic truth. That is, it calls for a sense of "methodological agnosticism" when one delves into metaphysical discussions. This "methodological agnosticism" implies that the process and results of thought engender an empirical conclusion rather than an a priori assumption about the questions under review. In his *Methodological Atheism, Methodological Agnosticism and Religious Experience*, Douglas V. Porpora illustrated how theologians may benefit from anthropologists by not taking truth-claims for granted but instead suspend belief in them long enough to investigate alternative explanations.

However, this suspension of belief should not be conflated with not considering the religious truth at all, which is known as "methodological atheism." Methodological agnosticism implies a sense of "provisional relativism" in order for the inquiry process to be "effective" and "genuine."[37] In this context, I find the Kantian distinction between the noumenon and the phenomenon quite enabling to this sort of "healthy agnosticism" and cultivates a sense of "intellectual humility" that is often lacking in dogmatic theologians who hasten to defend preconceived theological positions.

What is more, I see some resonance of this methodological agnosticism in the Qur'ān, whereby it encourages the methodological suspension of belief in a certain proposition until after the pursuit of truth is concluded. Taking this methodological agnosticism as a disciplinary premise, Q. 34:24–25 states, "Say [Muḥammad], 'Who provides for you from the heavens and the earth?' Say, 'God. And surely either we [Believers] or you [Disbelievers] are upon guidance *or* in manifest error.' " Some Qur'ān commentators, most notably al-Ṭabarī, argued that "or," which here translates the particle *aw*, means "and" and thus interpreted this verse to mean "And surely we (the believers) are guided and you (the disbelievers) are in manifest error."[38] Others, most notably al-Rāzī, took the verse at its face value and offered what can be termed a "Qur'ānic methodological agnosticism," maintaining that the verse means "Either we are astray or guided, *or* you are astray or guided," leaving us with this telling comment: "In this verse there is a divine instruction from God to Prophet Muḥammad to guide his scholarly and non-scholarly debates. Otherwise, if one of the debaters says to the other: 'what you say is faulty and you are mistaken,' he will get angry, and anger precludes constructive thinking. . . . However, if he says: 'let us, for the sake of Truth, practice reasoning to know which one of us is mistaken,' then his counterpart will be drawn further from prejudice."[39] I understand this slight and subtle point from al-Rāzī as a gentle invitation to embrace a genuine open-ended inquiry into the Truth that is free from any priori judgments.

Notwithstanding, I do not fully subscribe to the Kantian distinction between noumena and phenomena, for I believe that the Qur'ān gives us access to aspects of noumena, but this access is often clouded by the biases and subjectivities that accompany our quest for the Truth. Indeed, the famous parable of the elephant and the blind men may reveal two key subjectivities: "individual" subjectivities hampering the absorption of the Truth and subjectivities caused by the "context." To explain, the old allegory of the "elephant in darkness," which has its roots in the Buddhist tradition, provides a clear demonstration of the contextual deficiency. According to Rūmī's (d. 1273)[40] version of the story, a group of Hindus bring an elephant to a town at night. People of the town, impatient to wait until morning, go to the dark room where the elephant is kept. Unable to see the animal, they can only perceive it by touching it. Upon touching different parts of the elephant's body, each person describes the elephant differently. One, who has touched its ear, describes it as similar to a fan. Another, who has touched its trunk, says the elephant is like a gutter. A third man, who has touched its leg, describes the elephant as similar to a pillar. Finally, a person who has touched its back describes it as like a bed. If each of them had a candle at hand, there would be no difference in their statements.[41] That is the contextual deficiency, whereby the deficiency to conceive the reality of the elephant is not due to an inherent disability in the human mind per se, but due to the darkness/context surrounding it. This darkness caused by the night constitutes a thick veil preventing those approaching the elephant from the full comprehension of the truth.

While Rūmī's version of the story of the elephant indicates a contextual deficiency, al-Ghazālī's version shows an individual deficiency instead. While, in Rūmī's version, the visitors' inadequate perception of the elephant is due to the darkness of the room at night, al-Ghazālī described those visitors as "physically blind."[42] Therefore, one may conclude that, for al-Ghazālī, most humans are incapable of grasping Truth in its entirety due to individual subjectivities/inadequacies. Although they both differ as regard to the causes of such deficiencies, individual in the case of al-Ghazālī and contextual in the case of al-Rūmī, they both come to the same conclusion: that humans' quest for the Truth is, more often than not, clouded by individual and contextual deficiencies.

Taken together, I neither see the Islamic view of Truth as necessarily Exclusivist, nor do I see it as Inclusivist or Pluralist, but I see it as supporting the ongoing "seeking" of Truth, in tandem with "speaking" of it in the way one provisionally believes it to be. Therefore, Islamic Truth is not static, but dynamic and discursive, in line with Asad's theory of the "discursive tradition," mentioned at the outset of the monograph. The theological Truth that Islam pursues, preserves, and promotes is not necessarily "fully present" but is "provisionally" so. Simultaneously, Islam urges its followers to seek bits and pieces of this Truth wherever it may arise. Consequently, theology should be in the service of the Ultimate Truth, not the other way around.

4

"*Integrating*" *the* "*Tools*" *of* Maqāṣid al-Sharīʿa *into* Maqāṣid al-ʿAqīda

Definition and Transmission

Al-ḍarūriyyāt (the primaries), *al-ḥājiyyāt* (the complementaries), and *al-taḥsīniyyāt* (supplementaries) are basic tools in *Maqāṣid al-Sharīʿa*. As the word itself signifies, *ḍarūriyyāt* refers to things that are indispensable for human life from Islamic law's perspective. Essentially, Muslim jurists divided this zone into what is necessary to preserve one's soul, religion, wealth, mind, and lineage/offspring. That is, human life is in danger if people's "souls" are in danger. Hence, the *Sharīʿa* prohibits killing one another and sanctifies the human soul. Human life is in danger if one's "wealth" is in danger. Hence, *Sharīʿa* prohibits all forms of financial corruption and ordains deterring penalties for their protection. Human life is in danger if the "mind" is in danger. Hence, the *Sharīʿa* bans drinking alcohol and all other intoxicants. Human life is in danger if "lineage" is in danger. Hence, there exist many Islamic principles that regulate all aspects of lineage and offspring, ranging from marriage and divorce to promoting good education. These are considered *ḍarūriyyāt* because neglecting them would result in corruption, anarchy, and disruption.[1]

Ḥājiyyāt are designed to remove hardships and difficulties which are, however, less essential for human life than *ḍarūriyyāt*. Examples of these are commercial laws, means of transportation, and all ways of removing hardship from people's lives. Although the *Sharīʿa* maintains those complementaries, it recognizes that they are not matters of life and death, and that the lack of any of them does not jeopardize any of the above *ḍarūriyyāt*. Nevertheless, those *ḥājiyyāt* have the potential to move from the domain of *ḥājiyyāt* into

The Higher Objectives of Islamic Theology. Mohammed Gamal Abdelnour, Oxford University Press.
 DOI: 10.1093/oso/9780197648636.003.0004

the domain of *ḍarūriyyāt* if the lack of any of these complementaries became prevalent and pandemic.[2]

Taḥsīniyyāt are those that complement the other two, but in a manner of perfection and refinement. The distinction between the level of *taḥsīniyyāt* and that of the other two is best explained in the following manner. The preservation of life, which is a primary objective, cannot be maintained without the maintenance of a good healthcare system, such as hospitals and clinics. Hence, building decent hospitals and clinics becomes a complementary need. However, if one hospital is not enough to provide the needed services for a region, erecting another one is likely to participate in the complementary needs. Having erected a hospital equipped with primary and complementary means, it may then seem "eminently desirable to acquire the more advanced and up-to-date diagnostic equipment, as and when they become available."[3]

Illustrating the relation between the three levels, al-Shāṭibī stated that the *ḍarūriyyāt* are the basis for the other two. If the *ḍarūriyyāt* are disturbed, the other two will naturally be disturbed. However, if the other two are disturbed, the *ḍarūriyyāt* are not necessarily disturbed. Yet the loss of the other two naturally affects the well-being of the *ḍarūriyyāt*. Hence, when the *ḍarūriyyāt* are preserved, it is important to preserve the *ḥājiyyāt* as well, and when the *ḥājiyyāt* are preserved, it is important to pursue the *taḥsīniyyāt*.[4] Nevertheless, it is worthy of mention that the relations between those three zones are not watertight and that there is room for overlap. Hence, under necessities, *ḥājiyyāt* may move from their own realm into the realm of *ḍarūriyyāt* and vice versa.[5]

The question that needs to be asked, however, is whether this taxonomy is applicable to Islamic theology. I argue that it does apply to Islamic theology. Exploring the Qur'ān and the Sunna may provide us with examples that suggest its applicability. The Qur'ān indicates that not everything in the Islamic creed holds the same weight. For instance, the Qur'ān in several places reduces the requirements for salvation to three, as mentioned in Q. 2:62: belief in God, belief in the Last Day, and doing good deeds. However, Q. 3:85 expands such requirements to include belief in "Islam," leaving the term "Islam" unqualified and disputed by exclusivists, inclusivists, and pluralists. And in other places, such as Q. 2:285, it invites people to believe in God, His Angles, His Books, and His Messengers.

Due to this variety, there existed different views on the question of salvation: Exclusivists say that "there is only religious tradition or interpretation of that tradition that leads to salvation, while followers of other beliefs will be punished in hell"; Inclusivists believe that there is only one religion that is authentically salvific, yet "sincere outsiders who could not have recognized it as such will be saved"; and Pluralists believe that "regardless of the circumstances, there are several religious traditions or interpretations that are equally effective salvifically."[6] While exclusivist interpretations essentially appeal to Q. 3:85,[7] inclusivist ones often appeal to Q. 2:285, and pluralists often quote Q. 2:62.

Reconciling these various verses, classical Qur'ān commentators, who largely held the exclusivist interpretation, essentially resorted to either (1) subscribing to the theory of abrogation (*naskh*), stating that, for instance, Q. 2:62 is abrogated by Q. 3:85; or (2) specifying the generality of the more fluid verses, saying, for instance, that the acknowledged Christians and Jews in Q. 2:62 are only those who adhered to these religions before the advent of Prophet Muḥammad, but when Muḥammad came, they forsook their religion and followed his.[8]

In my estimation, both ways involve various degrees of arbitrariness and subjectivity. By "arbitrariness" I refer to the recourse to *naskh* when there is no decisive evident that any of these verses was revealed before or after the other, let alone the controversial nature of *naskh* itself as an exegetical device, as shall be expounded later. By "subjectivity" I refer to the imposition of the interpreter's view on the Qur'ān by deciding what was meant to be general and what was meant to be particular without a demonstrative proof that such is the case.

I argue that the taxonomy of *ḍarūriyyāt*, *ḥājiyyāt*, and *taḥsīniyyāt* may help reconcile these various, seemingly antithetical interpretations without appealing to arbitrary exercises of interpretation and therefore may also serve as an example of the applicability of this taxonomy to Islamic theology. To clarify, all these different interpretations agree on one level but disagree on different ones. So, simply, what they agree about should be included in the zone of *ḍarūriyyāt* and all other disputed requirements should be excluded from this zone but included in the zone of *ḥājiyyāt* or *taḥsīniyyāt*, depending on how they affect the primary purpose of Islamic theology, which is contextually contingent, as shall be clarified in the next section. To put this more basically, if Muslim theologians agree about the necessity to believe in God in order to be saved, then belief in God should alone be in the zone of *ḍarūriyyāt*. On the contrary, if not all of them believe in the notion of *al-firqa al-nājiya* (the saved denomination), this notion should not be included in the zone of *ḍarūriyyāt*, but rather in less important zones. If this approach is taken seriously, it has the potential to open a door for ecumenism in Islamic theology and can help develop an objective-oriented theology.

To further accentuate that not all creedal matters are equal in importance, let us look at Q. 3:7: "It is He who has sent down to you, [O Muḥammad], the Book; in it are verses [that are] beyond dispute—they are the foundation of the Book—and others are disputable/unclear." Taking the verse at face value, not every creedal matter is of the same quality in terms of clarity and, consequently, in terms of essentiality, inviting us to pursue the Qur'ān's *muḥkamāt* (decisive verses) and make them our starting point. I here equate *muḥkamāt* with *ḍarūriyyāt*, arguing that it is the duty of the believer to pursue what is central and essential and distinguish it from what is less central and less essential.

Another scriptural proof may help emphasize the point further. The Prophet once asked his Companion Muʿādh ibn Jabal (d. c. 639), "O Muʿādh, do you know what is the Right of God upon His worshippers, and what is the Right of His worshippers upon Him?" He replied: "God and His Messenger know better." Upon this, the Prophet said, "God's Right upon His worshippers is that they should worship Him Alone and associate no partners with Him, and His worshippers' right upon Him is that He should not punish one who does not associate a thing with Him." Muʿādh added: "I said to the Messenger of God: 'Shall I give [these] glad tidings to people?' The Prophet replied, 'Do not tell them this good news for they will depend on it alone.'"[9]

According to this *ḥadīth*, although the Prophet knew that worshiping God alone is the primary requisite for reaching salvation, he did not want this to be known publicly as it may well have incited believers to reduce their faith to the minimal level, i.e., the *ḍarūriyyāt*. Rather, he wished they would augment their faith with other complementary and supplementary matters. Hence, he prevented Muʿādh from spreading such news for fear that people would content themselves with only the level of *ḍarūriyyāt*. But to avoid the sin of concealing such knowledge, Muʿādh revealed the *ḥadīth* just before his death.

Furthermore, the Prophet highlighted the importance of other complementary and supplementary matters in other *ḥadīths*, as he aimed for the optimum and wished for the perfection of faith at all levels. He said in another authentic report, "[N]o one of you becomes a true believer until he likes for his brother what he likes for himself."[10] However, it is unanimously agreed by Muslim scholars that one's faith is still valid even if one does not like for one's brother what one likes for oneself. Reconciling these reports, the Prophet in Muʿādh's *ḥadīth* must have been referring to the level of *ḍarūriyyāt*, whereas in the second *ḥadīth* he was referring to the less important levels of *ḥājiyyāt* and *taḥsīniyyāt*. Another instance: the Prophet is reported to have said three times, "By God, he is not a believer! It was asked, 'Who is that?' He said, 'One whose neighbour does not feel safe from his evil.'"[11] If such *ḥadīths* are taken at face value, without measuring them against the above taxonomy, the potential of the excessive exercise of *takfir* (excommunication) is maximized. In fact, this is, more or less, what the Kharijites did. Contrary to orthodox Islamic theology, they advocated that a Muslim who had committed a sin had become an unbeliever (*kāfir*). The extreme ones would go as far as to say that such a sinner is an apostate, that his rights and possessions are to be taken from him and that it is permissible to shed his blood.[12]

Although none of the theologians consulted throughout this book used the taxonomy of *ḍarūriyyāt, ḥājiyyāt,* and *taḥsīniyyāt* in a theological context, "hints" of its usage exist. The Qur'ān asserts the Unity of God, for example, but it still speaks of His "hands" (Q. 38:75), His "eyes" (Q. 54:14), His "face" (Q. 55:27), and of His seating himself on His Throne (Q. 20:5). These ways of describing God, including speaking of a "Beatific Vision," imply that God has a body. While early Sunni theologians considered the Beatific Vision a matter of essentiality, the Muʿtazilites opposed such precepts, arguing that God is a simple essence, which led them to deny that God has a body or any of the characteristics of bodies. They therefore denied the Beatific Vision.[13] However, for lack of a criterion of what constitutes "essential" and what constitutes "inessential" in theology, the Muʿtazilites were denied orthodoxy.

However, with the maturity of Sunni theology by al-Ghazālī's time, we see that he attempted to redefine the weight of such questions according to his Fivefold Typology, to which we shall return in the next chapter. According to this typology, not only was the Muʿtazilite interpretation accepted as plausible, but the weight of the question of the Beatific Vision was demoted from the zone of *ḍarūriyyāt* to the zone of *taḥsīniyyāt*. In his *Fayṣal*, al-Ghazālī distinguished things with which one is deemed an "unbeliever" from things with which one is not. People who readily opt for metaphorical interpretations based on superficial proofs, al-Ghazālī argued, should not in every instance be labeled "unbelievers." Rather, one should investigate further. If their metaphorical interpretation is pertinent to an inessential creedal principle, they should not be deemed unbelievers. He addressed those who readily excommunicate their fellow Muslims on the basis of such questions, advising his readers in the following manner:

> If he [the theological opponent] claims that the definition of Unbelief is that which contradicts the Ashʿarite school, or the Muʿtazilite school, or the Ḥanbalite school, or any other school, then know that

> he is a gullible, dim-witted fellow who is stifled by his enslavement to blind following. In fact, he is blinder than the blind. So do not waste your time trying to reform him. For it would be enough to silence him that you compare his claim with those of his opponents, since he will not find any difference between him and the rest of those who blindly follow some other school in opposition to him. And it may be that, of all the schools, his patron (whom he follows) is inclined toward the Ashʿarite school, holding that to go against this school, even in the finest of details, is an incontrovertible act of Unbelief. Ask him, though, how he came to enjoy this monopoly over the truth, such that he could adjudge (the likes of) al-Bāqillānī to be an Unbeliever (*kāfir*) because the latter goes against him on the question of God's possessing the attribute of eternity, holding that this attribute is indistinct from the essence of God.
>
> Why should al-Bāqillānī be more deserving to be branded an Unbeliever for going against the Ashʿarite school than the Ashʿarite would be for going against al-Bāqillānī? Why should one of these parties enjoy a monopoly over the truth to the exclusion of the other? Is it on the basis of who preceded whom in time? If this be the case, then al-Ashʿarī was himself preceded by others like the Muʿtazilites. Let the truth, then, rest with precedence. Or is it on the basis of one possessing more virtue and knowledge than the other? But by what scale and by what measuring device is this knowledge and virtue to be quantified, such that it would be proper for him to claim that no one in existence is more virtuous than the one he has chosen to follow? If, on the other hand, it is permissible for al-Bāqillānī to go against the Ashʿarite school, why should this be denied to others? What is the difference between al-Bāqillānī and al-Karābīsī or al-Qalānisī and others?[14]

In this quotation, al-Ghazālī pointed out that theological bias and subjectivity may impact our definition of orthodoxy and our process of identifying what should go under *ḍarūriyyāt* and what is otherwise. Reproaching his fellow Ashʿarites, he argued that one should not prohibit for others what he allows for himself, and theologians need to figure out a bare minimum upon which they agree. By such theological bias al-Ghazālī referred to those who tolerate al-Bāqillānī's distancing from the Ashʿarite school on the question of God's eternity, claiming that this disagreement is excusable for it is only a minor one. Al-Ghazālī then lamented: On what basis, other than mere biasness, is this license limited to al-Bāqillānī alone? On the other hand, why should the Muʿtazilites be excommunicated while they fully acknowledge "that God is knowing and has knowledge of all things, and that He is powerful and has power over all possibilities."[15] Al-Ghazālī then said that if you are just, you will know that one who gives a theologian a monopoly over religious truth is himself closer to being guilty of *kufr*, for he puts this theologian's authority in the position of the Prophet, who alone occupies the position of infallibility.[16]

Another example is how some Sufis contend that what Abraham meant by seeing the stars, moon, and sun, accompanied by his comment, "This is my lord," is not the exoteric meaning of these entities but rather angelic entities, whose luminosity is intellectual rather than perceptual, arguing that Abraham was too noble to take these as his lord. Indeed, Abraham would not, they argue, have worshiped them even if they remained shining. They also say, "How was it feasible for the stars to be the first thing to catch his attention, when the sun is more prominent?" All these arguments, said al-Ghazālī, are anchored on "speculative presumption" (*ẓann*) and not on demonstrative proofs (*burhān*), and therefore he attempted to refute their proofs. As for their reference to Abraham's nobility, it is refuted by the fact that Abraham was a youth at the time. And yet there is nothing that is incredible about a future prophet once exercising such an intellectual endeavor only to forsake it shortly afterward. As for the stars captivating his attention before the sun, it has been reported that he had isolated himself in a cave and came out for the first time at "night." Be that as it may, all of these are nondemonstrative contentions about an "inessential" principle in theology; hence, theologians should be given the benefit of the doubt, just as Sunní theologians would often handle speculative matters among their fellow Ashʿarites. The proponents of such interpretations should not be labeled either unbelievers or heretics.[17]

Al-Ghazālī added a qualification with which we see how theological *ḥājiyyāt* and *taḥsīniyyāt* are contextually contingent, highlighting that these minority interpretations are tolerable, unless they influence the masses in a way that may jeopardize the zone of *ḍarūriyyāt*. If such is the case, charges of heresy (*bidʿa*), not unbelief, could be directed against them, with a view to protecting the masses.[18]

Having given an example of the nonessential matters of creed, al-Ghazālī moved to highlight the essential matters with which a person can either be deemed a believer or an unbeliever. He argued that "anyone who alters the apparent meaning of a text without a definitive logical proof must be branded an Unbeliever, like those who deny the resurrection of the body and the occurrence of sentient punishment in the Hereafter on the basis of speculative presumptions, suppositions, and assumed improbabilities in the absence of any definitive logical proof."[19] Similarly, those who say that God knows nothing apart from Himself and that He only knows the universals of the universe must be branded unbelievers for three reasons. First, there is no definitive proof to their claim of the impossibility of bodily resurrection. Second, if such ideas were to prevail, they would be harmful to the masses, as it would weaken their consciousness of God's presence and could lead to moral laxity and social disintegration. Third, these statements imply deeming what the Prophet taught to be a lie.[20]

Al-Ghazālī then gave his readers a rule of thumb that closely relates to our usage of *ḍarūriyyāt, ḥājiyyāt,* and *taḥsīniyyāt* in theology. He wrote that "speculative matters (*al-naẓariyāt*) are of two types. One is connected with the fundamental principles of creed, the other with secondary issues. The fundamental principles are acknowledging the existence of God, the prophethood of his Prophet, and the reality of the Last Day. Everything else is secondary."[21] Al-Ghazālī here clearly distinguished between the essential and the inessential creedal principles, asserting that *takfīr* should transpire only at the level of the *naẓariyāt* (which I name *ḍarūriyyāt*). If those fundamental matters are safe, one is safe in one's interpretation. An example of non-fundamental matters is the wrong ideas that theologians may hold about the caliphate and the status of the Companions.[22] It is worth quoting him at length here:

> Know, however, that error regarding the status of the Caliphate, whether or not establishing this office is a (communal) obligation, who qualifies for it, and related matters, cannot serve as grounds for condemning people as Unbelievers. Indeed, Ibn Kaysān denied that there was any religious obligation to have a Caliphate at all; but this does not mean that he must be branded an Unbeliever. Nor do we pay any attention to those who exaggerate the matter of the Imāmate and equate recognition of the Imām with faith in God and His Messenger. Nor do we pay any attention to those who oppose these people and brand them Unbelievers simply on the basis of their doctrine on the Imāmate. Both of these positions are extreme. For neither of the doctrines in question entails any claim that the Prophet perpetrated lies.[23]

Traditionally, theologians have used, however, the twofold dichotomy of *uṣūl al-ʿaqīda* (primaries of theology) versus *furūʿ al-ʿaqīda* (supplementaries of theology). So, one might ask, why not maintain the classical twofold pattern instead of the threefold taxonomy of *ḍarūriyyāt, ḥājiyyāt,* and *taḥsīniyyāt*? I am abandoning this twofold pattern, for it contributed, in one way or another, to the formulation of theological differences in an either/or scheme, whereby creedal matters were seen as either central or marginal; either primary or supplementary. However, the reality is that there are creedal matters that escape this twofold dichotomy by being less important than *uṣūl* but also more important than *furūʿ*. Additionally, the pattern of *uṣūl* versus *furūʿ* assumes that theology is a static subject that does not interact and speak to the context in which it emerges, whereas the threefold taxonomy of *ḍarūriyyāt, ḥājiyyāt,* and *taḥsīniyyāt* assumes a sense of dynamism in the theological tradition, where creedal matters may move from one zone to another depending on the theological development that accompanies the life of every theological system. Hence, Ibn Taymiyya rightly problematized this twofold typology in his *Fatāwā*, contending that it is not only scripturally baseless but also subjective and relative.[24]

Having established the extendibility of the threefold taxonomy to Islamic theology, we are now in a better position to put it into theological use by examining three key elements in Islamic theology: *al-firqa al-nājiya*, faith vis-à-vis deeds, and the role of the Prophet. In the remainder of this chapter, we will see how the notion of *al-firqa al-nājiya* began in early Sunnism, more particularly Ashʿarism, as part of the *ḍarūriyyāt* of Islamic theology, without which one cannot attain salvation or pursue truth. However, this notion was weakened and moved from the zone of *ḍarūriyyāt* to the *ḥājiyyāt* in classical Ashʿarism, and it became weaker in modern Ashʿarism, where it was largely considered part of the *taḥsīniyyāt*. The second notion (faith vis-à-vis deeds), interestingly, had the opposite journey. While in early Ashʿarism, deeds were largely seen not as essential to one's faith but rather part of *taḥsīniyyāt*, I argue that with al-Ghazālī's emphasis on deeds, they moved from the zone of *taḥsīniyyāt* to the zone of *ḥājiyyāt*. Although al-Ghazālī's position stood the test of time in modern Ashʿarism, the emergence of reformed Ashʿarism with ʿAbduh moved deeds further from the zone of *ḥājiyyāt* to the zone of *ḍarūriyyāt*. Indeed, this shift had a bearing on the religious value of the good deeds of non-Muslims. Regarding the place of Prophet Muḥammad, although it was never in the zone of *taḥsīniyyāt*, reformed Ashʿarism considered belief in Prophet Muḥammad as part of *ḥājiyyāt* rather than *ḍarūriyyāt*—unlike the place of God, which never departed the area of *ḍarūriyyāt* in Islamic theology. We shall now begin with the concept of *al-firqa al-nājiya*.

Al-Firqa al-Nājiya *in* al-Ḍarūriyyāt, al-Ḥājiyyāt, *and* al-Taḥsīniyyāt

Al-firqa al-nājiya (the saved denomination) is a theological notion that is grounded on the popular *ḥadith*, quoted earlier, that says, "[T]here will befall my nation (Muslims) what befell the children of Israel. The children of Israel divided into seventy-two religious' groups and my community will divide into seventy-three religious' groups, one more than they. All of them are in hellfire except one religious' group."[25] This form of the *ḥadīth* is found in Ibn Mājah (d. 886), Abū Dāwūd al-Sijistānī (d. 888), al-Tirmiḏī (d. 892), and al-Nasāʾī (d. 915), four of the six canonical Sunni collections of *ḥadīth*.[26] However, it does not exist in al-Bukhārī (d. 870) nor in Muslim (d. 875), the two most authentic *ḥadīth* collections in the Sunni tradition. This *ḥadīth* largely dominated the theological scene of early Islamic theology.

Starting with one of the key fathers of Sunni Islam, Ibn Ḥanbal (d. 855) took the above *ḥadīth* at face value and to a large degree grounded his theology on it. The eleventh-century historian Al-Khaṭīb al-Baghdādī (d. 1071)[27] mentioned in his *Sharaf Aṣḥāb al-Ḥadīth* (The Merits of the Folk of Traditions) that Ibn Ḥanbal commented on the ḥadīth with the following statement: "If they [the saved denomination] are not the people of *Ḥadīth*, then I do not know who they are!"[28]

Although Abū al-Ḥassan al-Ashʿarī, the eponymous founder of Ashʿarism, never mentioned the *ḥadīth*, neither in his magnum opus, *Maqālāt al-islāmiyyīn* (The Views of the Islamic Denominations), nor in his other works, this does not mean he considered all Muslim denominations to be valid paths to salvation. Rather, what emerges from his writings is that he considered only two Muslim denominations to be valid paths. George Makdisi pointed out that al-Ashʿarī accepted Atharism (practically: Ḥanbalism) as well as Ashʿarism as being salvifically effective paths. Makdisi put it this way:

> This makes Ashʿarī the follower of two middle roads: (1) that of the Pious Ancestors who were anxious to avoid two extremes: *ta'wīl* and *tashbīh*; and (2) that of the "kalām-using orthodox" who wanted to uphold the divine attributes, against the Muʿtazilites, and uphold the use of *ta'wīl* in order to avoid falling into *tashbīh*. The former attitude is regarded by the Ashʿarites as being *ṭarīq as-salāma*, the road of salvation, and the latter is regarded by them as being *ṭarīq al-ḥikma*, the road of wisdom; both of which roads were travelled by Ashʿarī himself.

> By virtue of Ashʿari's two middle roads, those who followed the one or the other were equally Ashʿarite, equally orthodox.[29]

However, it seems that the first pre-Ghazālian Ashʿarite to consolidate this denomination-based salvation was Abū Bakr al-Bāqillānī (d. 1013),[30] by using, if not probably coining, the term *Ahl al-Sunna wa-al-Jamāʿa* (the People of the Sunna and the Community/Unity).[31] Al-Bāqillānī frequently joined the term *Ahl al-Sunna wa-al-Jamāʿa* with the term *Ahl al-ḥaqq* (the people of truth),[32] which probably underlined his view that non-Ashʿarites are not among the people of truth. This category, that is, the people of truth, encompasses the two trajectories traveled by al-Ashʿarī previously. Al-Bāqillānī did not see any significant differences between the theology of the followers of al-Ashʿarī and that of Ibn Ḥanbal. In fact, on several occasions, he identified himself as a Ḥanbalīte, signing some of his epistles with the name Muḥammad ibn al-Ṭayyīb al-Ḥanbalī (the Ḥanbalīte).[33]

Notwithstanding, Abū Manṣūr ʿAbd al-Qāhir al-Baghdādī (d. 1037)[34] was apparently the first Ashʿarite theologian to coin the term *al-firqa al-nājiya*. He wrote several catechistic Ashʿarite treatises, among which is *al-Farq bayna al-firaq wa bayān al-firqa al-nājiya minhum* (Characteristics of Muslim Denominations and Identifying the Saved among Them), in which he dealt with the *ḥadīth* of the 73-schema, accepting it at face value and formulating his book according to a scheme of seventy-three groups; he went on to study and evaluate each denomination from an Ashʿarite standpoint, ending by condemning them as deviators from the straight path of *Ahl al-Sunna wa-al-Jamāʿa*. Following his predecessors, he saw *Ahl al-Sunna wa-al-Jamāʿa* as belonging to two categories: *Farīq al-raʾī* (the people of reasoning, i.e., the Ashʿarite theologians) and *Farīq al-ḥadīth* (the people of tradition, i.e., the Traditionists who follow Aḥmad Ibn Ḥanbal).[35] Indeed, the heaviness of al-Baghdādī's denomination-based theology appears in the following lengthy quotation, which he wrote in response to a questioner who asked him about the 73-tradition:

> You have asked me for an explanation of the well-known tradition attributed to the Prophet with regard to the division of the Moslim Community into seventy-three sects, of which one has saving grace and is destined for Paradise on High, whilst the rest are in the wrong, leading to the Deep Pit and the Ever-flaming fire. You requested me to draw the distinction between the sect that saves, the step of which does not stumble and from which grace does not depart, and the misguided sects which regard the darkness of idolatry as light and the belief in

truth as leading to perdition which sects are condemned to everlasting fire and shall find no aid in Allah. Therefore, I feel it incumbent upon me to help you along the line of your request with regard to the orthodox faith and the path that is straight how to distinguish it from the perverted heresies and the distorted views, so that he who does perish shall know that he is perishing and he that is saved that he is so saved through clear evidence.[36]

He proceeded to say:

The true view, according to us, is that the Ummat al-Islām comprises those who profess the view that the world is created, the unity of its maker, his preexistence, his attributes, his equity, his wisdom, the denial of his anthropomorphic character, the prophetic character of Muḥammad, and his universal Apostolate, the acknowledgment of the constant validity of his law, that all that he enjoined was truth, that the Koran is the source of all legal regulations, and that the Kaʿbah is the direction in which all prayers should be turned. Everyone who professes all this and does not follow a heresy that might lead him to unbelief, he is an orthodox Sunnite, believing in the unity of Allah.

If, to the accepted beliefs which we have mentioned he adds a hateful heresy, his case must be considered. And if he incline to the heresy of the Bāṭinīyah, or the Bayānīyah, or the Mughīrah, or the Khaṭṭābīyah, who believe in the divine character of all the Imāms, or of some of them at least, or if he follows the schools which believe in the incarnation of God, or one of the schools of the people believing in the transmigration of souls, or the school of the Maimūnīyah of the Khawārij who allow marriage with one's daughter's daughter or one's son's daughter, or follow the school of the Yazīdīyah from among the Ibāḍīyah with their teaching that the law of Islam will be abrogated at the end of time, or if he permits as lawful what the text of the Koran forbids, or forbids that which the text of the Koran allows as lawful, and which does not admit of differing interpretation, such an one does not belong to the Ummat al-Islām, nor should he be esteemed.

But if his heresy is like the heresy of the Muʿtazilites, or the Khawārij, or the Rāfiḍah of the Imāmīyah, or the Zaidīyah heresies, or of the heresy of the Najjārīyah, or the Jahmīyah, or the Ḍarārīyah, or the Mujassimah, then he would be of the Ummat al-Islām in some respects, namely: he would be entitled to be buried in the graveyard

> of the Moslems, and to have a share in the tribute and booty which is procured by the true believers in war with the idolators provided he fights with the true believers. Nor should he be prevented from praying in the mosques. But he is not of the Ummat in other respects, namely that no prayer should be allowed over his dead body, nor behind him (to the grave); moreover any animal slaughtered by him is not lawful food, nor may he marry an orthodox Moslem woman. It is also not lawful for an orthodox man to marry one of their women if she partake of their belief.[37]

Leaving al-Baġdādī, we move on to Abū al-Muẓaffar al-Isfarāyīnī (d. 1079), an Ashʿarite theologian and jurist who lived in present-day Afghanistan; who is another Ashʿarite theologian who employed the term *al-Firqa al-nājiya* quite frequently. In his *al-Tabṣīr fī al-dīn wa tamyyīz al-firqa al-nājiya ʿan al-firaq al-hālikīn* (The Enlightenment in Religion and Distinguishing the Saved Denomination from the Damned Ones), al-Isfarāyīnī provided a detailed discussion on the seventy-two damned groups, followed by a thorough account of the beliefs of the saved one, i.e., Ashʿarism with its traditionist parallel, asserting that *Farīq al-ḥadīth* held the same doctrines as *Farīq al-ra'i*. In fact, at times al-Isfarāyīnī called the Ashʿarites *Aṣḥāb al-ḥadīth* to highlight the unity of ends between the two trajectories.[38]

Imām al-Ḥaramayn al-Juwaynī is yet another pre-Ghazālian theologian who advocated denomination-based theology. Although his *Lumaʿ al-adilla fī qawāʿid ʿaqāʾid ahl al-sunna wa al-jamāʿa* (Illuminating Catechistic Proofs of the Doctrines of the People of the Sunna and the Community) did not make use of the above *ḥadīth*, the title as well as the content of the book do correspond to the idea of the saved group.[39] Similar to al-Bāqillānī, al-Juwaynī called the Ashʿarites *Ahl al-ḥaqq*.[40]

Having reached this point, it is worth noting, before we move into al-Ghazālī's contribution to this area, how the notion of *al-firqa al-nājiya* began in early Ashʿarism as part of the *ḍarūriyyāt* of Islamic theology, whereby its authority and authenticity were unquestioned. Early Ashʿarites and, by extension, early Muslim theologians saw truth and salvation as denomination-based, and this notion constituted an essential aspect of their theological paradigm.

However, with al-Ghazālī we see a different interpretation of the *ḥadīth*, demoting it out of the zone of *ḍarūriyyāt*. Al-Ghazālī lived in a critical time in which the exercise of *takfir* was at its peak. As a corollary to this, the question of who is to be regarded a Muslim and is on a valid path to salvation gained further momentum.[41] He produced and introduced a theory of *takfir* through which he deconstructed the scheme of the seventy-three divisions. In his *Fayṣal*, he explained this scheme further, arguing that although his version of this *ḥadīth* (assigning seventy-two denominations to damnation and entitling only one to salvation) is the most popular, another version says that only one of the seventy-three will be damned.[42]

Reconciling these two narrations, al-Ghazālī contended that each is concerned with a different class of people, and that the most popular version addresses the group of people who will neither be exposed to the Fire nor need intercession (*shafāʿa*); i.e., they will be saved by virtue of their own valid faith and righteous deeds. As for the less popular narration, he argued that it addresses the group(s) that will be exposed to Hellfire first and then will be admitted into Paradise after being purified in Hell. Hence, the *ḥadīth* calls such groups "damned" considering their initial state, for anyone who is admitted to Hell even for a short period of time cannot be called "saved," even if he is saved later. Based on this, the "damned" group in the less popular narration relates to the small group that is to be in Hell permanently.[43] As for the remaining seventy-two groups, he explained in one of his Persian letters how he viewed them:

> The cause of this diversity is that the community consists of three groups: the best, the worst and the middling. The best of the community are the *Sufis*, who have devoted all of their own personal will and desire to the will of God. The worst are the morally vicious, and those people who exercise oppression, drink wine and commit fornication, and give free rein to the desire for whatever they want and are able to do. They deceive themselves in thinking that Almighty God is generous and merciful, and they depend upon this (mercy). In the middle are the people among the masses of mankind who possess moral soundness (*salah*). So, every one of these divisions has twenty-four parts, and together they make seventy-two parts (*firaq*).[44]

Although early Ashʿarites did develop a system of toleration to accommodate the heterodox Muslim denominations, it was only with al-Ghazālī's canon of interpretation, to which we shall return in the following chapter, that this system became firmly established and epistemologically theorized. Frank Griffel outlined this Ghazālian contribution in the following:

> Al-Ghazālī understands that orthodoxy is in the eye of the beholder; from the viewpoint of an Ashʿarite, other Muslim groups such as the

Muʿtazilites or moderate Shīʿites are certainly not orthodox. Such heterodox groups, however, were not considered clandestine apostates from Islam, and they continued to enjoy legal status as Muslims. The Ashʿarites regarded them as tolerated groups within Islam. Distinguishing the criteria for apostasy from simple heterodoxy is one of al-Ghazālī's most important contributions to the legal discourse about unbelief and apostasy in Islam. He firmly establishes the legal status of tolerated heterodoxy, a category containing Muʿtazilites and most Shīʿites, for instance. According to this qualification, philosophers who avoid the three condemned teachings fall under this category of tolerated nonconformists or dissenters. Al-Ghazālī's distinction between taxing someone with unbelief (*takfīr*) and taxing someone with error (*takhṭi'a*), deviation (*taḍlīl*), or innovation (*tabdīʿ*) creates two different categories of deviators. The three latter judgements are mere pronouncements that the adversaries hold positions that are not correct and that will, in the opinion of al-Ghazālī, lead them toward punishment in the afterlife. Taxing someone with error, deviation, or innovation has no legal implication; in fact, it amounts to the declaration that the Muslim community tolerates such theological positions.[45]

Although the *ḥadīth* of the seventy-three denominations remained present in theological discussions after al-Ghazālī, different interpretations qualifying its exclusivism emerged. For instance, al-Rāzī engaged with the *ḥadīth* primarily in two places. In his commentary on Q. 21:92, which states, "Verily, this community of yours is one community and I am your Lord, so worship Me," he quoted the *ḥadīth* and considered it an authentic tradition, yet the interpretation he offered is inclusive. That is, he did not think the report is talking about the Hereafter, but rather the Here. Muslims will divide *in certain situations* in this world into seventy-three sects; the saved group is the one that sticks to the majority and does not deviate.[46] In his *Iʿtiqādāt firaq al-muslimīn wa-al-mushrikīn* (The Creeds of Muslim Denominations and Those of the Polytheists), al-Rāzī gave an apologetic account of the *ḥadīth*, asking, "What if someone said: How is it that the number of the denominations exceeded the number prophesied by the Prophet?" Al-Rāzī answered that the Prophet may have meant the "major" denominations rather than the "minor" ones. Another possibility, since the Prophet prophesied the number seventy-three, is that it cannot be less, but it could be more (Arabs use the seventies to exaggerate.)[47]

The great mediaeval theologian al-Ījī (d. 1413) discussed the *ḥadīth* in his magnum opus and arguably the most important Ashʿarite summa, *Kitāb al-mawāqif* (Book of Stations). Although he accepted the *ḥadīth* as an authentic tradition and considered it one of the signs of the prophethood of Prophet Muḥammad,[48] he neither practiced *takfīr* on its basis, nor did he condemn anyone to Hell. He wrote, "We do not practice *takfīr* against anyone of *Ahl al-qibla* except for those who deny the existence of the Omniscient Omnipotent Designer/Maker, or [believe/commit] polytheism, or den[y] prophethood, or what is known by necessity from Islam, or den[y] agreed upon matters such as breaking the boundaries of what is unlawful. As for deviation on other matters, deviators may be accused of heresy but not of unbelief."[49]

That said, before we move into modern Ashʿarism, it is important to note how the weight of the notion of *al-firqa al-nājiya* was dumbed down in Ghazālian and post-Ghazālian Ashʿarism, by questioning the authority of the *ḥadīth* upon which it is based and by offering more inclusive interpretations of it. In doing so, I argue, they moved the notion from the zone of *ḍarūriyyāt* to the zone of *ḥājiyyāt* in order to justify the legitimacy of other theological schools while remaining themselves Ashʿarites. The reason I emphasize that they moved it to the zone of *ḥājiyyāt,* not *taḥsīniyyāt,* is that they did not abolish its value completely, but rather still saw following the orthodox path, i.e., Ashʿarism, as safer for their theological orthodoxy.

This *ḥadīth*, however, did not have much influence in the modern Ashʿarite theological scene. In his *Ḥāshiya ʿalā sharḥ al-Dawwānī lil-ʿaqāʾid al-ʿaḍudiya* (Glosses on the Theological Commentary of Jalāl al-Dīn al-Dawwānī),[50] ʿAbduh[51] offered some significant insights into the *ḥadīth*, contending that the question about which group is leading a valid path is theologically problematic, for every group lays claim to it. Notwithstanding, the minute details of what the Prophet and his Companions believed remain undivulged; what is categorically known are only the basic tenets of their faith. Therefore, there is insufficient definitive knowledge to qualify any apodictic judgment to be pronounced. Furthermore, this *ḥadīth* challenges the Ashʿarite theology of *naẓar* (independent speculation), for the Ashʿarites are in unanimous agreement that the belief of blind followers is doubtful and undesirable, for it is not based on independent reasoning. However, subscribing to this *ḥadīth* would require dogmatically following a certain group.[52]

The appropriate way, said ʿAbduh, for the one who seeks to establish firm faith is to begin by verifying the sound proofs for the existence of God, followed by seeking proofs for the fact that God sends prophets, and then accept all of that which the Prophet conveys about the Unseen world and the Last Day. By doing this, ʿAbduh argued, man brings reason to meet with revelation, guiding him to the soundest proofs of faith. To obtain salvation in its most perfect form, one must accompany speculative inquiry with some form of Sufism, with which one purifies one's heart and seeks the perfection of one's soul. Anyone who takes the way of *naẓar* as well as the way of *sulūk* (Sufism) is indeed walking on the path of the Prophet and his Companions. The more one increases one's share of these two ways, the more one draws closer to the way of the Prophet, and the less one abides by these ways, the more one draws oneself closer to the way of the damned.[53]

Moving on to the twentieth century, some brief words on three popular Ashʿarite scholars may clarify how the *ḥadīth* was commonly received in that recent century. These three figures are Maḥmūd Shaltūt (d. 1963), Ibn ʿĀshūr, and ʿAbdel Ḥalīm Maḥmūd (d. 1979).[54] Although Shaltūt did not engage with the 73-divisions tradition, his practice attests to his view on it, as he played a—if not *the*—major role in Islamic ecumenism in the twentieth century. His efforts in dismantling the long-standing historical division between the Sunnis and the Shiites are remarkable and have been instrumental in making Egypt "the home of the only noticeable ecumenical society in modern Islam": *Jamāʿat al-taqrīb bayn'l-madhāhib al-islāmiyya* (Association for the Rapprochement of the Islamic Schools of Law).[55] About this Association Rainer Brunner wrote:

> The most spectacular result of this—as it soon turned out—brief honeymoon of Islamic ecumenism was a fatwa in 1959 by the JT's most prominent member, Mahmud Shaltut, who then served as rector of al-Azhar. In this fatwa, which was distilled from a newspaper interview, Shaltūt made it clear that Shiʿism was to be regarded as a legitimate fifth madhhab, alongside the four Sunni ones, and that it was legitimate to convert from Sunnism to Shiism and vice versa.[56]

As for Ibn ʿĀshūr's view, he did not differ significantly from Shaltūt. Although he did not deal with the *ḥadīth* at length, he tackled the question of Muslim denominations in passing in a paragraph in his *Uṣūl al-niẓām al-ijtimāʿī fil-Islām* (The Foundations of the Social System in Islam), arguing that it is up to each Muslim to choose which Muslim denomination to follow, be it Salafism, Ashʿarism, Māturīdism, Muʿtazilism, Khārijism, or even Imāmism. He further argued that the one who holds to the sound principles of reasoning will find his way to figure out the strengths and weaknesses of each Muslim denomination. The most important thing, said Ibn ʿĀshūr, is that Muslims do not accuse one another of infidelity based on these intratheological preferences. In that respect, Ibn ʿĀshūr is akin to al-Ghazālī and ʿAbduh in terms of allowing space for internal pluralism, though his personal affiliation lies with Ashʿarism.[57]

With respect to Ḥalīm, in his *al-Tafkīr al-falsafī fī al-islām* (Philosophical Thinking in Islam), he dedicated an entire section to critically engage with the *ḥadīth* of the 73-divisions. He began the discussion by lamenting traditional theologians' obsession with this *ḥadīth*, despite its questionable authenticity: "[I]t feels [like] those theologians believed that it is a duty upon themselves to exhaust the Islamic denominations in order to make them reach seventy-three, no matter whether this corresponds to reality or not."[58] He particularly took to task al-Sharastānī's (d. 1153) classification of Muslim denominations, due to his composition of his book of historiography on the basis of this tradition,[59] stating, "[N]ot only did historiographers count the denominations arbitrarily, but also theologians of each denomination were biased, picking anything that seems to give support to their views no matter how much truth it held."[60]

Ḥalīm consequently paused to question the epistemic value of the *ḥadīth* itself. He lamented that the *ḥadīth* that preoccupied the minds of many theologians and restricted their views is narrated neither in al-Bukhārī's nor in Muslim's collections. The *ḥadīth* is problematic not only in its *isnād* (chain of narration) but also in its *matn* (body of the text), for while in some collections of *ḥadīth*, the *matn* filters the to-be-saved group, in others it filters the to-be-damned group, as noted by al-Ghazālī earlier.[61] Ḥalīm then provided an example of how the *matn* of the *ḥadīth* was misused, mentioning that some Shiites considered "opposing others most ardently" as their criterion for identifying the saved group. If this criterion is pushed to its extreme, Ḥalīm said, it would denounce the Shiites themselves, for the only group that opposes others most ardently is Ashʿarism, for its fundamental principles contradict most non-Ashʿarite denominations.[62]

However, Ḥalīm in his *Hadhihi ḥayātī* (This Has Been My Life) showed some acceptance of the *ḥadīth*. Yet he almost ended up with the same conclusion as al-Ghazālī, that Sufism is the denomination that leads toward salvation and toward enjoying a spiritual union with the Divine even in this world before the other. Nevertheless, he remained far from taking that *ḥadīth* at face value; i.e., he consigned no Muslim denomination to Hellfire.[63]

The above presentation aimed to show that while the notion of *al-firqa al-nājiya* began in early Ashʿarism as part of the *ḍarūriyyāt* of Islamic theology, where its authority and authenticity were unquestioned, its weight was lowered in Ghazālian and post-Ghazālian Ashʿarism by its removal from the zone of *ḍarūriyyāt* to the zone of *ḥājiyyāt*. Additionally, it has become clear that in modern Ashʿarism the notion went even further down, to the zone of *taḥsīniyyāt*, with the likes of ʿAbduh and his school. However, this does not mean, in any way, that "all" modern Ashʿarite theologians abandoned the notion of *al-firqa al-nājiya*, but rather that mainstream Ashʿarite theology, represented in the key voices studied here, was moving further from it.

Faith vis-à-vis Deeds in al-Ḍarūriyyāt, al-Ḥājiyyāt, *and* al-Taḥsīniyyāt

The early Ashʿarite theology on this question is summarized by Ibn Fūrak (d. 1015).[64] According to him, early Ashʿarites believed that reward (*thawāb*) is initially granted by God's grace and not earned by believers' deeds. In fact, the believer's deeds come primarily through God's grace.[65] Hence, salvation itself is not *earned* through one's deeds, but rather is *granted* graciously by God. Deeds do not earn one's salvation; they are manifestations of one's gratitude to God and signs of one's acceptance of the Divine grace, so to speak. Al-Juwaynī too confirmed that the Salaf agreed that God's reward is by His grace, not by the believer's worthiness of this reward.[66] Those premises led to one key conclusion: correct faith is the essential requirement for salvation. Therefore, one can safely say that good deeds were not seen as part of the *ḍarūriyyāt* for attaining salvation but rather as part of the *taḥsīniyyāt*. The performance of good deeds had a supplementary role to one's attainment of reward, but deliverance from Hellfire is primarily anchored upon "correct faith".

This position had a bearing on whether the good deeds of non-Muslims are rewardable and meritorious in the Hereafter. In early Ashʿarism, the good deeds of non-Muslims had no religious value in the Hereafter, as they did not meet the necessary condition of correct faith. Since faith is about internal assent (*taṣdīq*), the good deeds of one who does not have that correct assent are of no value in the Hereafter. Deeds constituted a condition of *perfection* rather than *soundness* (*sharṭ kamāl lā sharṭ siḥḥa*). Thus, although one's faith may be imperfect if one does not strengthen it with good deeds, it remains sound.[67]

Although al-Ghazālī did not completely depart from the view that deeds do not pertain to the *ḍarūriyyāt*, it can plausibly be argued that he did not accept that deeds are part of *taḥsīniyyāt*; instead, he saw deeds as part of the zone of *ḥājiyyāt*, asserting that those who come to God only with mere abstract assent are at risk. Needless to say that he did not use the terminology of this taxonomy, but his theological orientation is clearly in line with it. In his short treatise *Ayyuhā al-walad* (O Beloved Disciple), al-Ghazālī engaged with a hypothetical counterpart, writing, "If it is said, 'He gets there [Paradise] by faith alone,' we reply: yes, but when will he get there? How many difficult obstacles must be overcome before arriving? And the first of these obstacles is that of faith [itself] and will he be safe from the denial of faith or not, and when he arrives, will he be unsuccessful and destitute?"[68] It is probably worth quoting at length:

> O disciple, be neither destitute of good deeds nor devoid of spiritual states, for you can be sure that mere knowledge will not help. It is as though a man in the desert had ten Indian swords and other weapons besides the man being brave and a warrior, and a huge, terrifying lion attacked him. What is your opinion? Will the weapons repel this danger of his from him without their being used and being wielded? It is obvious they will not repel unless drawn and wielded!
>
> Likewise, if a man studied a hundred thousand intellectual issues and understood them, but did not act on the strength of them, they would not be of use to him except by taking action. . . . [E]ven if you studied for a hundred years and collected a thousand books, you would not be eligible for the mercy of God the Exalted except through action. . . . [F]aith is a verbal declaration, consent by the heart and action in accordance with the [five] pillars; and the evidence of deeds is incalculable; even though *the worshipper attains Paradise by the bounty and grace of God the Exalted, nevertheless [this is] constituent to him being predisposed through obedience to him and worship of him, since "The Mercy of God is near to those who do good."*[69]

Having raised the status of "deeds" from the zone of *taḥsīniyyāt*, al-Ghazālī cautioned his readers that this does not mean that "deeds" are now part of the *ḍarūriyyāt*, highlighting that only "correct faith" lies in the zone of *ḍarūriyyāt*. He then quoted one of the popular statements of the Salaf that might imply that "deeds" are as important as "correct faith," and then refuted it. The statement says that "faith comprises inward assent, verbal confession, and good works." He responded in this poetic manner:

> It is not unlikely that good deeds be considered a part of faith, because they perfect and complete it, just as it is said that the head and hands are part of man. It is evident that a person will cease to be human if his head no longer exists; but he will not cease to be a human being if one of his hands is lost through amputation. Therefore, acceptance with the heart stands in relation to faith as does the head in relation to the existence of man. . . . [T]he remaining good deeds are like the limbs of the body, some are more important than the others.[70]

Having excluded good deeds from the zones of *ḍarūriyyāt* and *taḥsīniyyāt*, al-Ghazālī seems to have considered good deeds part of the *ḥājiyyāt*, whereby they facilitate what is necessary for sound faith. In his *Kitāb al-tawḥīd wa'l-tawakkul* (Faith in Divine Unity and Trust in Divine Providence), al-Ghazālī wrote, "Know that trust [in God] is a sub-branch of faith. All sub-branches of faith do not flourish except with [three requirements]: *ʿilm* (knowledge), *ḥāl* (spiritual state of consciousness), *ʿamal* (practice)."[71] By this al-Ghazālī meant that mere knowledge of God does not bring one to the state of reliance on Him, and consequently the attainment of true faith depends considerably on practice. He proceeded to show how faith flourishes when it goes beyond mere internal assent, whereby one will not observe other than God and aspire for none but Him. This will result in believing that no one has power to change an atom except by God, which explicitly adds to the soundness of one's faith.[72]

Moving to modern Ashʿarism, we see another shift to the value of deeds in relation to faith, whereby deeds move from the zone of *ḥājiyyāt* to the zone of *ḍarūriyyāt*. ʿAbduh is convinced that the cornerstone for salvation in all religions are three fundamental articles. Two of these articles have to do with correct faith, and one has to do with deeds. The first two are faith in the existence of God and faith in the Last Day. The third article is doing good deeds. Therefore, faith alone is not enough for one's salvation, and good deeds are part of the *ḍarūriyyāt*.[73] So here ʿAbduh went one step beyond al-Ghazālī on this question; although al-Ghazālī attempted to revisit the nature of the relation between faith and deeds, he still did not see them as of equal footing, but ʿAbduh did. ʿAbduh made use of one of the most often quoted traditions, which says that faith is what is firmly established in the heart and is verified by deeds (*al-īmān mā waqara fi-l-qalb wa-ṣaddaqahu al-ʿamal*). Neglecting deeds, ʿAbduh further argued, is what prompted Muslims to see non-Islamic religions as readily inferior to Islam, hence ended up "privatizing" and "racializing" Islam.[74]

Not only did ʿAbduh place good deeds on equal footing with faith, but he also de-linked good deeds from correct faith, arguing that a good deed is rewardable in the Hereafter whether or not accompanied by correct faith. ʿAbduh took Q. 99:7–8, "*Whoever* does an atom's weight of good, will see it. And *whoever* does an atom's weight of evil will see it," at face value, emphasizing that the alleged consensus of commentators on qualifying the generality of these verses should not be followed. He then proceeded to ask how these verses can be qualified when God says in Q. 21:47, "We will establish the scales of justice on the Day of Resurrection. No soul will suffer the least injustice. Even the equivalent of a mustard seed will be accounted for. We are the most efficient reckoners."[75]

ʿAbduh obviously was not alone in this; several theologians followed him. For instance, Muḥammad Abū Zahra (d. 1974)[76] grappled with the question: What is the fate of those non-Muslims who fail to meet the three requirements of salvation (faith in God, Last Day, and doing good deeds) but who did good deeds? Abū Zahra pointed out that the traditional position on this matter was that in Islam a good deed will be rewarded under two conditions: (1) the deed must be conducted in compatibility with God's law as revealed to Prophet Muḥammad; (2) the worshiper's intention has to be worshiping God through the performance of this good deed.[77] On the basis of these two conditions, non-Muslim good-doers were thought to be entitled only to a secular reward in the Here, but not in the Hereafter.[78]

Having offered the premises of the traditional view, Abū Zahra proceeded to offer his own argument. Taking part in a roundtable discussion to be published in the Al-Azhar mosque magazine in 1955, Abū Zahra walked against the traditional position, concluding that the good deeds of non-Muslims, performed for the sake of humanity and the spreading of goodness on earth, are religiously meritorious in and of themselves even if remote from correct faith, especially in situations in which the non-Muslim is not blamed for not adhering to Islam for whatever reason.[79]

Having reached this point, I hope to have succeeded in showing how the progression of the value of deeds vis-à-vis faith took place within the framework of *al-ḍarūriyyāt*, *al-ḥājiyyāt* and *al-taḥsīniyyāt*, even if it was never explicitly stated. While "deeds" began in early Ashʿarism as part of the *taḥsīniyyāt* of Islamic theology, its weight was promoted by al-Ghazālī, who moved it from the zone of *taḥsīniyyāt* to the zone of *ḥājiyyāt*, by arguing that deeds, though not "ends" in themselves, are indispensable "means" to the correct faith. The next step transpired with ʿAbduh's school, which promoted further the weight of deeds, moving it from the zone of *ḥājiyyāt* to the zone of *ḍarūriyyāt* on equal footing with correct faith.

The Prophet Muḥammad in al-Ḍarūriyyāt *and* al-Ḥājiyyāt

Beginning with early Ashʿarism, it goes without saying that since truth was *denomination*-based, questioning the necessity of belief in Prophet Muḥammad was out of the question. In his *Mujarrad*, Ibn Fūrak explained that "al-Ashʿarī believed that, if the Scripture is put aside, believing in God does not necessarily demand believing in Prophet Muḥammad."[80] Thus, a believer in God alone without believing in Prophet Muḥammad can still be considered a believer. Yet, since Scripture is perceived to link the two, non-Muslims cannot be called "believers." Hence, believing in Prophet Muḥammad was seen as an end in and of itself.

Furthermore, Islam was believed to have superseded non-Islamic religions. Al-Juwaynī devoted an entire chapter of his *Irshād* to the theory of supersessionism (*naskh*), where he summarized the Sunni supersessionistic view on non-Islamic religions. In this section, he responded to the Jews, who reject the Muslim theory of supersessionism. Al-Juwaynī contended that one of the most intelligent arguments of the Jews is that Muslims believe in the principle of supersessionism, yet they do not apply it to their own tradition. When the Jews ask Muslims, "What proof do you rely on to establish the eternality of your law?," Muslims respond that this is what Muḥammad has *informed* us. Then the Jews say, "Our Prophet [Moses] did the same; he *informed* us that his law is not to be superseded." Al-Juwaynī responded with two objections. First, if the claim of the Jews were true, God would not have revealed himself with the miracles of Jesus and Muḥammad, who came after Moses; since there were miracles after Moses, the Jews' tradition of supersessionism is invalidated by actual historical realities. Second, if it is truly said in the Torah that there is no prophet to come after Moses, why did those Jews who were contemporaneous with Muḥammad not show him this in their Scripture, even though they were keen on falsifying his prophethood? The fact that they did not suggests the falsity of their report.[81]

Al-Juwaynī is clearly not the first pre-Ghazālian theologian to rely on *naskh* in establishing the necessity of belief in Prophet Muḥammad for one to attain salvation. Al-Baghdādī, who died roughly fifty years before al-Juwaynī, argued on the same basis by offering a lengthy discussion on Islam's superseding non-Islamic religions in his *Kitāb usūl al-dīn*.[82] In fact, al-Ashʿarī himself, the founder of the school, believed that the finality of Prophet Muḥammad is established through the theory of *naskh*.[83] This tells us that believing in Prophet Muḥammad was considered part of the *ḍarūriyyāt* in early Ashʿarite theology and that it was essentially linked to belief in God, namely, that one cannot claim to believe in God without believing in Prophet Muḥammad. The next question, however, is whether it remained in the same zone in classical and modern Ashʿarism. The answer shall be sought in al-Ghazālī's genre.

Although al-Ghazālī, as we have seen, moved the notion of *al-firqa al-nājiya* from the zone of *ḍarūriyyāt* to the zone of *taḥsīniyyāt* and raised "deeds" from the degree of *taḥsīniyyāt* to the degree of *ḥājiyyāt*, for him Prophet Muḥammad remained in the zone of *ḍarūriyyāt*. In fact, he highlighted further the place of the Prophet and offered some new insights that are worthy of our attention. He taught that Muslim faith essentially means accepting the truthfulness of Prophet Muḥammad in everything that is authentically reported of him. In actuality, he introduced a sort of equalization between the Qur'ān (the word of God) and the *ḥadīth* traditions (the word of the Prophet), considering both as two types of revelation to be followed: one is recited (the Qur'ān), and the other is not (the *ḥadīth*/Sunna).[84] Furthermore, he believed in *naskh*, arguing that the law of Muḥammad superseded the laws of all previous prophets except whatever God affirmed to remain, and that God favored Muḥammad over all other prophets. Therefore, to him, believing in Muḥammad cannot be separated from believing in God.[85] Summarizing this move, Mohammed H. Khalil wrote:

> The prominent [Ashʿarite] theologian ʿAbd al-Qāhir al-Baghdādī (d. 1037) claimed that any Muslim who departs from the Ashʿarite orthodoxy risks not being counted among the believers. In response, Ghazālī argues that true unbelief consists in rejecting one of the three fundamental principles, that is, belief in one God, the Prophet, and the hereafter; or refusing to accept secondary doctrines derived from prophetic reports that are diffused and congruent (*mutawātir*)—in effect, a rejection of the Prophet's veracity. According to this standard, rationalists (*mutakallimūn*) within and without Ashʿarism, traditionalists (Ḥanbalītes), and Twelver Shi'ites could all be considered true Muslims, even if some of their views are problematic.[86]

What is more, al-Ghazālī considered Muḥammad "essential" not only for the authenticity of one's faith but also for one's salvation in the Hereafter. Let us examine the following text from his *Fayṣal*:

> But I say in addition that God's mercy will encompass many bygone communities as well, even if most of them may be briefly exposed to the Hellfire for a second or an hour or some period of time, by virtue of which they earn the title, "party of the Hellfire." In fact, I would say that, God willing, most of the Christians of Byzantium and the Turks of this age will be covered by God's mercy. I am referring here to those who reside in the far regions of Byzantium and Anatolia who have not come in contact with the message of Islam. These people fall into three categories: 1) A party who never heard so much as the name "Muhammad." These people are excused. 2) A party among those who lived in lands adjacent to the lands of Islam and had contact, therefore, with Muslims, who knew his name, his character, and the miracles he wrought. These are the blasphemous Unbelievers. 3) A third party whose case falls between these two poles. These people knew the name "Muhammad," but nothing of his character and attributes. Instead, all they heard since childhood was that some arch-liar carrying the name "Muhammad" claimed to be a prophet, just as our children heard that an arch-liar and deceiver called al-Muqaffaʿ falsely claimed that God sent him (as a prophet) and then challenged people to disprove his claim. This group, in my opinion, is like the first group. Even though they heard his name, they heard the opposite of what his true attributes were. And this does not provide enough incentive to compel them to investigate (his true status).[87]

Unpacking the quotation, we see that al-Ghazālī thought non-Muslims can be divided into three classes in the Hereafter based on whether they recognized Muḥammad's prophethood. One class is those whom the name of Prophet Muḥammad never reached: their unbelief is excused. The second comprises those who have heard his name and learned of his traits and miracles and lived alongside Muslims and interacted with them: their unbelief is not excused. The third contains those in between the previous two. Muḥammad's name has reached their ears, but they do not know his true personality. Instead, they have heard from the time they were young that a deceitful liar named Muḥammad claimed to be a prophet. Such people are excused like those in the first category, for while they have heard his name, they heard the opposite of his real qualities. And hearing such things would not normally rouse one to find out who he really was.

Based on the above discussion, believing in Prophet Muḥammad lies in the zone of *ḍarūriyyāt* in al-Ghazālī's higher theology, which remained the case in post-Ghazālian Ashʿarism. For instance, in his commentary on Q. 11:17,[88] al-Rāzī explicated the verse by quoting the following tradition: "By Him in Whose hand is the life of Muḥammad, he who amongst the community of Jews or Christians hears about me, but does not affirm his belief in that with which I have been sent and dies in this state (of disbelief), he shall be but one of the denizens of Hell-Fire."[89] Another occurrence is his engagement with verse Q. 2:62,[90] where he argued that the phrase "believes in God" necessarily demands belief in Prophet Muḥammad.[91] In other words, faith in God cannot be true if it is not accompanied by faith in Prophet Muḥammad.

The question remains, did the status of Muḥammad ever move out of the zone of *ḍarūriyyāt*? With ʿAbduh, we see a trend in modern Ashʿarite theology that took God, not Prophet Muḥammad, as its starting point. This centralization of God demanded that ʿAbduh revisit the theory of *naskh*, which saw Muḥammad's message as superseding previous messages, a leitmotif in earlier Ashʿarite thinking. While classical Ashʿarites largely presented *naskh* as a matter of "doctrine," ʿAbduh's school saw it merely as an "exegetical device" instead.[92] Therefore, they attempted to deconstruct the basis of this theory and denied that Islam's relation to Christianity and Judaism is one of replacement, but rather saw it as one of fulfillment.[93] ʿAbduh argued that Islam came primarily to *reform*, not to *revoke*, Christianity and Judaism. Hence, while Christians are invited to *acknowledge* the truth of Prophet Muḥammad, they are not required to *convert* to Islam in order to attain salvation. Appealing to Q. 3:64,[94] this reformation lies in inviting them to go back to the original message of their religions. Therefore, Islam's key message to Jews and Christians is one of "witness," as in Q. 2:243, which reads, "We have made you [Muslims] a just community that you will be witnesses over the people and the Messenger will be a witness over you."[95]

Having centralized the figure of God alone in the zone of *ḍarūriyyāt*, ʿAbduh was cautious on branding non-Muslim believers in God as *kuffār* (disbelievers) on account of their denial of Prophet Muḥammad. In his journal, *al-Manār* (The Lighthouse), Rashīd Riḍā, reflecting ʿAbduh's thought, argued that the word *kāfir* today applies exclusively to atheists and that Muslims cannot automatically regard non-Muslim believers as *kuffār* anymore. Anyone who calls a non-Muslim a *kāfir* is committing a blameworthy act that goes against the theological ethos of Islam.[96] This is indeed a paradigm shift on the usage of the term "believer" (*mu'min*). For a believer, previously, could only mean a Muḥammadan, but with ʿAbduh, anyone who believes in God and the Last Day is a believer no matter whether he is a Muḥammadan or otherwise.

Revisiting the role of Prophet Muḥammad, ʿAbduh introduced a sense of equality between Islam, on the one hand, and Christianity and Judaism, on the other, by basing his position on Q. 2:62,[97] reading it alongside Q. 4:123–125, which state:

> It will not be according to your hopes or those of the People of the Book: anyone who does wrong will be requited for it and will find no one to protect or help him against God; (123) anyone, male or female, who does good deeds and is a believer, will enter Paradise and will not be wronged by as much as the dip in a date stone (124). Who could be better in religion than those who direct themselves wholly to God, do good, and follow the religion of Abraham, who was true in faith? God took Abraham as a friend (125).

Explicating these verses, ʿAbduh quoted a *ḥadīth* that describes the revelatory occasion of Q. 4:123–125, which basically gives an account of the quarrel of groups of Jews, Christians, and Muslims, each asserting ultimate superiority. ʿAbduh proceeded "to sketch some of the implications of an excessive concern with sectarian allegiance. He feels that God's reproach is addressed to an imbalance, namely the imbalance that develops when an individual's interest in being identified with a religion outweighs the fervour with which he practises."[98]

Responding to those who equated Islam with Muḥammadanism, ʿAbduh appealed to Q. 3:85, which is often taken to mean that there is no path to God but through Muḥammad. The verse reads, "If anyone seeks a religion other than *islām*, it will not be accepted from him: he will be one of the losers in the Hereafter." ʿAbduh argued that confusing *islām* here with Islam is not only inaccurate but an act of theological racism. Salvation is based on *islām* rather than Islam. Living in a state of submission to God, and not merely belonging to the religion that is formally called Islam, is what puts one on the path of salvation. This is what is meant when the Qur'ān depicts Abraham (and other prophets as well) as being a *muslim*, or one who submits to God. Therefore, the Qur'ānic view of a "true" *muslim* is of one whose faith in God is pure and free from associating partners with Him.[99]

What essentially sets ʿAbduh's school apart from al-Ghazālī's is that they have different starting points and different understanding of what lies within the zone of theological *ḍarūriyyāt*. Starting his theology with God meant necessarily that ʿAbduh's theology would be a God-based theology, which means that all prophets are "means" to God and not "ends" in and of themselves. In contrast, by starting his theology with Prophet Muḥammad, it is only natural that al-Ghazālī concluded with a Muḥammadan-based theology. While, to al-Ghazālī, for one to attain salvation, one needs not only to believe in God but also to believe in Prophet Muḥammad, to ʿAbduh belief in God is the only necessity, apart from doing good deeds and believing in the Last Day. As a result, belief in Prophet Muḥammad lay in the area of *ḥājiyyāt* in ʿAbduh's theology, whereas it lay within the zone of *ḍarūriyyāt* for al-Ghazālī and earlier Ashʿarites' theology.

To conclude, examining *al-firqa al-nājiya*, faith vis-à-vis deeds, and the role of Prophet Muḥammad in Islamic theology showed that each question had a particular journey of either progression or regression in its theological weight. We saw, first, how the notion of *al-firqa al-nājiya* began in early Ashʿarism as part of the *ḍarūriyyāt* but moved to *ḥājiyyāt* in classical Ashʿarism, and moved even further in modern Ashʿarism to become part of the *taḥsīniyyāt*. The opposite journey applies to the second case. While in early Ashʿarism good deeds were largely seen as nonessential to one's faith, with al-Ghazālī's emphasis on deeds, they moved from *taḥsīniyyāt* to the zone of *ḥājiyyāt*. However, with ʿAbduh's further emphasis on good deeds, they moved progressively to the zone of *ḍarūriyyāt*, which had a significant bearing on the religious value of the good deeds of non-Muslims. As for the place of Prophet Muḥammad, although it was never in the zone of *taḥsīniyyāt*, modern Ashʿarism largely considered faith in Prophet Muḥammad as part of *ḥājiyyāt*, not *ḍarūriyyāt*, as a means to God but not as an end per se. What never departed from the area of *ḍarūriyyāt* in Ashʿarism is faith in God.

What does this signify? And how can this taxonomy help Islamic theology develop? I argue that if this taxonomy of *ḍarūriyyāt*, *ḥājiyyāt*, and *taḥsīniyyāt* is properly applied in Islamic theology, it can help develop a systematic theology of ecumenism not only at the intrafaith level but also at the interfaith level. To explain the intrafaith level, let us take the question of deeds vis-à-vis faith as an example. Classical Ashʿarism's marginalization of deeds is largely opposed by the vast majority of other Sunni schools, which look at deeds as part of the *ḍarūriyyāt*.[100] If ʿAbduh's view of deeds is considered seriously, not only will this naturally bring about more commonalities with other theological schools, but it will also revive a culture of "good practice" in the modern Muslim mind, a mind that has largely reduced Islam to a "faith system" that does not place much emphasis on deeds.

As for the interfaith level, if ʿAbduh's centralization of God alone in the area of *ḍarūriyyāt* is seriously considered, it will bring about more commonalities with other faith traditions and will also put limits on the usage of the term *kāfir*, which is still used, largely arbitrarily. To give an example, the most intense debate in which Al-Azhar engaged in 2017–2018 was whether Christians are *kuffār* or not. Some popular Azharite shaykhs publicly declared Christians to be *kuffār*, and although they strongly emphasized that this had nothing to do with respecting their rights of citizenship, the controversy did not end, necessitating the intervention of Al-Azhar, as the official voice of Sunni Islam in the country, which, in its turn, commissioned some Azharite professors to speak on TV shows to alleviate the heated debate. Instead of creating a space for revisiting such historical-theological stances, Al-Azhar concluded with a middle-stance manifesto, declaring that Muslims are not *in the position to* declare non-Muslims *kuffār*; this is left to God.[101]

The public noted how the discussants used Scripture in support of their two *opposing* views to endorse their theological positions. This led to some arbitrary and contradictory definitions of how Scripture uses the term *kuffār*. The heated debate on this term and its theological applications and implications indicates a critical need to produce hermeneutical rules that consider the context in which the term occurs in the Muslim Scripture, and also to ask what exactly are the *ḍarūriyyāt* of Islamic theology, the violation of which may allow *takfīr*.

In light of the above conclusions, we shall move to the last chapter, which will, hopefully, exemplify how a *maqāṣidī*-oriented approach to Islamic theology may well help tackle one of the key volatile areas in modern Muslim theology, that is, Sunni-Wahhabi-Shiite relations.

5

Why Does Maqāṣid al-ʿAqīda *Matter?*

NOTHING CAN BETTER attest to the need for approaching Islamic theology with a *maqāṣidī*-oriented approach than the contemporary Shiite-Wahhabi-Sunni conflict. The conflict started primarily around political issues, yet it undoubtedly had doctrinal facets to it, especially in relation to religious and political authority. The Shiites believed that ʿAlī—the Prophet's cousin and son-in-law—and his male descendants, namely the Twelver Imāms, had inherited Muḥammad's charisma, and consequently were entitled to be not only his political heirs but also the maintainers of his religious authority. But the majority, which later constituted the Sunni community, believed that the Prophet's heirs (caliphs) did not inherit Muḥammad's charisma, and hence held only his political power.[1] With the passage of time, these issues continued to evoke intense emotions and to be vigorously debated by both sides. Those heated disputes about the distant past, as Fred Halliday observed, have become crucial to present-day conflict so that both parties may answer two key questions: who a true Muslim is (religious facet) and who should dominate the Muslim world (political facet).[2]

At the heart of this conflict lies a popular argument that lumps Ibn Ḥanbal as well as Ibn Taymiyya together with Ibn ʿAbd al-Wahhāb as the key proponents of anti-Shiism and anti-Shiites in the Sunni tradition. That is, the roots of anti-Shiism in the Sunni tradition are not to be located only in the writings of Ibn ʿAbd al-Wahhāb, but also, probably more originally, in the writings of Ibn Ḥanbal and Ibn Taymiyya. Reflecting this common argument, Guido Steinberg wrote the following statement:

> With this treatise [Ibn ʿAbd al-Wahhāb's *al-Radd ʿala al-Rāfiḍa*], Ibn ʿAbd al-Wahhab *was in line with a long tradition of great Hanbali*

The Higher Objectives of Islamic Theology. Mohammed Gamal Abdelnour, Oxford University Press.
© Oxford University Press 2022. DOI: 10.1093/oso/9780197648636.003.0005

> *reformers.*[3] Ahmad bin Hanbal himself was a traditionist (i.e., a hadith scholar) and theologian rather than a lawyer, and seemingly had not intended to found a school of law at all. As a traditionist, his main interest was in collecting, criticising, and categorising hadith material. On the basis of the Qur'ān and of trustworthy hadith collections, Ibn Hanbal and fellow traditionists established what they regarded as true Islamic doctrine. These reports, however, had been transmitted by the companions of the Prophet (*sahaba*), many of whom are not regarded as reliable by the Shiʿis because of their role in the conflict over the rightful succession to the Prophet—the most important point of contention between Sunnis and Shiʿis. As a result of this conflict, the Shiʿis regarded many of these companions not only as untrustworthy but also claimed that they had in fact strayed from the true path of Islam. *By the very nature of his occupation, Ibn Hanbal had to develop a robust anti-Shiʿism.*[4]

However, Steinberg's observation calls for some revisitation, for although Ibn Ḥanbal considered the Sunnis to be the true followers of the Prophet, since ʿAlī, in his view, thought of himself as below Abū Bakr, ʿUmar, and ʿUthmān,[5] he never practiced blanket *takfir* or excommunication against the Shiites. He, and to a large degree Sunnis in general, would observe silence about the great conflict between ʿAlī and Muʿāwiya.[6] For instance, Ibn al-Jawzī (d. 1201)[7] in his *Manāqib al-Imām Aḥmad Ibn Ḥanbal* (The Merits of the Master Aḥmad Ibn Ḥanbal) reported that when a man from the Prophet's family asked about that divide between the early Sunnis and Shiites, Ibn Ḥanbal turned away from him. When he was asked why he turned away from a man from the family of Banū Hāshim (the Prophet's family), he recited, "That was a nation who has passed away. They shall receive the reward of what they earned and you of what you earn. And you will not be asked of what they used to do" (Q. 2:134).[8] Such statements have largely constituted the single most dominant attitude of Sunni scholars toward this early divide; an attitude that is often embodied in the statement of the eighth Umayyad caliph, ʿUmar ibn ʿAbd al-ʿAzīz' (d. 720), who, when asked about this divide, said, "That is a blood that God caused me to have no hand in shedding, and I do not want to dip my tongue in it [by talking about it]."[9]

On the contrary, Ibn Ḥanbal was one of the key defenders of ʿAlī's character whenever the latter was reviled during al-Mutawakkil's reign (847–861) of the Abbasid caliphate.[10] Ibn Taymiyya put it more clearly, when he said in his *Fatāwā* that Ibn Ḥanbal did not sway from his rejection of *takfir* against the Shiites. Even more distantly, not only did he refrain from practicing blanket *takfir* against them, but he also narrated many *ḥadīths* from Shiite *imāms* and scholars, which indicates that his stern statements, which shall be shown later, need to be contextualized. In his *Glimpses of Shiism in the Musnad of Aḥmad*, Sayyid al-Tabatba'i showed that one of the features of Aḥmad's *Musnad* is the wide space given to *ḥadīths* devoted to the merits of the Prophet's descendants, most of which are also confirmed from the viewpoint of Shiite Muslims. He further demonstrated that "compared to the other *ḥadīth* compendiums of the Sunnis, the *Musnad*'s emphasis on this subject is so pronounced that it has attracted the attention of orientalists and other researchers."[11]

Although Ibn Ḥanbal is sometimes critical of Shiism, this needs to not be overrated. By being critical I refer to reports attributed to him such as the following: "[T]hose who distance themselves from the Companions of Muḥammad, curse and belittle them; accuse the Companions of committing *kufr*, except four: ʿAlī, ʿAmmār, al-Miqdād and Salmān; they have nothing to do with Islam."[12] However, a holistic reading of his oeuvre will quickly show that these critical statements apply only to the Shiites that came to be later identified as the Bāṭinites/Ismāʿīlīs, in Ahmad's terms, the Rawāfiḍ (rejecters of Abū Bakr and ʿUmar).

In a similar vein, Ibn Taymiyya is often associated with marshaling antagonism against Shiites and Shiism.[13] Although most studies on Shiism describe him as pronouncing sweeping statements of *takfir* against the Shiites, a holistic reading of his writings will show that the case is not as straightforward as it may seem. This is partly because contemporary Wahhabis tend to quote his *Minhāj al-sunna* (Path of the Sunna), neglecting, for instance, his *al-Ṣārim al-maslūl ʿalā shātim al-rasūl* (The Loose Sword on the Insulter of the Prophet), even though, in the latter, he showed a more balanced position on Shiism. For example, he argued that if a person slanders the Prophet's Companions in a way that does not oppugn their religious faithfulness, instead describing them as being stingy or cowardly or lacking in knowledge, then we do not rule him to be a *kāfir* on such a basis. But if a person claims that they apostatized after the demise of the Prophet, apart from a small group that had Shiite inclinations, then there is no doubt that such a person is a *kāfir*, as he has denied what is established by the Qur'ān: that God was pleased with the Companions of His Prophet. More distantly, Ibn Taymiyya goes as far to say that whoever doubts that such a person is a *kāfir* is himself a *kāfir*, not by virtue of harboring a Shiite doctrine, but rather because this implies that those who transmitted the Qur'ān were not trustworthy and that the best generation of Muslims were mostly *kuffār* and hypocrites.[14] Thus, Ibn Taymiyya barely departed from Ibn Ḥanbal's take on this issue.

Notwithstanding, highlighting his stern statements only and taking them out of their context, many Wahhabis pass around the following quotation from Ibn Taymiyya: "[T]hey are more evil than most of the people of heresies, and they are more deserving of being killed than the Khārijites."[15] However, one needs to observe that what Ibn Taymiyya stated here does not apply to all Shiites or even all Rawāfiḍ (to use Ibn Ḥanbal's term), but only those who have specific beliefs which he described as saying that "the Companions became apostates after the death of the Prophet or that the majority of them were disobedient sinners."[16] The renowned scholar on Sunni-Shiite relations, Fathi Shaqaqi, confirmed this conclusion, accentuating that Ibn Taymiyya's severe statements on Shiism were, at any rate, directed at the Ismāʿīlīs and certainly not at Twelver Shiites. He proceeded to say that such statements were largely "utilised extensively by opponents of the Iranian revolution." To quote him at length:

> Prior to Ibn Taymiyya's time (d. 1328), fatwas such as his were not disseminated, despite the fact that the Shiʿa had by then been in existence for some 600 years. Furthermore, one had to take into account the threatening historical reality in which Ibn Taymiyya, and Muslim society as a whole, lived in the context of the Mongol invasion, which heightened zealous adherence to the Sunni creed.[17]

In his *al-ʿAqīda al-wāsiṭiyya* (The Creed to the People of Wāsiṭ), Ibn Taymiyya seemed even sanguine about Shiism in general, for he went further to say that the Prophet's Household should be honored, writing, "*Ahl al-Sunna* should love the Prophet's family, give them support, and honour the Prophet's will concerning them, as he said at Ghadīr Khumm twice: I ask you by God to take care of my family."[18] And then he explicitly stated that they reject only the rejectors (Rawāfiḍ) who reject the Companions and slander them, as well as the Nāṣibites, who insult *Ahl al-Bayt* in words and action.[19]

Shifting to the founder of Wahhabism, Muḥammad Ibn ʿAbd al-Wahhāb (d. 1792)[20] represented an unprecedented shift in the Sunni-Shiite conflict, for he was a polarizing figure. He threw sweeping statements of excommunication on Shiites, considering them to be heretics, and their veneration of their *imāms* as *shirk* (polytheism). Occupied by building up a new puritan society, he wrote a treatise titled *al-Radd ʿalā al-Rāfiḍa* (The Refutation of the Rejectionists). This treatise showed that Ibn ʿAbd al-Wahhāb's main issue with the Shiites was their "rejection" of the early Companions, which he saw as a threat to the foundation of his theological project. Therefore, he considered Shiites to be mostly unbelievers (*kuffār*) and, given that they claim to be Muslims, believed they are more harmful to the Muslim community "than Jews and Christians."[21]

It is important to notice here that at the heart of Ibn ʿAbd al-Wahhāb's ideology lay a belief in "a return to an Islam as practiced at the time of the Prophet and his original followers, the so-called ancestors (*Salaf*) from which the term Salafis is derived."[22] What naturally results from this ideology is that the Shiite rejectionism of the righteousness of the Prophet's Companions falls out of line with his capital beliefs and intended program of reform.[23]

On the other hand, the Shiite veneration of their *imāms* was, to him, tantamount to polytheism. It seems that the importance of tombs and graves in Shiite rituals must have incensed him, as someone "who fought similar practices, which had also become widespread among Sunnis. In many ways, Shiism ran counter to his message of radical monotheism (*tawḥīd*)."[24]

To support his program of reform, he drew selectively on the writings of Ibn Taymiyya in a way that largely abused the latter's views and took them out of context. According to Ibn ʿAbd al-Wahhāb's brother, Sulaymān (d. 1740), even though the former "did not concern himself with reading or understanding the works of the juristic predecessors," he "treated the words of some, such as Ibn Taymiyya . . . as if they were divinely revealed, not to be questioned or debated."[25] Additionally, Ibn Ḥumaydī (d. 1878), the key historiographer of the period, stated that Ibn ʿAbd al-Wahhāb was opportunistically selective about what he took from Ibn Taymiyya.[26] More dangerously, in his writings the term "Shiism" was loosely used, encompassing also the Twelvers, which includes the overwhelming majority of Shiites.[27] The term was never used in this way in pre-Wahhabi theology.

This "selectivity" got standardized in Wahhabi literature. Although Wahhabis arbitrarily picked the Ḥanbalite school as providing the exclusively authentic legal system in Islam, they were abusively selective of the writings and scholars of this school. In *The Great Theft: Wrestling Islam from the Extremists*, Abou El Fadl pointed out that, following the example of Ibn ʿAbd al-Wahhāb, Wahhabis have appropriated whatever they find in the writings of Ibn Taymiyya that are in harmony with their worldview, not only ignoring the rest of Ibn Taymiyya's writings but also never citing or referring to other Ḥanbalī jurists who were known for their rationalist and more liberal approaches, treating the views of the former as well as those of his close associate Ibn al-Qayyim "as immutable and beyond questioning."[28]

At the conceptual level, the concepts of *kufr* and *tawḥīd*, as Tarik K. Firro explained in his *Wahhabism and the Rise of the House of Saud*, were central to Ibn ʿAbd al-Wahhāb's project.[29] Drawing on those concepts, Ibn ʿAbd al-Wahhāb denounced many forms of public piety practiced by Muslims, mainly Sufi-oriented Muslims, assigning to his followers the mission of purifying Islam of all types of heresies, implying a denial of *tawḥīd* among many Muslims. He dedicated his *Kitāb al-tawḥīd* (Book of Monotheism) to refute the exegetical treatises of preceding and contemporary scholars, accusing them of having misled Muslims and caused them to internalize the customs of *shirk*. In his *Kashf al-shubuhāt fī al-tawḥīd* (Uncovering Misconceptions about Monotheism), he claimed that practices of *shirk* have permeated the Muslim world, comparing its prevalence to that which was practiced in the time of the Prophet and claiming that the number of the earliest polytheists was far less than those living in his age. Even more distantly, the polytheists of the day are even worse, for while the earlier ones prayed to God, the living have abandoned prayer.[30] Considering the veneration of graves and other sacred sites as pre-Islamic practices, he called for the uprooting of such customs, urging his allies to fight against such polytheists until they revert to monotheism.[31] Furthermore, due to the fact that such forms of public piety were widely practiced also by Shiites and that the Wahhabi movement expanded into areas inhabited by Shiites, Shiites were naturally not safe from excommunication.[32]

Having said that, it is crucial to note that such a radical understanding of *kufr* and *tawḥīd* does not emerge from the Ḥanbalī tradition (Atharism), despite its strictness, but rather departs from it.[33] That is, the Ḥanbalī tradition generally treated the question of *kufr* cautiously and accommodated commemoration rites for saints, including reading piety-related books at the grave of Ibn Ḥanbal. Ibn al-Jawzī's *Manāqib al-Imām Aḥmad Ibn Ḥanbal* offered extensive discussions detailing, with great admiration, the visitation ceremonies to Ibn Ḥanbal's grave.

While Ibn ʿAbd al-Wahhāb did not literally say that Shiites were outside the fold of Islam, his following generation did. For instance, ʿAbd al-Laṭīf Āl al-Shaykh (d. 1876),[34] counting the sects and locations of the infidels, denounced the heretical inclination of the Shiites, reiterating the principles of Ibn ʿAbd al-Wahhāb, which are elaborated in his *Risāla fī al-Radd ʿala al-Rāfiḍa*, and placing them outside the realm of Islam. In her *Saudi Clerics and Shīʿa Islam*, Raihan Ismail highlighted how he considered "the practices of praying to ʿAlī, Ḥusayn, ʿAbbās, and ʿAbd al-Qādir as acts of *shirk*, only to be pardoned following deep repentance."[35] Furthermore, he described the Shiites of Iraq as similar to Christians in faith as well as in practice on account of their divination of their *imāms*.[36] ʿAbdullah (d. 1826), Ibn ʿAbd al-Wahhāb's son, triggered by the above considerations and practices, wrote a lengthy book, *Jawāb Ahl al-Sunna fī naqd kalām al-Shīʿa wa-al-Zaydiyya* (The Response of the Sunnis in Refuting the Shiite and Zaydi Claims), deeming "all Shiites" deviators from Islam and in need of reverting to the straight path of the Religion.[37]

In light of the above discussion, I hope to have pointed out how lumping Ibn Ḥanbal as well as Ibn Taymiyya together with Ibn ʿAbd al-Wahhāb as key proponents of anti-Shiism is erroneous and that the former's statements on Shiism and Shiites were more deeply qualified than those of the latter. This will hopefully help us understand the real roots of the conflict and its nature.

Having said that, it is now apt to move to showing how a *maqāṣidī*-oriented approach to the current Wahhabi-Shiite divide may well help heal this breach. Drawing inspirations from al-Ghazālī's canon of interpretation, ʿAbduh's Theology of Unity, and Shaltūt's initiatives, I aim to demonstrate how such efforts may well serve as effective examples of how a *maqāṣidī*-oriented approach to Islamic theology is capable of constructing a Muslim theology of ecumenism.

The Maqāṣidī-*Oriented Approach and Treating the Wahhabi-Shiite Conflict*

The first lesson that al-Ghazālī has to teach us here is "precision." That is, although he wrote a number of treatises in which he attempted to refute the doctrines of Shiism, he was always clear that the object of his critique was not ordinary Shiites, but rather the Bāṭinites. The most detailed of these treatises is his *Faḍāʾiḥ al-baṭiniyya wa faḍāʾil al-mustaẓhiriyya* (The Infamies of the Bāṭinites and the Virtues of the Mustaẓhiriyya), more widely referred to as *Kitāb al-mustaẓhirī* (Exotericist). The purpose of this work was to systematically present, analyze, and critique the Ismaili doctrine of *taʿlīm* (authoritative instruction) of the alleged *imām* of the time. Those Ismaili Shiites were largely known as Bāṭinites and were proponents of the Fatimid counter-caliphate in Cairo.[38]

Al-Ghazālī's attempts to deal with the esoteric Ismaili Shiites and their erroneous interpretations amounted to defining the boundaries of religious pluralism in the Sunni tradition. Defining these boundaries resulted in what al-Ghazālī called *qanūn al-taʾwīl* (a canon of interpretation), which is part of his *Fayṣal.* There he said, "You should refrain from accusing any group of unbelief and from spreading rumours about the people of Islam—even if they differ in their ways—as long as they firmly confess that there is no god but God and that Muḥammad is His messenger, and as long as they hold this true and do not contradict it."[39]

Explaining this "canon of interpretation," al-Ghazālī contended that God sometimes decides to express Himself in metaphors rather than literal definitions. It then becomes the job of the interpreter to trace these metaphors back to their intended meaning. That said, there are five possible levels of meanings to a given word in a piece of revelation: (1) ontological (*dhātī*), (2) sensory (*ḥissī*), (3) conceptual (*khayālī*), (4) noetic (*ʿaqlī*), and (5) analogous (*shabahī*). These five degrees correspond to a descending scale of literalness, "with ontological (*dhātī*) being literal in the strict sense, sensory (*ḥissī*) representing the first level of figurative existence, and analogous (*shabahī*) representing the most remote."[40] When interpreting Scripture, one must start with the ontological degree. One cannot move to the following degree if the statement in question can be understood as true on that literal level. If otherwise, one must move to the closest degree. If the next degree cannot be sustained, one moves to the more remote degree.[41] To give an example, on the sensory degree, the sun appears to rise and set while revolving around the earth. Nevertheless, on the ontological degree, the earth revolves around the sun. Accordingly, a layman who is ignorant of astronomy would understand Q. 18:17[42] literally, while an astronomer would be justified in understanding this verse to be literally untrue and only sensorily true. Granted that both parties do not reject the truth of the verse on all levels without justification, neither of them can be accused of denying the truthfulness of Scripture.[43] With this canon of interpretation, al-Ghazālī managed to theorize for a plurality of understanding of the Scripture in order to avoid falling into the trap of *takfir*, which is often motivated by each denomination claiming a monopoly on religious truth.

Based on the inclusive interpretation of Islam initiated by al-Ghazālī, the non-orthodox schools of theology, including the Shiites, began to enjoy a level of acceptance. In fact, Twelver Shiites joined the Sunnis against the Bāṭinites of the Fatimid caliphate which ruled Egypt (969–1171).[44] Compare Ibn ʿAbd al-Wahhāb's maxims of *takfir* to what al-Ghazālī wrote in his *Bidāyat al-hidāya* (The Beginning of Guidance), for instance; you will see two different versions of Islam, whereby al-Ghazālī advises his readers not to engage in *takfir* or to curse humans or animals or even foods. He wrote:

> Take care never to curse anything that God has created, be it an animal or a type of food, let alone people. Nor to swear that one of the people of the Qibla (Muslims) is guilty of associating partners with God, or of unbelief, or of hypocrisy, for it is only God who has access to peoples' hearts. So, do not intervene between God and His subjects. More distantly, on the Day of Resurrection, you will neither be asked: why did you not curse So-and-So? Nor why were you silent about So-and-So? Even more distantly, if you have never cursed Satan once in your entire lifetime, you will not be asked about it. However, if you curse someone you will surely be taken into account for it.[45]

Moving from al-Ghazālī to ʿAbduh, it is interesting to note that, although Ibn ʿAbd al-Wahhāb and ʿAbduh both appealed to the notion of *tawḥīd* in their programs of reform, they developed radically different, if not opposing, conclusions. While the former developed a radical theology of "identity" that can barely tolerate co-Muslim denominations (let alone non-Muslims), the latter developed a theology of "unity" whose accommodation expanded beyond the Muslim community to include the Abrahamic faith traditions, arguing that belief in God's Unity should motivate believers in God to unite under His name and mold their community by the concept of Unity, considering this as one of the key objectives of Islamic theology, as has been clarified in the first chapter of this book.

ʿAbduh's project of reform came as a response to two types of decay in the Muslim world: intellectual and societal. That is, he contended that the Muslim "mind" had reached a state of intellectual ossification, and that the Muslim "community" had undergone an inner decay. This situation led to the emergence of protest responses, most notably the Wahhabi movement in the eighteenth and nineteenth centuries. While he believed in the legitimacy of the Wahhabi call in terms of challenging the prevalent sense of "traditionalism" prevalent in traditional circles of learning, he thought that Wahhabis were not intellectually competent to undertake such a reform because of their adoption of a literalist approach to the scriptures as well as lacking an understanding of the higher objectives that Islam came to fulfill and upon which it was built.[46] Furthermore, he was dissatisfied with their aggressive extremism and their loose practice of *takfīr*.[47]

Although ʿAbduh believed that Shiism too was in need of reform inasmuch as Sunnism was, he was far from harboring an extremist position on it. In this context, it is noteworthy that he took Bahaism as a Shiite denomination whose objective was to reform Shiism from within and to bring it in conversation with Sunni Islam.[48] When Riḍā raised the point that Bahaism believes in the validity of all religions and that they attempt to unite humanity around this belief, ʿAbduh responded, "Indeed, bringing religions together is of what Islam came to achieve," and then quoted Q. 3:64, which states, "Say, 'O People of the Scripture, come to a word that is equitable between us and you—that we will not worship except God and not associate anything with Him and not take one another as lords instead of God.' But if they turn away, then say, 'Bear witness that we are Muslims [submitting to Him].' "[49]

Appealing to sources of unity in the Islamic tradition, ʿAbduh gave a new lease on life to the notion of *tawḥīd* that is out of line with that of ʿAbd al-Wahhāb. As has been clarified earlier, in *Risālat al-tawḥīd*, ʿAbduh showed that disregarding a *maqāṣidī* approach to Islamic theology was a primary reason for Islamic theology's failure to do its ecumenical job, likening Muslim theological debates, present and past, to the situation of two groups of brothers who have been divided, even though they were heading to a shared goal.[50]

Practicing what he preached, ʿAbduh, in his exile in Beirut in the 1880s, presided over the *Jamʿiyyat al-taʾlīf wa al-taqrīb* (Society of Reconciliation and Ecumenism), which was a diverse society, having Christian, Jewish, and Muslim members from different denominations, with a view to furthering harmony between the three monotheistic religions and their internal denominations.[51] It seems that the Society worked on creating a global correspondence network instead of separate meetings. According to Riḍā, the Society also aimed at teaching Europeans about true Islam and its merits, depicting Islam as the natural continuation and evolution of Christianity and Judaism.[52] In light of this, had ʿAbduh's theology taken the lead in modern Muslim theology instead of Ibn ʿAbd al-Wahhāb's, I argue, the shape of the modern Muslim world would have been different.

Moving from ʿAbduh to Shaltūt, one may see the latter's efforts in this area serving as an example of practicalizing al-Ghazālī's law of interpretation and ʿAbduh's Theology of Unity. Indeed, the twentieth-century *Jamāʿat al-taqrīb bayn al-madhāhib al-islāmiyya*, with Shaltūt's leading role in it, can rightly be considered the first official attempt to bridge the gap between Sunnis and Shiites.[53] Although it faced challenges from Wahhabi-oriented scholars, at the end of the 1950s it managed to reach a wider public when the Egyptian president Gamal Abdel Nasser realized the usefulness of pan-Islamism for his foreign policy program.[54] The most thrilling outcome of this endeavor was a fatwa in 1959 by Shaltūt, in which he not only legitimized Shiism as a fifth *madhhab*, alongside the four orthodox schools, but also allowed mutual conversion from one to the other.[55] This fatwa has officiated the following:

1. Islam does not oblige any of its adherents to be affiliated with a specific madhhab. Rather, we say: Every Muslim has, first of all, the right to follow any of the legal schools that have been properly handed down and whose rules in their specific (legal) effects are laid down in writing. A person who follows one of these schools is entitled to turn to any other without being subjected to reproach.
2. In the sense of the religious law of Islam (*sharʿan*), it is allowed to perform the divine service (*taʿabbud*) in accordance with the rite of the *Jaʿfariyya*, which is known as *Shīʿa imāmiyya*, in the same way as in accordance with all schools of the Sunnis.[56]

However, and unfortunately, when Nasser cut off relations with Iran only one year later, following a diplomatic crisis over Iran's alleged recognition of Israel, this meant the end of the Association's activities and the rejuvenation of mutual polemics.[57] In addition to this, "Khomeini's triumph seemed to threaten the entire region, both politically and intellectually, and the 1980s in particular were marked by a multifaceted fear on all levels of an Iranian export of the revolution and by a fierce stepping up of anti-Shiʿi polemics, either through new publications or new editions of tried and tested older ones."[58] Furthermore, due to the large dissemination of Wahhabism for various reasons since the 1970s,[59] Wahhabi scholars undermined the achievements of *Jamāʿat al-taqrīb*.

After Shaltūt's recognition of Shiism as a valid *madhhab*, the Wahhabis made the fatwa an object of mockery[60] and turned the Wahhabi-Shiite conflict into a deeper theological divide. That is to say, the question that a Sunni layman would ask today normally is not whether or not a Sunni can worship according to a Shiite *madhhab*, but whether Shiites are even Muslims, which is a dangerous shift. In this context, the Sunni theological positions on Shiites today can loosely be grouped into three: (1) those who say that the Shiites are *kuffār*, (2) those who say that Shiites are Muslims, and (3) those who say that some Shiites are Muslims and others are *kuffār*. The first group is often condemned by the other two for pronouncing "sweeping statements" that will necessarily harden the hearts of common Shiites and turn them further away from Sunni Islam. Hence, they are often advised to differentiate between lay Shiites and their leaders, for the Shiite masses are being brainwashed by their leaders, and it is the responsibility of the Sunnis to "save" them.[61]

On the other hand, the third group accuses the second of obfuscating and compromising the truth, for they involve in intermarriages and co-worshiping with Shiites; such common activities will eventually lead the Shiites to assume that their way is approved by the Sunnis. On the Day of Judgment, says the third group, "these same Shiites will point fingers at us and ask us why we did not warn them of the *kufr* of their beliefs." Hence, they say that "it is very necessary to expose the *kufr* of the leaders of Shiʿism. They have declared war on the true Islam, both by word and by sword. Unity with them is not possible, and it is a part of their creed to accept the *Ahl al-Sunnah* externally but to oppose us internally. If we allow ourselves to be fooled by false slogans of (Muslim unity), we will only be left to one day deal with the Shia leaders stabbing us in the back, as has been the case historically."[62]

The third way, which is arguably the most dominant, contends that some Shiites are not *kuffār* because they are simply ignorant of the beliefs of Shiism which constitute *kufr*, but some others are *kuffār*. However, they argue, leniency toward the masses should not compromise the fact that Shiism is itself *kufr*. Hence, they pass condemnation in generic terms and abstain from condemning specific individuals. The exception to this rule is those Shiite leaders who "propagate" their views: it is necessary to condemn them publicly so that people are warned to keep away from them.[63]

To conclude, the most obvious finding to emerge by looking at these conflicts is the absence of a *maqāṣidī*-oriented approach to contemporary Muslim theological discourse. Even though this conflict has a lot more to it than the theological dimension, I believe that the proposed *Maqāṣid al-ʿAqīda* may well serve as a tool that may pave the way for the desired Islamic ecumenism. As we have seen, al-Ghazālī's and ʿAbduh's *maqāṣidī*-oriented approaches to theology, coupled with Shaltūt's attempts at theological ecumenism, may be taken as leading examples of theoretical and practical initiatives that could help bridge such widening gaps and bring the different parties to some mutual criterion for understanding Islamic theology. Confirming this posture, I would like to end this chapter with this enlightening Ghazālian advice:

> None of them should condemn the others as Unbelievers because he holds the latter to be mistaken in what they believe to be a logical proof; for rendering such judgements is no trifling matter that is easily

> substantiated. Instead, let them establish among themselves a mutually agreed-upon criterion for determining the validity of logical proofs that enjoys the recognition of them all. For if they do not agree on the scale by which a thing is to be measured, they will not be able to terminate disputes over its weight. We have cited the five (probative) scales in our book, *al-Qisṭās al-mustaqīm* [The Just Balance]. These are the scales regarding the validity of which it is inconceivable that anyone disagree, assuming that they have been properly understood. Indeed, everyone who understands these scales acknowledges them to be an absolute means to certainty. And for those who have mastered them, dispensing and exacting fairness, exposing (the subtleties of difficult) matters, and terminating disputes become matters of ease.[64]

Conclusions

THE PRIMARY MOTIVE behind this monograph was to address an epistemic gap in the study of the Islamic tradition, that is, the absence of a systematic theology of *Maqāṣid al-ʿAqīda* along the lines of the genre of *Maqāṣid al-Sharīʿa.* The monograph was also motivated by the overemphasis on *Maqāṣid al-Sharīʿa,* which has contributed to overshadowing not only the objectives of Islamic theology but also the objectives of (Islam) itself. This overshadowing involved an intellectual jump from the genus (Islam) to one of its particulars (Islamic *Sharīʿa*), a jump that contributed to the reduction of Islam to a set of legal codes, even though *Sharīʿa* (law) is only a subcategory of the Islamic tradition. This indicated a need to develop a theory/theories of not only *Maqāṣid al-ʿAqīda* but also, and more logically, a theory/theories of *Maqāṣid al-Islām.* This monograph attempted to address the former need, with a view to addressing the latter in a separate monograph.

The monograph is predicated on the idea that there are three key values that Islam aims to pursue, preserve, and promote: Truth, Justice, and Beauty. These three values correspond to three aspects of the Islamic tradition: theology, law, and Sufism. The monograph averred that while Islamic law's key objective is the pursuit, preservation, and promotion of Justice and Sufism's key objective is the pursuit, preservation, and promotion of Beauty, Islamic theology's key objective is the pursuit, preservation, and promotion of Truth. This value-based system draws inspiration from the well-known *ḥadīth* of *Jibrīl,* which consists of three constituents that offer the best summary of the essence of Islam, as explained at the outset of the monograph.

Having identified the pursuit, preservation, and promotion of *al-Ḥaqq* (Truth) as the general objective of Islamic theology, I addressed the question of why not *falāḥ* (success), or *najāh* (salvation), or any other outcome-based theories. I contended that such alternatives may well serve as a valid objective

The Higher Objectives of Islamic Theology. Mohammed Gamal Abdelnour, Oxford University Press.
 DOI: 10.1093/oso/9780197648636.003.0006

for Islam as a whole (which is a separate question), but not to "Islamic theology" per se.

In the process, some key pre-Ghazālian and post-Ghazālian contributions to *Maqāṣid al-ʿAqīda* were investigated, but al-Ghazālī's and ʿAbduh's contributions were given special treatment due to the fact that their writings planted the foundational seeds of the genre. However, the monograph identified six key causes that may well have precluded the fruition of such seeds: (1) the rejection of *taʿlīl* in orthodox theology, (2) confusing *maqṣad* (objective) with *ʿilla* (underlying cause) and *maṣlaḥa* (interest/benefit), (3) having traditions that discourage reflection on God and His actions, (4) lacking transdenominational theological maxims, (5) lacking epistemic probability in theology, and (6) separating Sufism from theology.

Grappling with questions of sources and methods, the second chapter identified the Qurʾān as the primary and undisputed source to this emerging genre, as expected, but also showed how the Sunna may be used, despite the complexities around its authenticity and authority in theology. More importantly, the chapter gave examples of what the derivation of *Maqāṣid al-ʿAqīda* from such sources may look like. Even more importantly, it implemented some tools that may be considered, if used cautiously, within the context of *Maqāṣid al-ʿAqīda*, such as *al-siyāq* (the context) and *istiqrāʾ* (inductive reasoning).

The third chapter attempted a theory of *Maqāṣid al-ʿAqīda*. While it began by "interrogating" the classical theory of *Maqāṣid al-Sharīʿa* on account of its *ḥudūd*-centeredness and its reducing of the function of *maqāṣid* to mere "preservation," as compared to functions of "acquisition" and "promotion," it hastened to demonstrate how to "generate" a theory of *Maqāṣid al-ʿAqīda*, by showing that the ultimate purpose of Islamic theology is embodied in the pursuit, preservation, and promotion of *al-Ḥaqq* (Truth). In doing so, it appealed to the Kantian distinction between the "phenomenon" (the way we see things) and the "noumenon" (the-thing-in-itself), with a view to drawing some "methodological" inspirations from it. Those premises led to the conclusion that the theological truth that Islam pursues, preserves, and promotes is not necessarily "fully present" but is "provisionally" so. Therefore, Islamic theology encourages "seeking" bits and pieces of this truth wherever it may arise, in tandem with "speaking" of it in its "provisional state." Consequently, Islamic theology becomes a dynamic discipline that is in the service of the ultimate truth and not a static one that is often in the service of "traditionalism," which is condemned by the scripture.

While the third chapter "interrogated" the classical theory of *Maqāṣid al-Sharīʿa*, the fourth chapter "integrated" some of its "tools" into the emerging

Maqāṣid al-ʿAqīda, i.e., the threefold taxonomy of *ḍarūriyyāt*, *ḥājiyyāt*, and *taḥsīniyyāt*. The chapter began by domesticating this taxonomy in theology and justifying its extendibility and applicability, in preference to the traditional twofold pattern of *uṣūl al-ʿaqīda* and *furūʿ al-ʿaqīda*. Having theorized the applicability of this threefold taxonomy, I showed its utility in theology by investigating three case studies (*al-firqa al-nājiya*, deeds vis-à-vis faith, and the place of Prophet Muḥammad in Islamic theology). This investigation showed how the notion of *al-firqa al-nājiya* began in early Ashʿarism as part of the *ḍarūriyyāt* of Islamic theology, without which one cannot attain salvation and pursue truth. However, the notion was weakened and moved from the zone of *ḍarūriyyāt* to the *ḥājiyyāt* in classical Ashʿarism, and it became even weaker in modern Ashʿarism, where it largely became part of the *taḥsīniyyāt* zone. The second case had the opposite journey. While in early Ashʿarism, good deeds were largely seen as nonessential to one's faith (constituting a condition of *perfection* rather than *soundness*/*sharṭ kamāl lā sharṭ siḥḥa*), with al-Ghazālī's emphasis on deeds, I contended, they moved from the zone of *taḥsīniyyāt* to the zone of *ḥājiyyāt*. With reformed Ashʿarism, as represented in ʿAbduh's school, deeds moved further from the zone of *ḥājiyyāt* to the zone of *ḍarūriyyāt*, a move that had a positive bearing on the religious value of the good deeds of non-Muslims. Regarding the place of Prophet Muḥammad, although it was never in the zone of *taḥsīniyyāt*, in modern Ashʿarism there emerged a school that considered belief in Prophet Muḥammad as part of *ḥājiyyāt* rather than *ḍarūriyyāt*: a means to God, as opposed to being viewed as an end.

The two key findings of the fourth chapter were, first, that the threefold taxonomy is one of the exegetical tools that *Maqāṣid al-ʿAqīda* can methodically benefit from *Maqāṣid al-Sharīʿa*, and that using it revealed not a few connections and correlations that would barely be brought to the fore if another approach were taken; second, that Islamic theology is a dynamic, living, and discursive entity that is inextricably linked to history and not contextually independent.

The fifth chapter showed how the lack of a *maqāṣidī*-oriented approach to Islamic theology contributed to the rejuvenation of the denomination-based theology predominant in early Islam. In doing so, it used the Shiite-Wahhabi conflict as an example of a theology that is wandering in uncharted territory in the modern era of Islam. This last chapter highlighted two important conclusions: (1) the need to distance the legacy of Ibn Ḥanbal and Ibn Taymiyya from that of Ibn ʿAbd al-Wahhāb in terms of their take on Shiism and (2) the need to revitalize al-Ghazālī's, ʿAbduh's and Shaltūt's *maqāṣidī*-oriented approach in theology toward the development of a Muslim theology of ecumenism.

The Way Forward

"So what?" is the question that arises at the end of this journey. What does the configuration of *Maqāṣid al-ʿAqīda* mean to the Islamic tradition? More particularly, to the genre of Islamic theology? To put it briefly, this project essentially means taking a step toward basing the Islamic tradition on a system of values instead of a system of *ḥudūd* (penalties). Throughout this monograph I pointed out how the genre of *Maqāṣid al-Sharīʿa* emerged as a positive corollary to the *ḥudūd*. Jurists felt there was a pressing need to explain those penalties, and *Maqāṣid al-Sharīʿa* offered itself as the best explanation. Had the genre of *Maqāṣid al-Sharīʿa* been a value-based system, I argue, different objectives may have been developed, and consequently how Islam is lived could have been influenced, if not determined, by such value-based outlooks. Furthermore, the marginalization of such values led to the marginalization of "ethical Islam" and the maximization of "legal Islam" and "political Islam." Therefore, this monograph is a move toward "ethicizing" the Islamic tradition and reintroducing balance between its various dimensions and core values: Truth, Justice, and Beauty.

What does the transplantation of the taxonomy of *ḍarūriyyāt, ḥājiyyāt,* and *taḥsīniyyāt* mean to Islamic theology? I argue that if this taxonomy is properly situated in Islamic theology, it can develop a systematic theology of ecumenism as well as a form of practical theology. I attempted to explain this theology of ecumenism in the final chapter, embodied in the Sunni-Shiite-Wahhabi relations and what a *maqāṣidī*-oriented approach to it can do at this platform. As for the theology of action, I gave an example of deeds in relation to faith, pointing out that classical Ashʿarism's marginalization of the role of good deeds in the soundness of one's faith, which is largely opposed by the vast majority of other Sunni theologies, contributed to minimizing the role that theology may well play in the "practice" of the faithful. With the many challenges facing our world today, most notably the preservation of the environment and the establishment of social justice, I hope this monograph will eventually lead to the practicalization of Islamic theology, which is often shunned as an impractical genre.

At an interfaith level, I argue that if the centralization of God alone in the area of *ḍarūriyyāt* is seriously considered, as ʿAbduh proposed, it will bring about more commonalities with other faith traditions and will also put limits on the usage of the term *kufr*, which is still used largely arbitrarily. I used al-Azhar's take on the practice of *takfīr* against Egyptian Christians in 2017–2018 to explain the urgency of this matter, and I aim to examine this area further from a *maqāṣidī* approach in future research, tackling questions such as the following: If belief in Prophet Muḥammad does not lie within the zone of *ḍarūriyyāt*, what does this mean for Islam's universal message? Will Islam still be directed to all mankind, as commonly perceived? Even more distantly, what does this mean to the question of *khatm al-nubuwwa* (seal of prophethood) and Islam's position on movements like the Aḥmadiya?

Last but not least, although much effort has been exerted in this monograph, I recognize that this is a suggestion and a work in progress that is far from being full-fledged. I conclude with what Abou El Fadl began with in his *Speaking in God's Name*: "[T]his book explores the idea of speaking for God without pretending to be God or, at least, without being perceived, for all practical purposes, as God. Dealing with God's law inevitably involves an intricate balance between the sovereignty of the Divine, human determinacy, and morality."[1] What I take from Abou El Fadl's statement is that if we take seriously God's Sovereignty and Omnipotence, we, as human representatives of God on earth, can never identify ourselves with God's intent "definitively" or claim to have "fully" comprehended His Knowledge. Therefore, the primary intention of the monograph is not to offer any "categorical conclusions" but to direct the attention of researchers to this area and set the scene for a much-neglected genre, offering a skeletal introductory framework to lay the foundation for deeper studies.

Notes

PRELIMS

1. This *ḥadīth* will be quoted verbatim in the third chapter.
2. The thirteenth-century jurist and traditionist al-Nawawī (d. 1277) mentioned that scholars of Islam considered this *ḥadīth* to be a foundational pillar (*aṣl*) of the Islamic tradition. Abū Zakariā Yaḥyā al-Nawawī, *al-Minhāj fī sharḥ Ṣaḥīḥ Muslim* (Amman and Riyadh: International Ideas Home, 2000), p. 83.
3. Fazlur Rahman, "The Post-Formative Developments in Islam—II:IV: The Philosophical Movement," *Islamic Studies* 2.3 (1963), p. 302.
4. Khaled Abou El Fadl, *Reasoning with God: Reclaiming Shariʿah in the Modern Age* (New York: Rowman and Littlefield, 2014), pp. 363–365.
5. Abū Ḥāmid Al-Ghazālī, *Jawāhir*, ed. Muḥammad R. R. Qabbānī (Beirut: Dār Iḥyāʾ al-ʿUlūm, 1986), p. 40.
6. Malek Bennabi, *Shurūṭ al-nahḍa*, trans. ʿAbdelṣabūr Shāhīn (Damascus: Dār al-Fikr, 1986), pp. 97–103.
7. Khaled Abou El Fadl, *The Search for Beauty in Islam: Conference of the Books* (Washington, DC: Rowman and Littlefield, 2006).
8. This is in the sense that other Islamic disciplines depend on theology, whereas theology does not depend on other Islamic disciplines. To clarify, to postulate the obligation of prayer, for instance, one must initially establish the existence of the Obligator Himself, i.e., God. Ḥassan al-Shāfiʿī discussed this question extensively in his *Al-Madkhal l'drāsat ʿilm al-kalām*, 2nd ed. (Karachi: Idārat al-Qurʾān wa al-ʿUlūm al-Islāmiyya, 2001), pp. 198–209.
9. Ibn ʿAbd al-Salām was a renowned *mujtahid* in Islamic law and a key Ashʿarite theologian. Sherman Jackson, *Islamic Law and the State: The Constitutional Jurisprudence of Shihab Al-Din Al-Qarafi* (Leiden: Brill, 1996), p. 10.
10. Al-Shāṭibī is an "Andalusian Maliki scholar and reformer. Wrote on a variety of subjects including usul al-fiqh, grammar, and poetry. Was critical of fiqh of his age and disagreed with Maliki contemporaries on many points, including taxation and

the significance of taqlid (precedent)." John L. Esposito, ed., *The Oxford Dictionary of Islam* (New York: Oxford University Press, 2003), p. 289.

11. Aḥmad al-Raysūnī, *Naẓariyyat al-maqāṣid ʿinda al-Imām al-Shāṭibī*, trans. Nancy Roberts (Herndon, VA: International Institute of Islamic Thought, 2006), p. 17.
12. Muḥammad al-Zuḥaylī, *Maqāṣid al-Sharīʿa: Asās li-huqūq al-insān* (Doha: Ministry of Awqāf and Islamic Affairs of Qatar, 2003), p. 70.
13. Al-Fāsī was a "Moroccan historian, teacher, poet, and political leader. Taught Islamic history at al-Qarawiyin University (1930). In 1934 he and other activists issued a Moroccan Reform Plan. Arrested and exiled to Gabon by the French (1937–46) but continued to influence the Moroccan reform movement. Upon return from Gabon, served as head of the Istiqlal (Independence) Party but in 1947 was forced to flee to Cairo and remained there until Moroccan independence in r 955." Esposito, *The Oxford Dictionary of Islam*, p. 83.
14. ʿAllāl Al-Fāsī, *Maqāṣid al-Sharīʿa al-Islāmiyya wa makārimuhā* (Casablanca: Maktabat al-Waḥda al-ʿArabiyya, n.d.), p. 3.
15. Ibn ʿĀshūr was born in Tunis in 1879. After receiving classical Islamic education, he joined the renowned Zaytuna University to become a teacher and remained there all his life. His masterpiece, *Maqāsid al-Sharīʿa al-Islāmiyya*, published in 1946, is a foundational work in the area of *Maqāsid al-Sharīʿa*. See Jonathan A. C. Brown, *Misquoting Muhammad: The Challenges and Choices of Interpreting the Prophet's Legacy* (London: Oneworld, 2014), pp. 278–280.
16. al-Ṭāhir Ibn ʿĀshūr, *Maqāṣid al-Sharīʿa al-Islāmiyya*, 2nd ed., ed. Muḥammad Ṭ. al-Mesāwī (Amman: Dār al-Nafāʾs, 2001), p. 251.
17. *Reasoning with God* is also a title of one of Khaled Abou El Fadl's books. Although this book does not address *Maqāṣid al-ʿAqīda* directly, it significantly contributed to the maturation of my thoughts here.
18. Muʿtazilism is a "rationalist" school of Islamic theology that flourished in the cities of Basra and Baghdad during the eighth to the tenth centuries. They are best known for denying the status of the Qurʾān as uncreated and co-eternal with God, accentuating that if the Qurʾān is the word of God, He logically "must have preceded his own speech." The philosophical underpinning of the Muʿtazilites centered on the notions of divine justice and divine unity. See Ludwig W. Adamec, *Historical Dictionary of Islam*, 3rd ed. (London and New York: Rowman, 2017), p. 315; Majid Fakhry, *A History of Islamic Philosophy*, 2nd ed. (New York: Columbia University Press, 1983), pp. 46–48.
19. Ashʿarism is the name of an Islamic philosophico-religious school of theological thought that developed during the tenth and eleventh centuries, attempting to lay down the foundation of an orthodox Islamic theology, as opposed to the rationalist theology of the Muʿtazilites, and in opposition to the radical literalist class. It made use of dialectical methods for the defense of the authority of divine revelation as applied to theological subjects. Founded by the theologian Abū al-Ḥasan

al-Ashʿarī (873–935), it is the most dominant theological school of Sunnī Islam which established an orthodox dogmatic guideline. Disciples of the school are known as the Ashʿarites. See Adamec, *Historical Dictionary of Islam*, p. 61.

20. David Johnston, "A Turn in the Epistemology and Hermeneutics of Twentieth Century Uṣūl al-Fiqh," *Islamic Law and Society* 11.2 (2004), p. 238.
21. Johnston, "A Turn in the Epistemology and Hermeneutics of Twentieth Century Uṣūl al-Fiqh," p. 238.
22. Johnston, "A Turn in the Epistemology and Hermeneutics of Twentieth Century Uṣūl al-Fiqh," p. 242.
23. Al-Āmidī was an "Ashʿarite theologian and Shafiʿi jurisprudent, and representative of a real commitment to Peripatetic philosophy as an essential aspect of how to undertake the Islamic sciences. Born in Amid, where he was first of all taught the principles of Hanbalism, he moved on to Baghdad to study with Ibn Fadlan, there becoming a Shafiʿi jurist. He also became interested in philosophy in Baghdad, and reports say he was instructed in this discipline by a Christian. He made the acquaintance of Suhrawardi on a visit to Syria, and then in 1196 he moved to Cairo to teach, and then fled to Damascus, where he died." Oliver Leaman, *The Biographical Encyclopedia of Islamic Philosophy* (London: Bloomsbury, 2015), p. 17.
24. Johnston, "A Turn in the Epistemology and Hermeneutics of Twentieth Century Uṣūl al-Fiqh," p. 242.
25. Frederick M. Denny, "Islamic Theology in the New World: Some Issues and Prospects," *Journal of the American Academy of Religion* 62.4 (1994), p. 1070.
26. Al-Ghazālī, *Jawāhir*, pp. 39–40.
27. Al-Dhahabī was a fourteenth-century Syrian historian, chronicler, and traditionist. See Fozia Bora, *Writing History in the Medieval Islamic World: The Value of Chronicles as Archives* (London: I. B. Tauris, 2019), p. 38.
28. Ibn Taymiyya was "born in Harran in northern Syria and educated in Damascus, he became a jurist of the Hanbalite school of law, teaching at Damascus and Cairo. His father and grandfather were famous authorities of the Hanbali school. . . . He condemned many practices of popular Islam as sinful innovations (bidʿah), was repeatedly imprisoned, and died in jail. His teachings have inspired revivalist movements, including 19th-century Wahhabism and present-day Islamists." Adamec, *Historical Dictionary of Islam*, p. 194.
29. Ahmed El Shamsy, *Rediscovering the Islamic Classics: How Editors and Print Culture Transformed an Intellectual Tradition* (Princeton, NJ, and Oxford: Princeton University Press, 2020), p. 214.
30. George Makdisi, "Law and Traditionalism in the Institutions of Learning of Medieval Islam," *Theology and Law in Islam,* ed. G. von Grunebaum (Wiesbaden: Otto Harrassowitz, 1971), p. 75.
31. Denny, "Islamic Theology in the New World," p. 1073.
32. Paul R. Powers, *Intent in Islamic Law* (Leiden and Boston: Brill, 2006), p. 2.

33. Marshall Hodgson, *The Venture of Islam: Conscience and History in a World Civilization*, vol. 1 (Chicago: University of Chicago Press, 1974), p. 238.
34. Shahab Ahmed, *What Is Islam? The Importance of Being Islamic* (Princeton, NJ, and Oxford: Princeton University Press, 2016). For this discussion, see especially the second chapter in the book: "Islam as Law, Islams-not-Islam, Islamic and Islamicate, Religion and Culture, Culture and Civilization," pp. 113–176.
35. See Michel Foucault, *Archeology of Knowledge and the Discourse on Language* (New York: Pantheon, 1972).
36. Mark Juergensmeyer, "2009 Presidential Address: Beyond Words and War: The Global Future of Religion," *Journal of the American Academy of Religion* 78.4 (2010), p. 891.
37. Ashk Dahlén, *Islamic Law, Epistemology and Modernity: Legal Philosophy in Contemporary Iran* (New York: Routledge, 2003), p. 348.
38. Franz Rosenthal, *Knowledge Triumph: The Concept of Knowledge in Medieval Islam* (Leiden and Boston: Brill, 2007), p. 2.
39. Talal Asad, *The Idea of an Anthropology of Islam* (Washington, DC: Centre for Contemporary Arab Studies, 1986), pp. 14–15.
40. *Mishkat al-maṣābīḥ*, book 2, *ḥadīth* 43.
41. Daniel W. Brown, *Rethinking Tradition in Modern Islamic Thought* (Cambridge: Cambridge University Press, 1999), p. 2.
42. This is a chapter of mine in the forthcoming *Oxford Handbook of Islam and Reform*, edited by Emad Hamdeh and Natana Delong-Bas.
43. Talal Asad, *Formations of the Secular: Christianity, Islam, Modernity* (Stanford, CA: Stanford University Press, 2003), p. 224.
44. Asad, *Formations of the Secular*, p. 222.
45. Asad, *Formations of the Secular*, p. 220.
46. This runs counter to Hallaq's argument, which "considers that taqlid not only functioned as an effective means of legal change but even more so than ijtihad itself because, unlike ijtihad, taqlid-based interpretations were seen as to be loyal to and continuous with the ongoing tradition." Adis Duderija, *The Imperatives of Progressive Islam* (New York: Routledge, 2017), p. 37.
47. For the difference between those approaches, see Duderija, *The Imperatives of Progressive Islam*.
48. Abdullah Saeed, *Reading the Qur'an in the Twenty-First Century: A Contextualist Approach* (New York: Routledge, 2014), p. 21.
49. Ebrahim Moosa, *Ghazālī and the Poetics of Imagination* (London and Chapel Hill: University of North Carolina Press, 2005), p. 265.
50. Moosa, *Ghazālī and the Poetics of Imagination*, p. 269.
51. Ibn Khaldūn was an "influential Arab historian, historiographer, and social philosopher. Held numerous public positions in Tunis; moved to Cairo in 1392, where he taught and served as a judge until his death. His major works are his autobiography (*Al-tarif b'Ibn Kholdun*), a candid evaluation of his career, and the *Muqaddimah*

(Introduction to history), which traces his thoughts on sedentary and desert populations, dynasties, and the caliphate. In the *Muqaddimah*, Ibn Khaldun stated that he had established a new science, *ilm al-umran* (science of social organization); he is accordingly regarded as the father of sociology." Esposito, *The Oxford Dictionary of Islam*, p. 128.

52. Montgomery Watt, *The Faith and Practice of Al-Ghazali* (New Delhi: Kitab Behavan, 1996), p. 27.
53. ʿAbd al-Raḥmān Ibn Khaldūn, *Muqaddima*, 1st ed., ed. ʿAbdullāh M. Al-Darwīsh, vol. 2 (Damascus: Maktabat al-Hidāya, 2004), p. 205.
54. Al-Farābī was the "founder of Islamic political philosophy and formal logic in the Islamic world. Wrote important commentaries on Aristotle and works of philosophy, the most famous of which addresses the question of the virtuous city, characterized by division and protection of all good things among people and by the relationship between (and mutual duties of) ruler and ruled. Also synthesized the political philosophy of Plato and Islamic political thought. Integrated religion and science in written works." Esposito, *The Oxford Dictionary of Islam*, pp. 80–81.
55. Al-Ījī was born at Ij, near Shiraz, where he served as judge and instructor. His main work was on Islamic theology, and his efforts here are noted for their systematization of the genre. Al-Iji penned a Quran commentary, and, in "*Mataliʿ al-Anwar* (*The Rising of the Lights*), a description of the scope of Kalam itself. Much more intricate than either of these works is his *Kitab al-Mawaqif* (*Book of Stations*) which divides theology into six topics (stations): epistemology, ontology, the theory of essence, the accidents that characterize that substance, the nature of the soul, and, finally, religious issues such as eschatology and the nature of prophecy." Leaman, *The Biographical Encyclopedia of Islamic Philosophy*, p. 237.
56. Iqbāl was a poet in Persian and Urdu, a philosopher, and a founding father of Pakistan. He had a doctorate from Munich, and he taught Arabic, history, and economics at the Oriental College at Lahore. "He held that Islam properly understood and rationally interpreted is not only capable of moving along with the progressive and evolutionary forces of life, but also of directing them into new and healthy channels in every epoch. . . . He favoured the partition of India to protect the culture of Muslims in what would have been a predominantly Hindu state." Adamec, *Historical Dictionary of Islam*, p. 207.
57. Muhammad Iqbal, *The Reconstruction of Religious Thought in Islam*, ed. Javed Majeed (Stanford, CA: Stanford University Press, 2012), p. 3.
58. *Takfir* is a controversial term in Islamist discourse, as one Muslim is declaring another a nonbeliever (*kāfir*). Contemporary uses of the term have their roots in the twentieth-century Islamist Sayyid Qutb's advocacy of *Takfirism* (theology of excommunication) against the state or society that is deemed *Jāhilī* (being in a state of ignorance and disbelief). This practice is widely held and applied by Jihadist organizations to varying degrees. Mainstream Islam holds that excommunication against those who profess their Islamic faith is not sanctioned by Islam and that an

ill-founded *takfir* accusation is a major sin. Adamec, *Historical Dictionary of Islam*, p. 125.

59. Quoting the verse: "Indeed, those who believed [Muslims] and those who were Jews or Christians or Sabeans—those who believed in God and the Last Day and did righteousness—will have their reward with their Lord, and no fear will there be concerning them, nor will they grieve."
60. The verse states, "And whoever seeks a way other than Islam as religion—never will it be accepted from him, and he, in the Hereafter, will be among the losers." On the usage of the typology of Exclusivism, Inclusivism, and Pluralism in an Islamic context, see M. G. Abdelnour, *A Comparative History of Catholic and Aš'arī Theologies of Truth and Salvation: Inclusive Minorities, Exclusive Majorities* (Leiden and Boston: Brill, 2021).
61. Mohammad H. Khalil, *Islam and the Fate of Others: The Salvation Question* (Oxford: Oxford University Press, 2012), p. 7.
62. Khalil, *The Fate of Others*, p. 7.
63. Khalil, *The Fate of Others*, p. 7.
64. *Naskh* is "the repeal of a revelation by another. . . . This refers to changes in legal and practical matters, such as the prayer direction (*qiblah*), matters of inheritance, and penalties for adultery." Adamec, *Historical Dictionary of Islam*, pp. 25–26.
65. In her *Qur'anic Christians*, Jane McAuliffe traces the different interpretations of Q. 2:62 across ten Qur'ān commentaries, classical and modern. *Qur'anic Christians: An Analysis of Classical and Modern Exegesis* (Cambridge: Cambridge University Press, 1991), pp. 93–128.
66. Al-Tirmidhī was a Sunni jurist, traditionist, and *mutakallim* (theologian) of Khorasan, even though he is mostly known for his foundational works in Sufism. Bernd Radtke, "A Forerunner of Ibn al-Arabi: Hakim Tirmidhi on Sainthood," *Journal of the Ibn Arabi Society* 8 (1989), pp. 42–49.
67. Al-Qummī was the "most eminent of traditionists and a jurist of the school of Qom. His *Kitab al-tawhid* tries to show the compatibility of the imamate traditions with God's unity and justice. He held a position between the Ghulat and Mu'tazilite Shi'ite collector of hadith. Educated by his father, he continued his studies at Rayy with noted scholars and traveled widely in the Islamic world. Author of one of the Shi'ite Four Books of hadith (*Kutub al-arba'a*), he was the last prominent member of the Shi'ite traditionist school of Qom. His Shi'ite Creed (*Risalat al-i'tiqadat*) shows the doctrinal development of Shi'ism. Most of his 200 publications are lost." Adamec, *Historical Dictionary of Islam*, p. 184.
68. Al-'Āmirī was born in Khurasan (today's Iran) in the early tenth century and died in Nishapur in 992. He was also an Iranian "pupil of al-Kindi. He went to the court at Rayy where philosophy was officially supported by the Buyid vizier Ibn al-'Amid. Apparently, he made visits to Baghdad but was not highly regarded there given his provincial background, and he did not stay long. Toward the end of his life he came into favour in Khurasan and Transoxiania with the Samanid regime, lived in

the capital city Bukhara, and died in its most important city Nishapur. Al-ʿAmiri is known to have written at least twenty-five books, for which we have the titles, and six of these survive. Although it is true that al-Kindi did not often write on religious topics, it is also true that he argued there was no discrepancy between religion and philosophy. This is a point that his pupil takes up vigorously in his *al-Iʿlām bi-manāqib al-islām* (Exposition of the Merits of Islam), arguing that Islam is a supremely rational faith, a faith that repays rational examination." Leaman, *The Biographical Encyclopedia of Islamic Philosophy*, p. 21.

69. Al-Zāhid al-Bukhārī was "a Ḥanafi jurist (*faqīh*), theologian (*mutakallim*), and commentator of the Qurʾān (*mufassir*). He is one of those Islamic scholars who were well known and appreciated during their lifetimes and for a time afterwards but then fell into oblivion." Angelika Brodersen, "al-Bukhārī, ʿAlāʾ al-Dīn," *Encyclopaedia of Islam, THREE*, ed. Kate Fleet et al. (Leiden: Brill, 2013).
70. Al-Rāzī is "one of the last encyclopedic writers of Islam. He was an adherent of the Ashʿarite school and a violent opponent of Muʿtazilism. His most important works are The Résumé (*Kitab al-muhassal*), about philosophical and theological ideas, as well as the commentary on the Quran, titled The Key to God's Secret (*Mafatih al-Ghayb*). Ibn Khallikan described Razi as 'the pearl of the age, a man without a peer; he surpassed all his contemporaries in scholastic theology, metaphysics, and philosophy' (II, 652). He was born in Rayy and died in Herat in present-day Afghanistan." Adamec, *Historical Dictionary of Islam*, p. 366.
71. Al-Dehlawī was an eighteenth-century Muslim polymath: traditionist, reformer, historiographer, bibliographer, and theologian. See Brown's *Misquoting Muhammad*.
72. Riḍā was an Islamic reformist thinker. Born near Tripoli, he left for Egypt in 1897 and collaborated with ʿAbduh "in publishing the monthly journal called The Lighthouse (*Al-Manar*) in Cairo. The journal demanded reform and the revitalization of Islam and Islamic society. . . . His teachings inspired both moderates and conservatives." Adamec, *Historical Dictionary of Islam*, pp. 371–372.
73. See Immanuel Kant, *Critique of Pure Reason* (Cambridge: Cambridge University Press, 1999); Veli-Matti Karkkainen, *An Introduction to the Theology of Religions: Biblical, Historical and Contemporary Perspectives* (Westmont, IL: InterVarsity Press, 2003), p. 292.
74. See Abdullah Saeed, *Islamic Thought: An Introduction*, 1st ed. (London and New York: Routledge, 2006), pp. 67–70; Sherman Jackson, *Islam and the Problem of Black Suffering* (Oxford: Oxford University Press, 2009), p. 80.
75. Ibn Ḥanbal was a Muslim "scholar and eponymous head of the Hanbali school of law. He was a student of al-Shafiʿi, founder of the Shafiʿite school of law. His is the most conservative, but smallest, of the four Sunni schools." Adamec, *Historical Dictionary of Islam*, p. 187.
76. Shaltūt "was born in a delta village in Buḥayrah Province in 1893. He memorized the Quran, attended the Al-Azhar–affiliated Religious Institute in Alexandria, and graduated as an ʿĀlim from Cairo's Al-Azhar. He became an immediate disciple

of Muṣtafā al-Marāġī (d. 1945) who drew his inspiration from ʿAbduh's intellectual reservoir and briefly became the Grand Imām of Al-Azhar in 1928–1929, until his reformist plans brought about his swift downfall. Šaltūt briefly taught Islamic jurisprudence (*fiqh*) at Al-Azhar before losing his post in 1931 in a purge of al-Marāġī's reformist group. When al-Marāġī returned as the Grand Imām of Al-Azhar in 1935, Šaltūt came with him as vice-dean of the Sharia College. To his disappointment, exile had extinguished Marāġī's reformist enthusiasm. Šaltūt nevertheless continued to support overarching reform of Al-Azhar, and in 1958 Naṣer appointed him as the Grand Imām 'before forcing its reorganization three years later.'" Abdelnour, *A Comparative History of Catholic and Aš'arī Theologies of Truth and Salvation*, p. 148.

77. Walter Hooper, *Selected Literary Essays*, 3rd ed. (Cambridge: Cambridge University Press, 1980), p. 2.

CHAPTER 1

1. Denny, "Islamic Theology in the New World," p. 1073.
2. Denny, "Islamic Theology in the New World," p. 1073.
3. Denny, "Islamic Theology in the New World," p. 1073.
4. Radtke, "A Forerunner of Ibn al-Arabi," pp. 42–49.
5. Al-Dhahabī, *Tadhkirat al-ḥuffāẓ*, vol. 2, ed. ʿAbel Raḥmān al-Maʿlamī (Hyderabad: Dār al-Maʿarif al-Osmānia, 1958), p. 645.
6. Al-Ḥakīm al-Tirmidhī, *Ithbāt al-ʿilal*, 1st ed., ed. Khalid Zahrī (Ribat: Kulliyat al-Adāb wa'l-ʿUlūm al-Insāniya, 1998), pp. 67–68.
7. Al-Tirmidhī, *Ithbāt al-ʿilal*, p. 80.
8. Al-Tirmidhī, *Ithbāt al-ʿilal*, pp. 80–81. For the five objectives of Islamic law, see Adis Duderija, ed., *Maqāṣid al-Sharīʿa and Contemporary Reformist Muslim Thought: An Examination* (New York: Palgrave Macmillan, 2014), p. 3.
9. Al-Tirmidhī, *Ithbat al-ʿilal*, p. 80.
10. Al-Tirmidhī, *Ithbāt al-ʿilal*, pp. 82–85.
11. Al-Tirmidhī, *Al-Ḥajj wa asrāru*, 1st ed., ed. Ḥosny Zidān (Cairo: Maṭbaʿat al-Saʿāda, 1969), p. 13.
12. Al-Tirmidhī, *Al-Ḥajj*, pp. 119–120.
13. Adamec, *Historical Dictionary of Islam*, p. 184.
14. Ibn Bābawayh al-Qummī, *ʿIlal*, 1st ed. (Beirut: Dār al-Murtaḍā, 2006), p. 16.
15. Ibn Bābawayh, *ʿIlal*, pp. 16–17.
16. Ibn Bābawayh, *ʿIlal*, p. 246.
17. Ibn Bābawayh, *ʿIlal*, p. 250.
18. Ibn Bābawayh, *ʿIlal*, p. 121.
19. Ibn Bābawayh, *ʿIlal*, pp. 190–191.
20. Abū Zayd al-Balkhī "was a member of the Imamiyya sect, and it was to explore more of the theoretical basis of that sect that he traveled along the pilgrim route

on foot to Baghdad. He was a pupil of al-Kindi's disciple, Ahmad b. al-Tayyib al-Sarakhsi (d. 286/899), and an important writer on a wide range of topics. . . . He lived to be around eighty years old, and his religious works are no longer extant, but the praise for them by many authorities remains." Leaman, *The Biographical Encyclopedia of Islamic Philosophy,* pp. 48–49.

21. Al-Tawḥīdī "was a Persian man of letters, a scribe and courtier who gives precious information about the religious, political, and cultural milieu of fourth-/tenth-century Iraq." Leaman, *The Biographical Encyclopedia of Islamic Philosophy,* pp. 476–477.
22. Ibn Miskawayh "was part of the intellectual elite of his time, and this was a period often labeled as that of 'Islamic humanism,' in that there was a certain commitment to reason and universality among the educated community. Miskawayh numbered among his friends and colleagues al-Tawhidi, al-'Amiri, Ibn Sa'dan, al-Sahib ibn 'Abbad, Abu Sulayman al-Sijistani al-Mantiki, Badi' al-Zaman, Abu Bakr al-Khwarazmi, and many others. He studied the works of the great historian Ibn Tabari with Ibn Kamil, who had been the historian's student. Working in the Islamic Neoplatonic tradition, Miskawayh placed a great deal of importance on ethics." Leaman, *The Biographical Encyclopedia of Islamic Philosophy,* p. 324.
23. Al-Kindī is known as the philosopher of the Arabs. He lived around the beginning of the ninth century and was known for his deep familiarity with Greek sciences. See Leaman, *The Biographical Encyclopedia of Islamic Philosophy,* pp. 278–279.
24. Everett K. Rowson, "Al-ʿĀmirī," in *History of Islamic Philosophy*, ed. Seyyed H. Nasr and Oliver Leaman, vol. 1 (London and New York: Routledge, 1996), pp. 405–415.
25. Abū al-Ḥassan Al-ʿĀmirī, *al-Iʿlām bi-manāqib al-islām,* 1st ed., ed. Aḥmad Ghorāb (Riyadh: Dār al-Aṣāla, 1988), p. 60. Those *dimensions* can be taken as a forerunner of Ninian Smart's theory of the Seven Dimensions of Religion. These seven dimensions are (1) ritual, (2) narrative and mythic, (3) experiential and emotional, (4) social and institutional, (5) ethical and legal, (6) doctrinal and philosophical, (7) material. See Ninian Smart, *The World's Religions: Old Traditions and Modern Transformations* (Cambridge: Cambridge University Press, 1989).
26. Paul L. Heck, "The Crisis of Knowledge in Islam (I): The Case of al-Amirī," *Philosophy East and West* 56.1 (2006), p. 109.
27. Heck, "The Crisis of Knowledge in Islam," p. 122.
28. Heck, "The Crisis of Knowledge in Islam," p. 123.
29. Al-ʿĀmirī, *al-Iʿlām*, p. 129.
30. Al-ʿĀmirī, *al-Iʿlām*, p. 130.
31. Heck, "The Crisis of Knowledge in Islam," p. 123.
32. Al-ʿĀmirī, *al-Iʿlām*, pp. 133–135.

33. Al-ʿĀmirī, *al-Iʿlām*, p. 128.
34. See Al-ʿĀmirī, *al-Iʿlām*, p. 128.
35. Al-Juwaynī was a Persian Ashʿarite theologian, commonly known as Imām al-Ḥaramayn (leading master of the two holy cities), that is, Mecca and Medina. He taught and studied there in Hijaz for four years, hence his epithet. He gained a large following and was invited back to Nishapur by the founder of the Shāfiʿite Madrasa, Niẓām al-Mulk (d. 485/1092). Upon his return, al-Juwaynī was appointed to teach the doctrine of the Ashʿarites at the Niẓamiyya until his death. Al-Ghazālī is his most renowned student. He "engaged in the study of theological principles, spent his life deciphering between what a Muslim ought and ought not to do. . . . A Persian, he held the view that the caliphate need not be held by a member of the Quraysh." Adamec, *Historical Dictionary of Islam*, p. 234.
36. Khalil, *The Fate of Others*, p. 26.
37. See, for instance, Duderija, *Maqāṣid al-Sharīʿa and Contemporary Reformist Muslim Thought*; Wael B. Hallaq, *A History of Islamic Legal Theories: An Introduction to Sunni Usul al-Fiqh* (Cambridge: Cambridge University Press, 1997).
38. Muḥammad ʿAbdu, *Maqāṣid al-ʿaqīda ʿinda al-Ghazālī* (Ribat: Arab Network for Research and Publishing, 2002).
39. Al-Ghazālī, *Jawāhir*, pp. 41–42.
40. Abū Ḥāmid al-Ghazālī, *al-Mustaṣfā min ʿilm al-uṣūl*, 1st ed. (Beirut: al-Risāla, 1997), p. 33.
41. Abū Ḥāmid al-Ghazālī, *al-Mustaẓhiri*, trans. Richard J. McCarthy (Woodbridge, UK: Twayne, 1980), p. 237.
42. Abū Ḥāmid al-Ghazālī, *Shifāʾ*, ed. Ḥamad al-Kabīsī (Baghdad: Al-Irshād, 1971), pp. 204–205.
43. Abū Ḥāmid al-Ghazālī, *Iḥyāʾ ʿulūm al-dīn*, 1st ed. (Beirut: Dār Ibn Ḥazm, 2005), p. 1354.
44. Abū Ḥāmid al-Ghazālī, *al-Maqṣad*, trans. David B. Burrell and Nazih Daher, 6th ed. (Cambridge: Islamic Texts Society, 2007), p. 1.
45. Al-Ghazālī, *al-Maqṣad*, p. 2.
46. Al-Ghazālī, *Jawāhir*, p. 23.
47. Al-Ghazālī, *al-Maqṣad*, p. 2.
48. Al-Ghazālī, *al-Maqṣad*, p. 2.
49. See Richard Frank, *Al-Ghazālī and the Ashʿarite School* (London and Durham, NC: Duke University Press, 1994).
50. Frank, *Al-Ghazālī and the Ashʿarite School*, pp. 76–77.
51. Al-Ghazālī, *al-Maqṣad*, p. 30.
52. Al-Ghazālī, *al-Maqṣad*, p. 31.
53. Al-Ghazālī, *al-Maqṣad*, p. 31.
54. Al-Ghazālī, *al-Maqṣad*, p. 31.
55. Al-Ghazālī, *al-Maqṣad*, p. 31.

56. Al-Ghazālī, *al-Maqṣad*, p. 67.
57. Al-Ghazālī, *al-Maqṣad*, p. 67.
58. Al-Ghazālī, *al-Maqṣad*, p. 67.
59. Al-Ghazālī, *Iḥyā'*, p. 1419.
60. Al-Ghazālī, *al-Maqṣad*, pp. 53–54.
61. Al-Ghazālī, *al-Maqṣad*, pp. 54–55.
62. Abū Ḥāmid al-Ghazālī, *al-Iqtiṣād*, trans. Dennis Morgan Davis Jr. (PhD diss., University of Utah, 2005), p. 156.
63. Al-Ghazālī, *al-Iqtiṣād*, p. 156.
64. Al-Ghazālī, *al-Iqtiṣād*, pp. 157–160.
65. Al-Ghazālī, *al-Iqtiṣād*, p. 161.
66. Al-Ghazālī, *al-Iqtiṣād*, pp. 160–161.
67. Al-Shāfiʿī is the founder of the Shāfiʿī school of law. He was born in Gaza and buried in Cairo. He "was arguably the first to formulate the classical theory of the bases of Islamic law. Today, Shāfiʿites are found mainly in Syria, the southern part of the Arabian Peninsula, East Africa, and Southeast Asia. See Adamec, *Historical Dictionary of Islam*, p. 398.
68. Abū Ḥāmid al-Ghazālī, *Iljām al-ʿawām ʿan ilm al-kalām*, trans. Abdullah H. Ali (Philadelphia, PA: Lamp Post, 2008), p. 28.
69. Al-Ghazālī, *Iljām al-ʿawām*, pp. 28–29.
70. Al-Ghazālī, *Iljām al-ʿawām*, pp. 51–52.
71. Al-Ghazālī, *al-Iqtiṣād*, pp. 52–53.
72. Abū Ḥāmid al-Ghazālī, *Fayṣal*, trans. Sherman Jackson, in Jackson, *On the Boundaries of Theological Tolerance in Islam* (New York and Oxford: Oxford University Press, 2002), p. 93.
73. Al-Ghazālī, *Fayṣal*, p. 94.
74. Al-Ghazālī, *al-Maqṣad*, pp. 92–93.
75. Al-Ghazālī, *Iḥyā'*, p. 1432.
76. Al-Ghazālī, *Iḥyā'*, pp. 1432–1437.
77. *Sunan Ibn Māja*, h, vol. 1, book 1, *ḥadith* 85.
78. Abū Ḥāmid al-Ghazālī, *Minhāj al-qāṣidīn* (Beirut: Dār al-Kutub al-ʿIlmiyya, 1988), pp. 123–133.
79. Al-Ghazālī, *al-Maqṣad*, p. 90.
80. Al-Ghazālī, *al-Maqṣad*, p. 54.
81. Al-Ghazālī, *al-Maqṣad*, p. 56.
82. Al-Ghazālī, *al-Maqṣad*, pp. 56–57.
83. See Martin Wittingham, *Al-Ghazālī and the Qur'ān: One Book, Many Meanings* (New York: Routledge, 2007), p. 66.
84. Wittingham, *Al-Ghazālī and the Qur'ān*, p. 71.
85. Al-Ghazālī, *Iljām al-ʿawām*, p. 61.

86. Al-Ghazālī, *Iljām al-ʿawām,* pp. 61–64.
87. Abū Isḥāq al-Shāṭibī, *al-Muwāfaqāt,* trans. Imran A. K. Nyazee, vol. 2 (Reading, UK: Garnet, 2014), pp. 67–68.
88. Al-Ghazālī, *Iljām al-ʿawām,* pp. 95–96.
89. Al-Ghazālī, *Iljām al-ʿawām,* pp. 94–97.
90. Al-Ghazālī, *Iljām al-ʿawām,* pp. 94–97.
91. Al-Zāhid al-Bukhārī, *Maḥāsin al-islām* (Cairo: Maktabat al-Quds, 1938), p. 6.
92. Imran A. K. Nyazee, *Theories of Islamic Law* (Islamabad: Federal Law House, 2007), p. 56.
93. Fakhr al-Dīn al-Rāzī, *al-Maḥṣūl fī ʿilm uṣūl al-fiqh,* 2nd ed., vol. 5, ed. Ṭāhā J. al-Alwānī (Beirut: Mu'ssasat al-Risāla, 1992), p. 186.
94. For a comprehensive treatment of al-Rāzī's corpus, see Tareq Jaffer, *al-Rāzī: Master of Qur'ānic Interpretation and Theological Reasoning* (Oxford and New York, Oxford University Press, 2015).
95. Fakhr al-Dīn al-Rāzī, *Tafsīr al-fakhr al-Rāzī,* 1st ed., vol. 2 (Cairo: Dār al-Fikr, 1981), pp. 47–54.
96. Al-Rāzī, *Tafsīr,* vol. 32, p. 171.
97. Al-Rāzī, *al-Maḥṣūl,* p. 189.
98. See ʿIzz al-Dīn Ibn ʿAbd al-Salām, *Maqāṣid al-ʿibādāt,* 1st ed., ed. ʿAbd al-Raḥīm A. Qamḥiyya (Homs: Maṭbʿat al-Yamāma, 1995).
99. Denny, "Islamic Theology in the New World," p. 1074.
100. Aḥmad ibn ʿAbdel Ḥ . . . Ibn Taymiyya, *Majmuʿ al-fatāwā,* 3rd ed., vol. 32 (Al-Manṣūra: Dār al-Wafā', 2005), pp. 146–147.
101. Aḥmad dhātibn ʿAbdel Ḥalīm Ibn Taymiyya, *al-Jawāb al-ṣaḥīḥ li-man baddala dīn al-Masīḥ,* vol. 1 (Riyadh: Maṭābʿat al-Majd, n.d.), p. 22.
102. Shāh Walīullāh Al-Dehlawī, *Ḥujjat Allāh al-bāligha,* 1st ed., vol. 1, ed. Seyyed Sābiq (Beirut: Dār al-Jīl, 2005), p. 122.
103. Al-Dehlawī, *Ḥujjat,* vol. 1, p. 132.
104. Al-Dehlawī, *Ḥujjat,* vol. 1, p. 133–134.
105. See Felicitas Opwis, "Maṣlaḥa in Contemporary Islamic Legal Theory," *Islamic Law and Society* 12.2 (2005), pp. 182–223.
106. See Rashīd Riḍā, *al-Waḥy al-Muḥammadī,* 3rd ed. (Beirut: Maktabat ʿIzz al-Dīn, 1986).
107. Al-Azhar is an Islamic university in Egypt established by the Fātimids in 972 as a center of Islamic learning, based mainly in Cairo. It is today, arguably, the most significant Islamic university in the Muslim world. According to Adamec, *Historical Dictionary of Islam,* it began "as a Shiʿite college for the propagation of the Ismaʿili sect. After the Ayyubids conquered Egypt, the country reverted to Sunni Islam, and Al-Azhar eventually became the dominant orthodox institution and a model also for European universities. The famous historian/sociologist Ibn Khaldun lectured at Al-Azhar in the 14th century, and by the 18th century it dominated the educational scene in the Islamic world" (pp. 67–68).

108. Adamec, *Historical Dictionary of Islam*, p. 23. For a comprehensive treatment of ʿAbduh's life and thought, see Rashīd Riḍā, *Tārīkh al-imām Muḥammad ʿAbduh*, 2nd ed. (Cairo: Dār al-Faḍīla, 2006) and Muḥammad ʿImāra (d. 2020), *al-Aʿmāl al-kāmila li'l-imām Muḥammad ʿAbduh* (Cairo: Dār al-Shurūq, 1993).
109. On ʿAbduh's intellectual relation with al-Afghānī and Riḍā, see my forthcoming chapter "Muḥammad ʿAbduh and the False Divorce between Tradition and Modernity." For a study of each of the three figures and their influence upon one another, see Albert Hourani, *Arabic Thought in the Liberal Age 1798–1939* (London: Oxford University Press, 1962); Ammeke Kateman, *Muḥammad ʿAbduh and His Interlocutors: Conceptualizing Religion in a Globalizing World* (Leiden and Boston: Brill, 2019).
110. Muḥammad ʿAbduh, *The Theology of Unity*, trans. Isḥāq Musaʿad and Kenneth Crag (London: George Allen and Unwin, 1966), p. 57.
111. Muḥammad ʿAbduh, *Risālat al-tawḥīd*, ed. Muḥammad ʿImāra (Beirut and Cairo: Dār al-Shurūq, 1994), pp. 56–57.
112. ʿAbduh, *Risālat al-tawḥīd*, p. 17.
113. ʿAbduh, *Risālat al-tawḥīd*, pp. 77–78.
114. ʿAbduh, *Risālat al-tawḥīd*, pp. 78–79.
115. ʿAbduh, *Risālat al-tawḥīd*, p. 109.
116. ʿAbduh, *Theology of Unity*, pp. 124–125.
117. ʿAbduh, *Theology of Unity*, p. 126.
118. Hourani, *Arabic Thought*, pp. 151–152.
119. For the most substantial systematic practice of this principle in the premodern tradition, that which took place within the *qāḍī* framework under the Mamluks, see Yossef Rapoport, "Legal Diversity in the Age of *Taqlīd*: The Four Chief Qāḍīs under the Mamluks," *Islamic Law and Society* 10.2 (2003), pp. 210–228.
120. Hourani, *Arabic Thought*, pp. 151–152.
121. ʿAbduh, *Theology of Unity*, p. 130.
122. ʿAbduh, *Risālat al-tawḥīd*, pp. 145–146.
123. ʿAbduh, *Theology of Unity*, pp. 130–131
124. ʿAbduh, *Theology of Unity*, p. 134.
125. ʿAbduh, *Theology of Unity*, pp. 134–135.
126. Riḍā, *Tārīkh al-imām Muḥammad ʿAbduh*, vol. 1, pp. 819–830.
127. Kateman, *Muhammad ʿAbduh and His Interlocutors*, p. 89.
128. Canon of York in late Victorian England who had correspondence with ʿAbduh. They both helped initiate the Society of Harmony of Reconciliation between the three Abrahamic religions during ʿAbduh's exile in Beirut. Kateman, *Muhammad ʿAbduh and His Interlocutors*, p. 90.
129. Kateman, *Muhammad ʿAbduh and His Interlocutors*, p. 133.
130. Ahmad Hasan wrote, "*Qiyās* is a systematic form of reasoning in law. Before it developed into a sophisticated doctrine in the post-Shāfiʿī period, it was simply used to show a resemblance between two parallel cases or institutions. It started with

the use of personal opinion (*ra'y*) in cases not covered by an explicit text (*naṣṣ*). The employment of sound personal opinion (*ra'y*) to settle important matters was not uncommon in pre-Islamic Arabia. Men of opinion (*dhū'-l-ra'y*) and men weak in mind (*mufannad*) were two distinct categories of people in respect of reasoning. The exercise of *ra'y* was therefore not something novel in Islam. The Qur'ān of course alludes to its use by the Prophet, and points to its significance in ancient history. The Qur'ān lays great stress on the use of rational faculty. Its recurrent insistence upon (thinking) and (reflection), and its sporadic mention of ratio (*ʿillah*), and purpose of injunctions made for the exercise of *ra'y* and ultimately *qiyās* in Islamic jurisprudence." Ahmad Hasan, "The Principle of Qiyās in Islamic Law: An Historical Perspective," *Islamic Studies* 15.3 (1976), p. 201.

131. Abū Isḥāq al-Shāṭibī, *al-Muwāfaqāt fi uṣūl al-Sharīʿa* (The Reconciliation of the Fundamentals of Islamic Law), trans. Imran A. K. Nyazee, vol. II (Reading, UK: Garnet. 2014), p. 35.
132. See: Richard C. Martin, Mark Woodward, and Dwi S. Atmaja, *Defenders of Reason in Islam: Mu'tazilism: From Medieval School to Modern Symbol* (Oxford: Oneworld, 1997); Oussama Arabi, *Studies in Modern Islamic Law and Jurisprudence* (Leiden: Brill, 2001).
133. See his discussion of the Muʿtazilite engagement with the theory of atomism in Josef V. Ess, *The Flowering of Muslim Theology*, trans. Jane M. Todd (Cambridge, MA: Harvard University Press, 2006), pp. 79–115.
134. Iqbal, *The Reconstruction of Religious Thought in Islam*, p. 3.
135. Jackson, *Islam and the Problem of Black Suffering*, pp. 75–76.
136. Jackson, *Islam and the Problem of Black Suffering*, p. 76.
137. Al-Ghazālī, *Iḥyā'*, p. 1799.
138. Mohammed H. Kamali, "Goals and Purposes Maqāṣid al-Sharīʿa: Methodological Perspectives," *The Objectives of Islamic Law: The Promises and Challenges of Maqāṣid al-Sharīʿa*, ed. Idris Nassery, Rumee Ahmed, and Muna Tatari (London: Lexington, 2018), p. 11.
139. Roy P. Mottahedeh, "Pluralism and Islamic Traditions of Sectarian Divisions," *Diversity and Pluralism in Islam: Historical and Contemporary Discourses amongst Muslims,* ed. Zulfikar Hirji (London and New York: I. B. Tauris and Institute of Ismaili Studies, 2010), p. 32.
140. For a survey of the nature of such denominations and its impact on the formation of Islamic theology, see Josef van Ess's quartet of *Theology and Society in the Second and Third Centuries of the Hijra: A History of Religious Thought in Early Islam* (Leiden and Boston: Brill, 2016).
141. Aḥmad A. Duwayyish, *Fatāwā al-Lajna al-Dā'ima li'l-Buḥūth al-ʿIlmiya wa'l-Iftā*, vol. 2, ed. Aḥmad A. al-Duwayyish (Riyadh: Dār al-Mu'ayyad, 1424 H), p. 152.
142. He was a leading Muslim polymath from the celebrated al-Subkī family of Shāfiʿī ʿulamā, in the Mamluk era. See Jonathan P. Berkey and Marlis J. Saleh (eds.), "Al-Subkī and His Women," *Mamluk Studies Review* 14: 8.

143. Ḥassan al-Shāfiʿī, *Muqaddima taʾsīsiya l-ʿilm al-qawāʿid al-ʿitiqādiyya* (Cairo: Dhakhāʾir al-Warrāqīn, 2016), p. 32.
144. He was a Yemeni Shiite Zaidiyya scholar, with a special interest in defending the Sunna of the Prophet. See Jonathan A. C. Brown, *The Canonization of al-Bukhārī and Muslim: The Formation and Function of the Sunnī Ḥadīth Canon* (Leiden: Brill, 2007), p. 314.
145. Al-Shāfiʿī, *Muqaddima taʾsīsiya*, pp. 35–36.
146. He is a contemporary Egyptian scholar and a leading authority on Islamic theology, philosophy, and spirituality. He is a lecturer at Dār al-ʿUlūm, University of Cairo, and one of the senior scholars of Al-Azhar.
147. Al-Shāfiʿī, *Muqaddima taʾsīsiya*, p. 45.
148. Nuraan Davids and Yusef Waghid, *Ethical Dimensions of Muslim Education* (London: Palgrave Macmillan, 2016), p. 109.
149. Al-Ghazālī, *al-Maqṣad*, p. 2.
150. Toby Mayer, "Theology and Sufism," *The Cambridge Companion to Classical Islamic Theology*, ed. Tim Winter (Cambridge: Cambridge University Press, 2008), p. 271.
151. Paul L. Heck, review of *Sufism and Theology*, ed. Ayman Shihadeh, *Journal of Qur'anic Studies* 10.1 (April 2008), p. 129.
152. Ayman Shihadeh, *Sufism and Theology* (Edinburgh: Edinburgh University Press, 2007).
153. Heck, review of *Sufism and Theology*, p. 129.

CHAPTER 2

1. Ibn al-Qayyem was a "Hanbali jurist from Baghdad. Disciple of Ibn Taymiyyah and compiler of his works. Critic of popular religion and the excesses of Sufism. Member of Qadiri Sufi order. Compiled a collection of hadith of Muhammad's medical practices." John L. Esposito, John L. *The Oxford History of Islam* (New York: Oxford University Press, 1999), p. 128.
2. Ibn al-Qayyim, *Iʿlām al-muwaqqiʿīn ʿan Rabb al-ʿĀlamīn*, vol. 2, ed. Mashhūr b. Ḥasan Āl Salmān (Riyadh: Dār Ibn al-Jawzī, 1423/2002), p. 333.
3. Mohammed H. Kamali, "Issues in the Legal Theory of Uṣūl and Prospects for Reform," *Islamic Studies* 40 (2001), p. 13.
4. Aḥmad Ibn ʿAjība, *al-Baḥr al-madīd fī tafsīr al-Qurʾān al-majīd*, vol. 1, ed. Aḥmed A. Q. Raslān (Cairo: al-Hayaʾ al-Maṣriyya al-Āmma lil-Kitāb, 1999), pp. 591–592.
5. Ibn ʿAjība "was born in the village of al-Khamis on the Moroccan coast. His early education was in the Islamic sciences. He later on went to Fez to get his ijaza from Tawdi ibn Suda and Muhammad Bannis. When he was about thirty he returned to Tetuan, and his orientation changed toward tasawwuf, apparently after reading the works of Ibn 'Ata' Allah. Ibn 'Abjiba was a prolific author, and he covers the usual wide range of Islamic literature. In philosophy he wrote a number of fairly

brief texts on metaphysics, covering the range of issues that arise within Sufism." Leaman, *The Bibliographical Encyclopaedia of Islamic Philosophy*, p. 162.

6. Fakhr al-Dīn al-Rāzī, *al-Tafsīr al-kabīr*, 1st ed., vol. 11 (Cairo: Dar al-Fikr, 1981), pp. 112–113.
7. Al-Zamakhsharī was a theologian and philologist of Persian origin. He "was born at Zamakhshar and died at Korkanj in Transcaspia. Ibn Khallikan says of him, 'The great master (imam) in the sciences of Koranic interpretation, the Traditions, grammar, philology, and rhetoric, was incontrovertibly the first imam of the age in which he lived.' He was a Muʿtazilite, supporting the createdness of the Koran and, in spite of his origin, an opponent of the anti-Arab *shuʿubiyyah* movement. His Koran commentary *The Revealer* (*al-Kashshaf*) was original, and his Arabic grammar (*al-mufassal*) is still used as a reference work today." Adamec, *Historical Dictionary of Islam*, p. 489.
8. Ibn ʿUmar al-Zamakhsharī, *al-Kashshāf ʿan ghawāmiḍ ḥaqāʾiq al-tanzīl wa ʿuyūn al-aqāwīl fī wujūh al-taʾwīl*, ed. Khalil M. Shiḥa (Beirut: Dar al-Maʿrifa, 2009), p. 272.
9. Ibn ʿAjība, *al-Baḥr al-madīd*, vol. 3, p. 506.
10. Al-Ṭabarī was an "Islamic scholar from Tabaristan, present Iran, whose *Annals of Prophets and Kings* (*Tarikh al-rusul wa'l-muluk*) is a history of the world from its creation to the 10th century. It is the first history of the world in Arabic and an important source for the early history of the caliphate. He also produced a 30-volume commentary (tafsir) on the Koran. The Annals have been translated into English, German, and French." Adamec, *Historical Dictionary of Islam*, p. 425.
11. Muḥammad Ibn Jarīr al-Ṭabarī, *Jāmiʿ al-bayān ʿan taʾwīl āy al-Qurʾān*, ed. Bashshār ʿAwwād and ʿIṣām F. al-Hiristānī (Beirut: al-Risāla, 1994), p. 287.
12. Seyyed H. Nasr et al., *The Study Qurʾān: A New Translation and Commentary*, 1st ed. (New York: HarperCollins, 2015), p. 1265.
13. Al-Zamakhsharī, *al-Kashshāf*, pp. 477–478.
14. Al-Rāzī, *al-Tafsīr al-kabīr*, vol. 17, p. 195.
15. Al-Rāzī, *al-Tafsīr al-kabīr*, vol. 27, p. 140.
16. Nasr et al., *Study Qurʾān*, p. 2667.
17. Nasr et al., *Study Qurʾān*, pp. 1034–1035.
18. Nasr et al., *Study Qurʾān*, pp. 1034–1037.
19. Ibn ʿAjība, *al-Baḥr al-madīd*, vol. 2, p. 279.
20. Nasr et al., *Study Qurʾān*, p. 261.
21. Al-Ghazālī, *Iljām al-ʿawām*, pp. 71–73.
22. See Ibrāhīm al-Bāijūrī, *Ḥashiya ʿalā matn burdat al-Buṣayrī* (Amman: Prince Ghazi Trust for Qurʾānic Thought, 2012), pp. 130–131.
23. See Ibn ʿAbd al-Shakūr al-Bahārī's *Fawātiḥ al-Raḥamūt bi-Sharḥ Musallam al-thubūt*, 1st ed., vol. 2 (Beirut: Dār al-Kutub al-ʿlmiyya, 2002), pp. 120–136.
24. Khaled Abou El Fadl, *Speaking in God's Name: Islamic Law, Authority and Women* (Oxford: Oneworld, 2001), p. 209.

25. Abou El Fadl, *Speaking in God's Name*, p. 193.
26. Jalāl al-Dīn al-Suyūṭī, *Miftāḥ al-jannah fī al-iʿtiṣām bil-Sunnah* (Cairo: Dār al-Kutub, 1987), p. 35.
27. Duderija, *The Imperatives of Progressive Islam*, p. 202; see also Salwa Al-Awa, *Textual Relations in the Qur'an: Relevance, Coherence and Structure* (London: Routledge, 2006).
28. Feisal Abdul Rauf, ed., *Defining Islamic Statehood: Measuring and Indexing Contemporary Muslim State* (London: Palgrave Macmillan, 2015), p. 208.
29. Al-Ghazālī, *Iljām al-ʿawām*, pp. 91–92.
30. Abū Ḥāmid al-Ghazālī, *Qawāʿd al-ʿaqāʾd*, 2nd ed., trans. Nabih A. Faris (Lahore: Ashraf Printing Press, 1999), p. 35.
31. Ibn ʿAbbās was the "son of ʿAbbas ibn ʿAbd al-Muttalib, the uncle of the Prophet. He was a Companion of the Prophet and Islamic scholar, the first to produce a commentary of the Qur'ān. Originally a partisan of ʿAli, who appointed him governor of Basra, he made peace with the Umayyads. He participated in many campaigns, acted as an adviser to caliphs, and retired to Ta'if, where he died. Saʿd ibn Abi Waqqas said: I have never seen someone who was quicker in understanding, who had more knowledge and greater wisdom than Ibn Abbas. I have seen ʿUmar summon him to discuss difficult problems in the presence of veterans of Badr from among the Muhajirin and Ansar. Ibn Abbas would speak and ʿUmar would not disregard what he had to say." Adamec, *Historical Dictionary of Islam*, p. 182.
32. Al-Ghazālī, *Qawāʿd*, pp. 37–39.
33. Al-Ghazālī, *Qawāʿd*, pp. 39–40.
34. For a comprehensive treatment of this subject, see Safaruk Chowdhury, *Islamic Theology and the Problem of Evil* (Cairo: AUC Press, 2021).
35. Al-Ghazālī, *Qawāʿd*, pp. 41–42.
36. Al-Ghazālī, *Qawāʿd*, pp. 44–45.
37. Al-Ghazālī, *Qawāʿd*, pp. 44–45.
38. Al-Ghazālī, *Qawāʿd*, pp. 46–47.
39. Al-Ghazālī, *Qawāʿd*, p. 36.
40. Al-Ghazālī, *Qawāʿd*, p. 47.
41. Al-Ghazālī, *Qawāʿd*, pp. 47–52.
42. Al-Ghazālī, *Qawāʿd*, pp. 37–53.
43. Abū Ḥāmid al-Ghazālī, *Mishkāt*, vol. 19, trans. W. H. T. Gairdner (London: Royal Asiatic Society, 1924), pp. 137–139.
44. Bāṭinites is a "generic term for groups and sects, mostly Shiʿites, who distinguish the inner (batin) esoteric interpretation of the Koran and Islamic law from the outer (zahir) exoteric form. The esoteric doctrine consists of two main parts: the allegorical interpretation (taʿwil) of the Koran and the Traditions (Sunnah), and the truths (haqaʾiq), a system of philosophy and science coordinated with religion. Ismaʿilis and Qarmatians favored this interpretation and devised levels of initiation

according to the comprehension of the believer. Among Sunnis, some Sufi orders also accept allegorical interpretation." Adamec, *Historical Dictionary of Islam*, p. 81.

45. Al-Ghazālī, *Mishkāt*, p. 137.
46. Al-Ghazālī, *Mishkāt*, p. 137.
47. Al-Ghazālī, *Mishkāt*, pp. 139-140.
48. Al-Ghazālī, *Qawā'd*, p. 53.
49. See al-Ghazālī's introduction to his *Tahāfut al-falāsifa*. See also Muḥammad Ā. al-Jābirī, *Bunyat al-'aql al-'arabī: dirāsa taḥlīliya naqdiya l'nuẓum al-ma'rifa fi'l-thaqāfa al-'arabiya* (Beirut: Markaz Dirāsāt al-Waḥda al-'Arabiya, 1990), p. 22.

CHAPTER 3

1. Abdul Rauf, *Defining Islamic Statehood*, p. 27.
2. The verse states, "There shall be no compulsion in religion. True guidance has become distinct from error."
3. The verse says, "And had your Lord willed, those on earth would have believed—all of them entirely. Then, [O Muhammad], would you compel the people in order that they become believers?"
4. *Ridda* normally translated as "apostasy" and "is forbidden in Islam. An apostate has become an infidel (kafir); he may lose his property and is considered divorced from his wife because a Muslim woman may not be married to a non-Muslim. Some radical sects, like the seventh-century Kharijites, would even kill an apostate and his family. After the death of Muhammad, some of the Arab tribes considered their alliance with the Prophet terminated, and the caliphate of Abu Bakr (632–634) was devoted to forcing them to renew their loyalty and convert others in what came to be known as the 'Riddah Wars.' During European colonial occupation, Islamic laws of apostasy could not be enforced, and missionary activity, though with little success, was permitted. After independence, many Muslim states adopted Western legal institutions and, although apostasy was considered forbidden, they did not enforce punishments." Adamec, *Historical Dictionary of Islam*, p. 371.
5. al-Shāfi'ī, *al-Madkhal l'drāsat 'ilm al-kalām*, pp. 198–209.
6. Duderija, *The Imperatives of Progressive Islam*, p. 125.
7. 'Allāl al-Fāsī, *Maqāṣid al-Sharī'a al-islāmiyya wa makārimuha*, 5th ed.)Beirut: Dār al-Gharb al-Islāmī, 1993), p. 11.
8. Aḥmad Raysūnī, *Maqāṣid al-maqāṣid* (Beirut: al-Shabaka al-'Arabiyya, 2013).
9. Abdul Rauf, *Defining Islamic Statehood*, p. 27.
10. Al-Nawawī, *al-Minhāj sharḥ ṣaḥīḥ Muslim*, p. 83.
11. *Ṣaḥīḥ Muslim*, book 1, *ḥadīth*.
12. Ṭāhir al Ibn 'Āshūr, *Maqāṣid al-Sharī'ah al-Islamiyya*, trans. Mohamed T. El-Mesawi (London and Washington, DC: III, 2006), p. 73.
13. Ibn 'Āshūr, *Maqāṣid al-Sharī'a al-Islamiyya*, p. 72.

14. Elsaid M. Badawi and Muhammad Abdel Haleem, *Arabic-English Dictionary of Qur'anic Usage* (Leiden and Boston: Brill, 2008), pp. 225–226.
15. Al-Ghazālī, *al-Maqsad*, p. 125.
16. Al-Ghazālī, *al-Maqsad*, p. 125.
17. Nasr, *Study Qur'ān*, p. 2058.
18. *Ṣaḥīḥ al-Bukhārī*, book 80, *ḥadīth* 14.
19. Nasr, *Study Qur'ān*, p. 1042.
20. Nasr, *Study Qur'ān*, p. 1881.
21. Nasr, *Study Qur'ān*, p. 118.
22. Abū Ḥāmid Al-Ghazālī, *Kitāb sharḥ 'ajā'ib al-qalb*, trans. Walter J. Skellie (Louisville, KY: Fons Vitae, 2010), pp. 3–5.
23. Abū Isḥāq Al-Shāṭibī, 1st ed., vol. 2, *al-Muwāfaqāt*, ed. Abdullāh Dirāz (Beirut: Dār al-Kutub al-'Ilmyiyya, 2004), p. 168.
24. Al-Shāṭibī *al-Muwāfaqāt*, p. 170.
25. Al-Shāṭibī *al-Muwāfaqāt*, pp. 170–172.
26. This threefold typology has been defined in the introduction to this monograph, and a critical analysis of it is offered in my book *A Comparative History of Catholic and Aš'arī Theologies of Truth and Salvation*.
27. Rifat Atay, "Religious Pluralism and Islam: A Critical Examination of John Hick's Pluralistic Hypothesis" (PhD diss., University of St. Andrews, 1999), pp. 28–29.
28. Esra A. Dag, *Christian and Islamic Theology of Religions: A Critical Appraisal* (Oxford: Routledge, 2017), pp. 90–91.
29. See the second chapter in Khalil's *Islam and the Fate of Others*.
30. Atay, "Religious Pluralism," p. 37.
31. See Mohammed Arkoun, *Rethinking Islam: Common Questions and Uncommon Answers*, trans. Robert D. Lee (Oxford: Westview Press, 1994), pp. 16, 33; Atay, "Religious Pluralism," pp. 45–46.
32. Farid Esack, *Qur'an, Liberation and Religious Pluralism* (Oxford: Oneworld, 1996), pp. 155–180.
33. Dag, *Theology of Religions*, pp. 109–110. See also Reza S. Kazemi, *The Other in the Light of the One: The Universality of the Qur'an and Interfaith Dialogue* (Cambridge, UK: Islamic Texts Society, 2006).
34. See Immanuel Kant, *Critique of Pure Reason* (Cambridge: Cambridge University Press, 1999); Veli-Matti Karkkainen, *An Introduction to the Theology of Religions: Biblical, Historical and Contemporary Perspectives* (Westmont, IL: InterVarsity Press, 2003), p. 292.
35. See John Hick, *God and the Universe of Faiths* (London: Fount/Collins, 1973).
36. Andrew Chignell, "As Kant Has Shown," *Analytic Theology: New Essays in the Philosophy of Theology*, ed. Oliver Crisp and Michael C. Rea (Oxford and New York: Oxford University Press, 2009), p. 119.
37. Douglas V. Porpora, "Methodological Atheism, Methodological Agnosticism and Religious Experience," *Journal for the Theory of Social Behaviour* 36.1 (2006), 57–75.

38. See the interpretations of this verse in al-Ṭabarī's *Jāmiʿ al-bayān ʿan taʾwīl āy al-Qurʾān.*
39. al-Rāzī, *al-Tafsīr*, vol. 25, p. 258.
40. He is regarded as "the greatest of all Sufi poets, called Shaykh al-Akbar, the 'Greatest Master' (or *mawlana*) by his supporters. Born in Balkh, in present-day Afghanistan, he moved with his father to Konya in Turkey, called Rum at the time; hence, his name Rumi. He received a traditional education, and at age 15 he experienced his mystical 'unveiling.' He studied at the Nizamiyyah in Baghdad and traveled widely in the Islamic world. His masterpiece, the *Masnawi*, written in Persian, is a six-volume work of spiritual teachings. He is the founder of the Mevlevi order, also known as the 'Whirling Dervishes.' Jalal al-Din is buried in Konya." Adamec, *Historical Dictionary of Islam*, p. 225.
41. Cyrus Masroori, *An Islamic Language of Toleration: Rumi's Criticism of Religious Persecution* (London: Sage, 2010), p. 250.
42. See Abū Ḥāmid Al-Ghazālī, *The Alchemy of Happiness* (Tehran: Elmi va Frahanji, 2004).

CHAPTER 4

1. Mohammed H. Kamali, "Goals and Purposes Maqāṣid al-Sharīʿa: Methodological Perspectives," *The Objectives of Islamic Law: The Promises and Challenges of Maqāṣid al-Sharīʿa*, ed. Idris Nassery, Rumee Ahmed, and Muna Tatari (London: Lexington, 2018), p. 13.
2. Kamali, "Goals and Purposes Maqāṣid al-Sharīʿa," p. 13.
3. Kamali, "Goals and Purposes Maqāṣid al-Sharīʿa," p. 13.
4. Al-Shāṭibī, *al-Muwāfaqāt*, pp. 13–14.
5. Al-Shāṭibī, *al-Muwāfaqāt*, p. 14.
6. Khalil, *The Fate of Others*, p. 7.
7. The verse says, "And whoever desires other than Islam as religion—never will it be accepted from him, and he, in the Hereafter, will be among the losers."
8. See full discussion on the exegeses of Q. 2:62 in Jane McAuliffe, *Qur'anic Christians: An Analysis of Classical and Modern Exegesis* (Cambridge: Cambridge University Press, 1991), pp. 93–128.
9. *Riyāḍ al-Ṣāliḥīn*, Introduction, *ḥadīth* 426.
10. *Riyāḍ al-Ṣāliḥīn*, Introduction, *ḥadīth* 183.
11. *Riyāḍ al-Ṣāliḥīn*, Introduction, *ḥadīth* 305.
12. Ibn Taymiyya, *Majmuʿ al-fatāwā*, vol. 19, p. 42.
13. See George Hourani, *Reason and Tradition in Islamic Ethics* (Cambridge: Cambridge University Press, 1985), pp. 120–121.
14. Al-Ghazālī, *Fayṣal*, pp. 88–89.
15. Al-Ghazālī, *Fayṣal*, pp. 89–90.
16. Al-Ghazālī, *Fayṣal*, p. 91.

17. Al-Ghazālī, *Fayṣal,* pp. 107–109.
18. Al-Ghazālī, *Fayṣal,* pp. 107–109.
19. Al-Ghazālī, *Fayṣal,* pp. 109–110.
20. Al-Ghazālī, *Fayṣal,* pp. 109–110.
21. Al-Ghazālī, *Fayṣal,* p. 112.
22. Al-Ghazālī, *Fayṣal,* pp. 112–113.
23. Al-Ghazālī, *Fayṣal,* p. 113.
24. Ibn Taymiyya, *Fatāwā al-ṣalah,* ed. ʿAlī al-Ṭahṭawī (Beirut: Dar al-Kutub al-ʿIlmiyya, n.d.), pp. 565–566.
25. Roy P. Mottahedeh, "Pluralism and Islamic Traditions of Sectarian Divisions," *Diversity and Pluralism in Islam: Historical and Contemporary Discourses amongst Muslims*, ed. Zulfikar Hirji (London and New York: I. B. Tauris and Institute of Ismaili Studies, 2010), p. 32.
26. Mottahedeh, *Diversity and Pluralism in Islam*, p. 32.
27. He was a Sunni Muslim scholar and historian who loved in Baghdad. See Brown, *The Canonization of al-Bukhārī and Muslim*, p. 187.
28. Al-Khaṭīb al-Baghdādī, *Sharaf aṣḥāb al-ḥadīth*, 1st ed., ed. ʿAmr A. Selīm (Cairo: Maktabat Ibn Taymīyya, 1996), p. 61.
29. George Makdisi, "Ashʿarī and the Ashʿarites in Islamic Religious History I," *Studia Islamica,* no. 17 (1962), p. 52. While in his *Ibāna*, al-Ashʿarī took a clear Atharī position; in his *al-Lumaʿ fī al-radd ʿala ahl al-zaygh wa-al-bidaʿ* (The Sparks: A Refutation of Heretics and Innovators) he clearly came across as a typical Ashʿarite theologian. See Abū al-Ḥassan al-Ashʿarī, *al-Lumaʿ,* ed. Ḥammūda Ghurāba (Cairo: Maṭbaʿat Maṣr, 1955), p. 5.
30. Al-Bāqillānī is an early Ashʿarite theologian and Mālikite jurist; he spent much of his life defending and consolidating orthodox Sunnite Islam. A man of letters and master orator, he was highly regarded for his expertise in debating anti-orthodox views and hence often given the title "Sayf al-Sunna" (Sword of the Prophetic Way). He is said to have been educated by two of the direct students of al-Ashʿarī. See Adamec, *Historical Dictionary of Islam*, p. 76; Montgomery Watt, *Islamic Philosophy and Theology: An Extended Survey*, 2nd ed. (Edinburgh: Edinburgh University Press, 1985), p. 76.
31. It is worth mentioning that al-Ashʿarī used the term *Ahl al-Sunna wa-al-Istiqāma* across his *Maqālāt*, but in generic terms.
32. Abū Bakr al-Bāqillānī, *al-Inṣāf fimā yajibu ʿitiqāduhu wa-lā yajūzu al-Jahl bihi fī ʿilm al-kalām,* 2nd ed., ed. Muḥammad Z. al-Kawtharī (Cairo: Maktabat al-Azhar, 2000), p. 105.
33. Ibn Taymiyya, *Darʾ al-taʿāruḍ bayna al-ʿaql wa-al-naql,* vol. 1, ed. Muḥammad R. Sālim (Cairo: al-Hay'ia al-Miṣriyya al-ʿAmma lil-Kitāb, 1971), p. 270.
34. Al-Baghdādī was an Ashʿarite theologian and legist born and raised in Baghdad. He received his education in Nishapur and is buried in Isfarayn (present-day Iran). According to the historian Ibn Ḥallikān (d. 1282), "He possessed great riches,

which he spent on the learned (in the law) and on the treatises on different sciences and surpassed his contemporaries in every branch of learning. . . . [H]e gave lessons there, which were assiduously attended by doctors of the greatest eminence." Adamec, *Historical Dictionary of Islam*, pp. 73–74; Nuh Keller, *Reliance of the Traveller: A Classic Manual of Islamic Sacred Law* (Beltsville, MD: Amana, 1997), p. 1021.

35. ʿAbd al-Qāhir al-Baghdādī, *al-Farq*, 1st ed., Muḥammad ʿO. al-Khusht (Cairo: Maktabat Ibn Sīnā, 1988), pp. 26–28; Muḥammad Z. al-Kawtharī, *Muqaddimāt*, 2nd ed. (Damascus and Beirut: Dār al-Thurayya, 1997), pp. 147–155.
36. ʿAbd al-Qāhir al-Baghdādī, *al-Farq bayna al-firaq*, vol. 1, trans. Kate C. Seelye (New York: Columbia University Press, 1920), p. 19.
37. Al-Baghdādī, *al-Farq bayna al-firaq*, pp. 29–30.
38. Abū al-Muẓaffar al-Isfarāyīnī, *al-Tabṣīr fī al-dīn*, ed. Muḥammad Z. al-Kawtharī (Cairo: al-Maktabat al-Azhariyya, 2010), pp. 157–160.
39. ʿAbd al-Malik al-Juwaynī, *Lumaʿ al-adilla*, 2nd edn., ed. Fawqiyya Ḥ. Ḥammūda (Beirut: ʿĀlam al-Kutub, 1987), p. 85.
40. Al-Juwaynī, *Lumaʿ*, p. 95.
41. Abū Ḥāmid al-Ghazālī, *Mizān al-ʿamal*, 1st edn., ed. Suliemān Dunyā (Cairo: Dār al-Maʿārif, 1964), pp. 9–10.
42. Al-Ghazālī, *Fayṣal*, pp. 81–85.
43. Al-Ghazālī, *Fayṣal*, pp. 81–85.
44. Abū Ḥāmid al-Ghazālī, *Faḍāʾil al-anām min rasāʾil ḥujjat al-islām*, trans. Nūruddīn ʿAlī (Tunisia: Dār Tūnisiah, 1972), p. 147. See also Abū Ḥāmid al-Ghazālī, *Fadāʾiḥ al-bāṭiniyya* (Cairo: al-Dār al-Qawmiyya, 1964), pp. 146–160.
45. Frank Griffel, *Al-Ghazālī's Philosophical Theology* (New York: Oxford University Press, 2009), p. 105.
46. Fakhr al-Dīn al-Rāzī, *Tafsīr al-fakhr al-Rāzī*, 1st ed., vol. 22 (Beirut: Dār al-Fikr, 1981), p. 219.
47. Fakhr al-Dīn al-Rāzī, *Iʿtiqādāt firaq al-muslimīn wa-al-mushrikīn*, ed. Muṣtafa ʿAbdel Rāziq (Cairo: al-Nahḍa al-Miṣriyya, 1938), pp. 74–75.
48. ʿAḍud al-Dīn al-Ījī, *Kitāb al-mawāqif* (Beirut: Ālam al-Kutub, n.d.), p. 414.
49. Al-Ījī, *al-Mawāqif*, p. 430.
50. There is a robust debate over whether this work is actually ʿAbduh's or instead the work of his mentor, al-Afghānī. While most scholars ascribe the book to ʿAbduh, ʿImāra, unconvincingly in my view, defended the other view. See Muḥammad ʿAbduh, *Ḥāshiya ʿalā sharḥ al-dawwānī lil-ʿaqāʾid al-ʿaḍudiya*, ed. Muḥammad ʿImāra (Cairo: Maktabat al-Shurūq, 2002). See also Ḥassan al-Shāfiʿī, *Qawl fī al-tajdīd* (Cairo: Dār al-Quds al-ʿArabī, 2016).
51. In the sixth chapter of *A Comparative History of Catholic and Aš'arī Theologies of Truth and Salvation*, I demonstrate in what way I classify ʿAbduh as an Ashʿarite.
52. ʿAbduh, *Ḥāshiya*, pp. 160–162.
53. ʿAbduh, *Ḥāshiya*, pp. 164–165.

54. ʿAbd al-Ḥalīm Maḥmūd (d. 1978) "was the 40th Grand Imām of Al-Azhar. Just as al-Ġazālī wrote an autobiography in *The Deliverer from Error*, Ḥalīm also did in *al-Ḥamdu li-llāh! hadihi ḥayātī* (All Praise is Due to God: This Has Been my Life). In this work he relates that he was born into a renowned wealthy family that had many philanthropists and memorizers of the Quran. Doing Islamic studies at his birthplace (Sharqiyah governorate, 45 kilometres north east of Cairo), he joined Al-Azhar's neighbourhood institute in 1923. He was the youngest to be awarded ʿĀlimiyyah (a master's degree) in the history of Al-Azhar. Ḥalīm then headed to Paris, France, to study at the Sorbonne at his own expense (ḤHḤ 1985: 113–14). During his time in France, World War II raged, yet Ḥalīm continued with his PhD under the supervision of Massignon (ḤHḤ 1985: 125–126), whose influence can best be seen in how Ḥalīm then read al-Ḥallāj's controversy and how he justified such views (ABM 1969: 140). Upon returning to Egypt, he took a post at Al-Azhar University. In 1973, he was appointed Shayḫ Al-Azhar, the highest religious position in Egypt." Abdelnour, *A Comparative History of Catholic and Aśʿari Theologies of Truth and Salvation*, p. 152.
55. The Association was founded in Cairo in January 1947 "by the young Iranian cleric Muhammad Taqi al-Qummi, [and] can be rightly regarded as the first organized and systematic attempt to bridge the gap between Sunnis and Shiis. Although its protagonists—several of whom were high-ranking scholars of Al-Azhar University—tried hard to avoid open discussion of sectarian conflicts within Islam, the activities of the association were from the very beginning accompanied by polemical criticism from mainly Sunni Salafi circles. At the end of the 1950s, it nevertheless managed to reach a wider public, as the Egyptian president Nasser discovered the usefulness of pan-Islamism for his foreign policy." Rainer Brunner, "Interesting-Times: Egypt and Shi'ism at the Beginning of the Twenty-First Century," in *The Sunnah and Shiʿa in History: Division and Ecumenism in the Muslim Middle East*, ed. Meir Litvak and Ofra Bengio (New York: Palgrave Macmillan, 2011), p. 223.
56. See: Rainer Brunner, *Islamic Ecumenism in the 20th Century: The Azhar and Shiism between Rapprochement and Restraint* (Leiden and Boston: Brill, 2004).
57. Ibn ʿĀshūr, *Uṣūl*, 2nd ed. (Tunis: al-Dār al-Tūnisīyya, n.d.), p. 172.
58. ʿAbd al-Ḥalīm Maḥmūd, *al-Tafkīr al-falsafī fī al-islām*, 2nd ed. (Cairo: Dār al-Maʿārif, 1989), p. 72.
59. Ḥalīm, *al-Tafkīr*, pp. 72–73.
60. Ḥalīm, *al-Tafkīr*, p. 73.
61. Ḥalīm, *al-Tafkīr*, p. 75.
62. Ḥalīm, *al-Tafkīr*, pp. 73–74.
63. ʿAbd al-Ḥalīm Maḥmūd, *al-Ḥamdu li-llāh! hadhihi ḥayātī*, 3rd ed. (Cairo: Dār al-Maʿārif, 1985), pp. 136–141.
64. Ibn Fūrak was a significant figure in the early Ashʿarite tradition. He "started his education in Isfahan where he learned Shafiʿite *fiqh*, then he moved first to

Basra, then to Baghdad where he studied *kalam* with Abu al-Hasan al-Bakhili and Ibn Mujahid al-Tai, both were the students of al-Ashʿari. In Baghdad he also met with Baqillani and Isfaraini. At around 360 H/970 CE, he returned to his hometown and became a leading proponent of the Ashʿarite theology." Leaman, *The Biographical Encyclopedia of Islamic Philosophy*, p. 181.

65. Al-Ḥassan Ibn Fūrak, *Mujarrad maqālāt al-shaykh Abū al-Ḥassan al-Ashʿarī*, ed. Daniel Gimaret (Beirut: Dār al-Mashriq, 1987), pp. 150–163.
66. Al-Juwaynī, *Lumaʿ*, p. 122.
67. Ibn Fūrak, *Mujarrad*, pp. 150–153.
68. Abū Ḥāmid al-Ghazālī, *Ayyuhā al-walad*, trans. Tobias Mayor (Cambridge, UK: Cambridge Islamic Texts Society, 2005), pp. 8–10.
69. Al-Ghazālī, *Ayyuhā al-walad*, pp. 8–10.
70. Al-Ghazālī, *Iḥyā'*, p. 140.
71. Al-Ghazālī, *Iḥyā'*, p. 1603.
72. Al-Ghazālī, *Iḥyā'*, pp. 1604–1606.
73. Muḥammad ʿAbduh and Rashīd Riḍā, *Tafsīr al-manār*, 2nd ed., vol. 1 (Cairo: Dār al-Manār, 1367/1947), p. 336.
74. ʿAbduh and Riḍā, *Tafsīr al-manār*, pp. 336–337.
75. Muḥammad ʿImāra, *al-Aʿmāl al-kāmila li-i-imām Muḥammad ʿAbduh*, vol. 5 (Cairo: Dār al- Shurūq, 1993), p. 463.
76. Abū Zahra was a renowned twentieth-century public intellectual and religious scholar at Al-Azhar. He wrote over a dozen books on different areas, ranging from international relations in Islam to Islamic legal theories. Of these are *Lectures in Comparative Religion*, delivered in 1940 and published in 1965, and *Lectures on Christianity*, which were held and published in 1942. His "views are of capital importance to the modern study of Islam. This importance owes a lot to him being a 'critical insider' in the full sense of the two words. Thanks to an insider criticality, his views travelled far and wide across the Muslim world. In 2001, a British nonprofit educational foundation was established and named after him (Abu Zahra Foundation), aiming to revive this sense of criticality in the minds of Muslims living in the West. Abu Zahra died in 1974." Mohammed G. Abdelnour, "Muhammad Abu Zahra's Muslim Theology of Religions," in *Religious Imaginations: How Narratives of Faith Are Shaping Today's World*, ed. James Walters (London: Gingko Library, 2018), pp. 111–112.
77. Mohammad H. Khalil, *Between Heaven and Hell: Islam, Salvation, and the Fate of Others* (Oxford: Oxford University Press, 2013), p. 46.
78. Abdelnour, "Muhammad Abu Zahra's Muslim Theology of Religions," pp. 111–112.
79. Khalil, *Between Heaven and Hell*, p. 46.
80. Ibn Fūrak, *Mujarrad maqālāt*, p. 153.
81. ʿAbd al-Malik Al-Juwaynī, *al-Irshād ilā qawāṭʿ al-adilla*, ed. Aḥmad al-Sāyiḥ and Tawfīq Wahba (Cairo: Maktabat al-Thaqāfa al-Dīniyya, 2009), pp. 271–272.

82. ʿAbd al-Qāhir al-Baghdādī, *Kitāb uṣūl al-dīn*, 1st ed. (Beirut: Dār al-Kutub al-ʿIlmiyya, 2002), pp. 184–185.
83. Ibn Fūrak, *Mujarrad maqālāt*, pp. 174–180.
84. Griffel, *Al-Ghazali's Philosophical Theology*, p. 106.
85. Abū Ḥāmid Al-Ghazālī, *Iḥyāʾ ʿulūm al-dīn*, vol. 1 (Cairo: Dār al-Bayān al-ʿArabī, 1990), pp. 84–85.
86. Khalil, *The Fate of Others*, p. 31.
87. Al-Ghazālī, *Fayṣal*, p. 126.
88. The verse says, "As for those who are given solid proof from their Lord, reported by a witness from Him, and before it, the book of Moses has set a precedent and a mercy, they will surely believe. As for those who disbelieve among the various groups, Hell is awaiting them. Do not harbour any doubt; this is the truth from your Lord, but most people disbelieve."
89. Al-Rāzī, *Tafsīr*, vol. 17, p. 211.
90. The verse states, "Surely, those who believe, those who are Jewish, the Christians, and the converts; anyone who (1) believes in God, and (2) believes in the Last Day, and (3) leads a righteous life, will receive their recompense from their Lord. They have nothing to fear, nor will they grieve."
91. Al-Rāzī, *Tafsīr*, vol. 3, pp. 111–114.
92. For a comprehensive study on Abrogation, see John Burton, *The Sources of Islamic Law: Islamic Theories of Abrogation* (Edinburgh: Edinburgh University Press, 1990).
93. For a more detailed discussion of ʿAbduh's critique of this theory of ***naskh***, see Abdelnour, *A Comparative History of Catholic and Ašʿarī Theologies of Truth and Salvation*, pp. 140–142.
94. The verse states, "Say, 'People of the Book, let us arrive at a statement that is common to us all: we worship God alone, we ascribe no partner to Him, and none of us takes others beside God as lords.' If then they turn back, say ye: 'Bear witness that we (at least) are Muslims (submitting to God).'"
95. ʿAbduh and Riḍā, *Tafsīr al-manār*, vol. 2, pp. 5–6.
96. Rashīd Riḍā, *Majallat al-manār*, 2nd ed., vol. 1 (Cairo: Matbaʿat al-Manār, 1327/1910), pp. 17–19.
97. The verse says, "Indeed, those who believed [Muslims] and those who are Jews or Christians or Sabeans—those who believed in God and the Last Day and did righteousness—will have their reward with their Lord, and no fear will there be concerning them, nor will they grieve."
98. McAuliffe, *Qurʾānic Christians*, p. 118. See also ʿAbduh and Riḍā, *Tafsīr al-manār*, vol. 5, pp. 432–433.
99. ʿAbduh and Riḍā, *Tafsīr al-manār*, vol. 3, pp. 360–361.
100. Ibn Taymiyya, *Majmuʿ al-fatāwā*, vol. 7, pp. 103–104.
101. Aḥmed al-Beḥerī, *Al-Azhar lā yamlik takfīr al-nās* (Al-Azhar does not have the Authority to Excommunicate People), available at https://www.almasryalyoum.com/news/details/1132163 (accessed 14 March 2022).

CHAPTER 5

1. Meir Litvak and Ofra Bengio, *The Sunnah and Shi'a in History: Division and Ecumenism in the Muslim Middle East* (New York: Palgrave Macmillan, 2011), p. 2.
2. Fred Halliday, "Orientalism and Its Critics," *British Journal of Middle Eastern Studies* 20.2 (1993), p. 153.
3. Emphasis is mine.
4. Bengio and Litvak, *The Sunna and Shi'a in History*, p. 167.
5. Christopher Melchert, *Ahmad Ibn Hanbal* (Oxford: Oneworld, 2006), p. 91.
6. For a comprehensive study of the historiographical tradition around this event, see Erling L. Petersen's *ʿAlī and Muʿāwiya in Early Arabic Tradition: Studies on the Genesis and Growth of Islamic Historical Writing until the End of the Ninth Century* (Copenhagen: Scandinavian University Books, 1964).
7. He was an Arab Muslim polymath who lived in twelfth-century Baghdad and played an instrumental role in propagating the Hanbali school of orthodox Sunni jurisprudence. See Jonathan A. C. Brown, "Faithful Dissenters: Sunni Skepticism about the Miracles of Saints," *Journal of Sufi Studies* 1 (2012), pp. 123–168.
8. Ibn al-Jawzī, *Manāqib al-imām Aḥmad* (Beirut: Dar Hajr, 1973), p. 126.
9. Zakariyyā al-Ansārī, *Fatḥ al-Bāqī, bi-Sharḥ Alfiyat al-ʿIrāqī*, ed. ʿAbd al-Laṭīf al-Hamīm and Māhir Y. Faḥl, vol. 2, 1st ed. (Beirut: Dar al-Kutub al-ʿIlmiyya, 2002), p. 191. See also Abū Bakr Ibn al-ʿArabī, *Al-ʿawāṣim min al-qawāṣim*, ed. Maḥmūd M. al-Istanbūlī et al., 6th ed. (Cairo: Maktabat al-Sunna, 1412 H), p. 182.
10. Muḥammad Abū Zahra, *Aḥmad Ibn Ḥanbal: ḥayātuhu wa ʿaṣruhu, arāʾu al-fiqhiya* (Cairo: Dār al-Fikr al-ʿArabī, n.d.), pp. 170–171.
11. Sayyid M. H. al-Tabatba'i, *Glimpses of Shiism in the Musnad of Ibn Hanbal*, trans. Sayyid Shahbaz (Qom: Ahl al-Bayt World Assembly, n.d.), p. 3.
12. Aḥmad Ibn Ḥanbal, *al-Sunna*, 4th ed., ed. Muḥammad al-Qāḥṭānī (Riyadh: Dār ʿĀlam al-Kutub, 1996), p. 548.
13. See Yossef Rapoport and Shahab Ahmed, *Introduction in Ibn Taymiyya and His Times* (Karachi: Oxford University Press, 2010), p. 6.
14. Ibn Taymiyya, *Al-Ṣārim al-maslūl*, ed. Muḥammad M. ʿAbdel Ḥamīd (Riyadh: Dār al-Ḥaras al-Waṭanī, 1983), pp. 590–591.
15. Ibn Taymiyya, *Majmuʿ al-fatāwā*, vol. 28 (Riyadh: Wazārat al-Awqāf, 2004), p. 482.
16. Ibn Ḥanbal, *al-Sunna*, p. 548.
17. Bengio and Litvak, *The Sunna and Shiʿa in History*, p. 210.
18. Aḥmad dhātibn ʿAbdel Ḥalīm Ibn Taymiyya, *al-ʿAqīda al-wāsitiyya*, 2nd ed., ed. Ashraf ʿAbd al-Maqṣūd (Riyadh: Aḍwāʾ al-Salaf, 1999), p. 118.
19. Ibn Taymiyya, *al-ʿAqīda al-wāsitiyya*, p. 119.
20. He was born in ʿUyayna, which was a small village in the Najd region of central Arabia. He "studied theology with his father and then travelled widely in Arabia, Iran, and Iraq before going to Medina to study Islamic law and theology. . . . He

was shocked by what he considered sinful innovations in the great cities of Islam and allied himself with Muhammad ibn Saʿud of Dariya in Central Arabia to propagate his reformist ideas. ʿAbd al-Wahhab presented his ideas in The Book of Unity (*Kitab al-tawhid*), in which he attacked as sinful innovations the doctrines of Sufism, saint cults, and intercession and demanded the Koran and Traditions (Sunnah) as the sole bases of Islamic theology and jurisprudence. He was able to gain a considerable following among the Arab tribes, and, although initially defeated, the alliance between the Islamist reformer and the clan of Al Saʿud led to the conquest of Arabia and the establishment of Wahhabism in what came to be the Kingdom of Saudi Arabia." Adamec, *Historical Dictionary of Islam*, p. 23.

21. Jonah Steinberg, *Ismaʿili Modern: Globalization and Identity in a Muslim Community* (Chapel Hill: University of North Carolina Press, 2011), pp. 160–161.
22. Geneive Abado, *The New Sectarianism: The Arab Uprising and the Rebirth of Sunni-Shi 'a Rebirth*, Oxford Scholarship Online, 2016, p. 4.
23. Abado, "The New Sectarianism," p. 4.
24. Bengio and Litvak, *The Sunna and Shi'a in History*, p. 165.
25. Sulaymān ibn ʿAbd al-Wahhāb, *al-Ṣawāʿiq al-ilāhiyya fi'l-radd ʿalā al-Wahhābiyya*, 3rd ed. (Istanbul: Kusak, 1979), p. 4.
26. Ibn Ḥumaydī, *al-Suḥub al-wābila ʿala ḍarā'iḥ al-Ḥanābila* (Beirut: Maktabat al-Imām Aḥmad, 1989), p. 275.
27. Bengio and Litvak, *The Sunna and Shiʿa in History*, pp. 165–166.
28. Khaled Abou El Fadl, *The Great Theft* (San Francisco, CA: Harper, 2005), p. 152.
29. See also Tarik K. Firro, "The Political Context of Early Wahhabi Discourse of Takfir," *Middle Eastern Studies* 49.5 (2013).
30. Muḥammad Ibn ʿAbd al-Wahhāb, *al-Taʿlīqāt ʿala Kashf al-Shubuhāt*, ed. A. Ibn S. al-ʿUthaymīn (Beirut: Dār Auwlī al-Nuhā, 1996), p. 64.
31. Muḥammad Ibn ʿAbd al-Wahhāb, *Kashf al-shubuhāt fi al-tawḥīd*, ed. M. al-Dīn al-Khaṭīb (Cairo: al-Maṭbaʿa al-Salafiyya, 1965), pp. 9–14, 37–43.
32. Firro, "The Political Context of Early Wahhabi Discourse," p. 776.
33. Firro, "The Political Context of Early Wahhabi Discourse," pp. 771–772.
34. He "was prominent during the second Saudi state, and his publications were compiled by Shaykh Sulaymān Ibn Sahmān (a prominent *ʿālim* who lived during the second and early third Saudi states) in *Majmūʿ al-Rasāil wa-Masāil al-Najdīyyah* [The Najdī Compilation of Epistles and *Fatāwā*]. ʿAbd al-Laṭīf dedicated a significant portion of his work to attack *shirk* and its practices." Raihan Ismail, *Saudi Clerics and Shīʿa Islam* (New York: Oxford University Press, 2016), p. 58.
35. Ismail, *Saudi Clerics and Shīʿa Islam*, p. 58.
36. Firro, "The Political Context of Early Wahhabi Discourse," p. 783.
37. Firro, "The Political Context of Early Wahhabi Discourse," p. 776.
38. See Farouk Mitha, *Al-Ghazālī and the Ismailis: A Debate on Reason and Authority in Medieval Islam* (London and New York: I. B. Tauris, 2001). For a history

of the Ismailis, see Farhad Daftary, *The Isma'ilis: Their History and Doctrines* (Cambridge: Cambridge University Press, 1990).

39. Griffel, *Al-Ghazali's Philosophical Theology*, p. 106.
40. Al-Ghazālī, *Fayṣal*, p. 50.
41. Al-Ghazālī, *Fayṣal*, pp. 50–51.
42. The verse says, "And [had you been present], you would see the sun when it rose, inclining away from their cave on the right, and when it set, passing away from them on the left, while they were [laying] within an open space thereof."
43. Al-Ghazālī, *Fayṣal*, p. 50.
44. Bengio and Litvak, *The Sunna and Shiʿa in History*, p. 6.
45. Al-Ghazālī, *Bidāyat*, ed. Muḥammad al-Ḥajjār, 9th ed. (Beirut: Dār al-Bashā'r, 2001), pp. 170–171.
46. Muḥammad ʿAbduh, *al-Islām wa al-naṣrāyniyya*, 3rd ed. (Beirut: Dār al-Hadātha, 1988), pp. 127–128.
47. ʿImāra, *al-Aʿmāl al-kāmila*, vol. 3, p. 561.
48. ʿImāra, *al-Aʿmāl al-kāmila*, vol. 3, p. 561.
49. ʿImāra, *al-Aʿmāl al-kāmila*, vol. 3, p. 562.
50. Muḥammad ʿAbduh *The Theology of Unity*, trans. Isḥāq Musaʿad and Kenneth Crag (London: George Allen and Unwin, 1966), p. 57.
51. Riḍā, *Tārīkh al-imām Muḥammad ʿAbduh*, vol. 1, pp. 819–830.
52. Kateman, *Muhammad ʿAbduh and His Interlocutors*, p. 89.
53. For a comprehensive study of this association and its history, see Rainer Brunner, *Islamic Ecumenism in the 20th Century: The Azhar and Shiism between Rapprochement and Restraint* (Leiden and Boston: Brill, 2004).
54. Bengio and Litvak, *The Sunna and Shiʿa in History*, pp. 223–224.
55. Bengio and Litvak, *The Sunna and Shiʿa in History*, pp. 223–224.
56. Brunner, *Islamic Ecumenism*, pp. 289–290. See it also in Abu Umar F. Ahmad, *Theory and Practice of Modern Islamic Finance: The Case Analysis from Australia* (Boca Raton, FL: Brown Walker Press, 2010), pp. 81–82; Mahmud Shaltut, "Shaykh Mahmud Shaltut's Fatwa about Shia Madhab (1959)," https://www.icit-digital.org/articles/shaykh-mahmud-shaltut-s-fatwa-about-shia-madhab-1959 (accessed 15 March 2022).
57. Brunner, *Islamic Ecumenism*, p. 235.
58. Werner Ende, "Sunni Polemical Writings on the Shiʿa and the Iranian Revolution," in *The Iranian Revolution and the Muslim World*, ed. David Menashri (Boulder, CO: Westview, 1990), pp. 219–232.
59. For an exploration of such reasons see Brunner, *Islamic Ecumenism*, pp. 388–389; Bengio and Litvak, *The Sunna and Shiʿa in History*, p. 224.
60. See, for instance, ʿAbdullāh ibn Yābis, *Iʿlām al-anām bi-mukhālafāt shaykh al-Azhar Shaltūt lil-Islām* (Riyadh: Kalbānī Publications, n.d.).
61. See "Are the Shia Considered Muslims? A Balanced Answer," *Le Chiisme Duodécimain*, http://www.chiite.fr/en/islam_02.html (accessed 16 March 2022).

62. See "Are the Shia Considered Muslims?
63. See "Are the Shia Considered Muslims?"
64. Al-Ghazālī, *Fayṣal*, p. 106.

CONCLUSIONS

1. Fadl, *Speaking in God's Name*, p. 11.

Bibliography

ARABIC SOURCES

ʿAbduh, Muḥammad and Riḍā, Rashīd. 1367/1947. *Tafsīr al-manār*, 2nd ed. Cairo: Dār al-Manār.

ʿAbduh, Muḥammad. 1966. *The Theology of Unity*, trans. Isḥāq Musaʿad and Kenneth Crag. London: George Allen and Unwin.

ʿAbduh, Muḥammad. 1988. *al-Islām wa al-naṣrāyniyya*, 2nd ed. Beirut: Dār al-Hadātha.

ʿAbduh, Muḥammad. 1994. *Risālat al-tawḥīd*, 1st ed., ed. Muḥammad ʿImāra. Beirut and Cairo: Dār al-Shurūq.

ʿAbduh, Muḥammad. 2002. *Ḥāshiya ʿalā sharḥ al-dawwānī lil-ʿaqāʾid al-ʿaḍudiya*, ed. Muḥammad ʿImāra. Cairo: Maktabat al-Shurūq al-Dawliyya.

ʿAbdu, Muḥammad. 2002. *Maqāṣid al-ʿaqīda ʿinda al-Ghazālī*. Ribat: Arab Network for Research and Publishing.

Abū Zahra, Muḥammad. 1958. *Uṣūl al-fiqh*. Cairo: Dār al-Fikr al-ʿArabī.

Abū Zahra, Muḥammad. n.d. *Aḥmad Ibn Ḥanbal: ḥayātuhu wa ʿaṣruhu, arāʾuh al-fiqhiyya*. Cairo: Dār al-Fikr al-ʿArabī.

Al-ʿĀmirī. 1988. *al-Iʿlām bi-manāqib al-islām*, 1st ed., ed. Aḥmad Ghorāb. Riyadh: Dār al-Aṣāla.

al-Ansārī, Zakariyyā. 2002. *Fatḥ al-Bāqī, bi-Sharḥ Alfiyat al-ʿIrāqī*, 1st ed., vol. 2, ed. ʿAbd al-Laṭīf al-Ḥamīm and Māhir Y. Faḥl. Beirut: Dar al-Kutub al-ʿIlmiyya.

al-Ashʿarī, Abū al-Ḥassan. 1955. *al-Lumaʿ*, ed. Ḥammūda Ghurāba. Cairo: Maṭbaʿat Maṣr.

al-Ashʿarī, Abū al-Ḥassan. 1977. *al-Ibāna*, 1st ed., ed. Fawqiyya H. Ḥammūda. Cairo: Dār al-Anṣār.

al-Ashʿarī, Abū al-Ḥassan. 2002. *Risāla ilā ahl al-thaghr*, 2nd ed., ed. ʿAbd Allāh S. al-Junaidī. Medina: Maktabat al-ʿUlūm wa-al-Ḥikam.

al-Ashʿarī, Abū al-Ḥassan. 2009. *Maqālāt al-islāmīyyīn wa-ikhtilāf al-musallīn*, ed. Naʿīm Zarzūr. Beirut: al-Matkaba al-ʿAṣriyya.

al-Baghdādī, ʿAbd al-Qāhir. 1988. *al-Farq byna al-firaq*, 1st ed., ed. Muḥammad ʿO. al-Khusht. Cairo: Maktabat Ibn Sīnā.

al-Baghdādī, ʿAbd al-Qāhir. 2002. *Kitāb uṣūl al-dīn*, 1st ed. Beirut: Dār al-Kutub al-ʿIlmiyya.

al-Baghdādī, al-Khaṭīb. 1996. *Sharaf aṣḥāb al-ḥadīth*, 1st ed., ed. ʿAmr A. Salīm. Cairo: Maktabat Ibn Taymīyya.

al-Bahārī, Ibn ʿAbd al-Shakūr. 2002. *Fawātiḥ al-Raḥamūt bi-Sharḥ Musallam al-thubūt*, 1st ed., vol. 2. Beirut: Dār al-Kutub al-ʿlmiyya.

al-Bājūrī, Ibrāhīm. 2002. *Tuḥfat al-murīd ʿalā jawharat al-tawḥīd*, ed. ʿAlī Jomʿa. Cairo: Dār al-Salām.

al-Bājūrī, Ibrāhīm. 2012. *Ḥashiya ʿalā matn burdat al-Buṣayrī*. Amman: Prince Ghazi Trust for Qurʾānic Thought.

al-Bāqillānī, Abū Bakr. 2000. *al-Inṣāf fīmā yajibu iʿtiqāduhu walā yajūzu al-jahl bihi fī ʿilm al-kalām*, 2nd ed., ed. Muḥammad Z. al-Kawtharī. Cairo: Maktabat Al-Azhar.

Bennabi, Malek. 1986. *Shurūṭ al-nahḍa*, trans. ʿAbdelṣabūr Shāhīn. Damascus: Dār al-Fikr.

al-Bukhārī, al-Zāhid. 1938. *Maḥāsin al-islām*. Cairo: Maktabat al-Quds.

al-Dehlawī, Shāh Walīullāh. 2005. *Ḥujjat Allāh al-bāligha*, 1st ed., vol. 1, ed. Seyyed Sābiq. Beirut: Dār al-Jīl.

al-Dhahabī, Shams al-Dīn. 1958. *Tadhkirat al-ḥuffāẓ*, vol. 2., ed. Abel Raḥmān al-Maʿlamī. Hyderabad: Dār al-Maʿārif al-Osmānia.

Duwayyish, Aḥmad A. 1424 H. *Fatāwā al-Lajna al-Dāʾima liʾl-Buḥūth al-ʿIlmiya waʾl-iftāʾ*, vol. 2. Riyadh: Dār al-Muʾayyad.

al-Fāsī, ʿAllāl. 1993. *Maqāṣid al-Sharīʿa al-islāmiyya wa makārimuhā*, 5th ed. Beirut: Dār al-Gharb al-Islāmī.

al-Fāsī, ʿAllāl. n.d. *Maqāṣid al-Sharīʿa al-islāmiyya wa makārimuhā*. Casablanca: Maktabat al-Waḥda al-ʿArabiyya.

al-Fawzān, Ṣāliḥ. 2005. *Sharḥ nawāqiḍ al-islām*, 3rd ed. Riyadh: Maktabat al-Rushd.

Fūda, Saʿīd. 2009. *Majmūʿat muʾallafāt al-ustādh al-mutakallim Saʿīd Fūda fī ʿilm al-kalām*. Amman: Dār al-Fatḥ.

al-Ghazālī, Abū Ḥāmid. 1961. *Fayṣal al-tafriqa bayna al-islām wa-al-zandaqa*, ed. Sulaymān Dunyā. Cairo: ʿĪsā al-Bābī al-Ḥalabī.

al-Ghazālī, Abū Ḥāmid. 1964. *Faḍāʾiḥ al-bāṭiniyya*. Cairo: al-Dār al-Qawmiyya.

al-Ghazālī, Abū Ḥāmid. 1964. *Mizān al-ʿamal*, 1st ed., ed. Suliemān Dunyā. Cairo: Dār al-Maʿārif.

al-Ghazālī, Abū Ḥāmid. 1971. *Shifāʾ al-ʿalīl*, ed. Ḥamad al-Kabīsī. Baghdad: al-Irshād.

al-Ghazālī, Abū Ḥāmid. 1972. *Faḍāʾil al-anām min rasāʾil ḥujjat al-islām*, trans. Nūruddīn ʿAlī. Tunisia: Dār Tūnisia.

al-Ghazālī, Abū Ḥāmid. 1972. *Tahāfut al-falāsifa*, 6th ed., ed. Suliemān Dunyā. Cairo: Dār al Maʿārif.

al-Ghazālī, Abū Ḥāmid. 1986. *Jawāhir al-Qurʾān*, ed. Muḥammad R. R. Qabbānī. Beirut: Dār Iḥyāʾ al-ʿUlūm.

al-Ghazālī, Abū Ḥāmid. 1988. *Minhāj al-qāṣidīn*. Beirut: Dār al-Kutub al-ʿIlmiyya.

al-Ghazālī, Abū Ḥāmid. 1990. *Iḥyā' 'ulūm al-dīn*, vol. 1. Cairo: Dār al-Bayān al-'Arabī.

al-Ghazālī, Abū Ḥāmid. 1993. *Fayṣal al-tafriqa bayna al-islām wa-al-zandaqa*, 1st ed., ed. Maḥmūd Bījū. Cairo: n.p.

al-Ghazālī, Abū Ḥāmid. 1994. *Majmū'at rasā'il al-Ghazālī*. Beirut: Dār al-Kutub al-'Ilmiyya.

al-Ghazālī, Abū Ḥāmid. 1997. *al-Mustasfā min 'ilm al-uṣūl*, 1st ed. Beirut: al-Risāla.

al-Ghazālī, Abū Ḥāmid. 2001. *Bidāyat al-hidāya*, 9th ed., ed. Muḥammad al-Ḥajjār. Beirut: Dār al-Bashā'r.

al-Ghazālī, Abū Ḥāmid. 2005. *Iḥyā' 'ulūm al-dīn*, 1st ed. Beirut: Dār Ibn Ḥazm.

al-Ghazālī, Abū Ḥāmid. 2009. *al-Iqtiṣād fī al-i'tiqād*, ed. Muṣṭafā 'Omrān. Cairo: Dār al-Baṣā'ir.

Ibn 'Abd al-Salām, 'Izz al-Dīn. 1995. *Maqāṣid al-'ibādāt*, 1st ed., ed. 'Abd al-Raḥīm A. Qamḥiyya. Homs: Maṭb'at al-Yamāma.

Ibn 'Abd al-Wahhāb, Muḥammad. 1965. *Kashf al-shubuhāt fi'l-tawḥīd*, ed. M. al-Dīn al-Khaṭīb. Cairo: al-Maṭba'a al-Salafiyya.

Ibn 'Abd al-Wahhāb, Muḥammad. 1996. *al-Ta'līqāt 'ala kashf al-shubuhāt*, ed. A. Ibn Ṣ. al-'Uthaymiyyn. Beirut: Dār Auwlī al-Nuha.

Ibn 'Abd al-Wahhāb, Sulaymān. 1979. *Al-Ṣawā'iq al-ilāhiyyah fi'l-radd 'alā al-Wahhābiyya*, 3rd ed. Istanbul: Kusak.

Ibn 'Ajība, Aḥmad. 1999. *al-Baḥr al-madīd fī tafsīr al-Qur'ān al-majīd*, ed. Aḥmed A. Q. Raslān. Cairo: al-Haya'a al-Maṣriyya al-'Āmma lil-Kitāb.

Ibn al-'Arabī, Abū Bakr. 1412 H. *al-'Awāṣim min al-qawāṣim*, 6th ed., ed. Maḥmūd M. al-Istanbūlī et al. Cairo: Maktabat al-Sunna.

Ibn 'Asākir, 'Ali ibn al-Ḥasan. 1929. *Tabyīn kadhib al-muftarī fīmā nusiba ilā al-imām abī al-Ḥassan al-Ash'arī*. Damascus: Maṭba'at al-Taufiq.

Ibn 'Āshūr, Ṭāhir al. 2001. *Maqāṣid al-Sharī'a al-Islāmiyya*, 2nd ed., ed. Muḥammad Ṭ. al-Missāwī. Amman: Dār al-Nafā's.

Ibn 'Āshūr, Ṭāhir al. n.d. *Uṣūl al-niẓām al-ijtimā'ī fil-Islām*, 2nd ed. Tunis: al-Dār al-Tūnisīyya.

Ibn Fūrak, al-Ḥassan. 1987. *Mujarrad maqālāt al-shaykh Abū al-Ḥassan al-Ash'arī*, ed. Daniel Gimaret. Beirut: Dār al-Mashriq.

Ibn Ḥanbal, Aḥmad. 1996. *al-Sunna*, 4th ed., ed. Muḥammad al-Qāḥṭānī. Riyadh: Dār 'Ālam al-Kutub.

Ibn Ḥumaydī, Muḥammad b. 'Abd Allāh b. 1989. *al-Suḥub al-wābila 'ala ḍarā'iḥ al-Ḥanābila*. Beirut: Maktabat al-Imām Aḥmad.

Ibn al-Jawzī, Abū al-Faraj. 1973. *Manāqib al-imām Aḥmad*. Beirut: Dar Hajar.

Ibn Khaldūn, 'Abd al-Raḥmān. 2004. *Muqaddima*, 1st ed., ed. Abdullāh M. Darwīsh. Damascus: Maktabat al-Hidāya.

Ibn al-Qayyim. 1423/2002. *I'lām al-muwaqqi'īn 'an Rabb al-'Ālamīn*, ed. Mashhūr b. Ḥ. Āl Salmān. Riyadh: Dār Ibn al-Jawzī.

Ibn Rushd, Abū al-Walīd. 1998. *Tahāfut al-tahāfut*, 1st ed.n, ed. Muḥammad 'Ābid al-Jābirī. Beirut: Markaz Dirasāt al-Waḥda al-'Arabiyya.

Ibn Shahbah, Aḥmad M. U. 1987. *Ṭabaqāt al-Shāfiʿiyya*, ed. ʿAbd al-ʿAlīm Khān. Beirut: ʿĀlam al-Kutub.

Ibn Taymiyya, Aḥmad ibn ʿAbdel Ḥalīm. 1971. *Darʾ al-taʿāruḍ bayna al-ʿaql wa al-naql*, ed. Muḥammad R. Sālim. Cairo: al-Hayʾia al-Miṣriyya al-ʿAmma lil-Kitāb.

Ibn Taymiyya, Aḥmad ibn ʿAbdel Ḥalīm. 1983. *Al-Ṣārim al-maslūl*, ed. Muḥammad M. Abdelḥamīd. Riyadh: Dār al-Haras al-Waṭanī.

Ibn Taymiyya, Aḥmad ibn ʿAbdel Ḥalīm. 1998. *Iqtiḍāʾ al-ṣirat al-mustaqīm*, 2nd ed., ed. Nāṣir A. al-ʿAql. Riyadh: Dār Ishbīliya.

Ibn Taymiyya, Aḥmad ibn ʿAbdel Ḥalīm. 1999. *al-ʿAqīda al-Wāsiṭiyya*, 2nd ed., ed. Ashrafʿ Abd al-Maqṣūd. Riyadh: Aḍwā al-Salaf.

Ibn Taymiyya, Aḥmad ibn ʿAbdel Ḥalīm. 2004. *Majmuʿ al-fatāwā*, vol. 28. Riyadh: Wazārat al-Awqāf.

Ibn Taymiyya, Aḥmad ibn ʿAbdel Ḥalīm. 2005. *Majmuʿ al-fatāwā*, 3rd ed., vol. 32. Al-Manṣūra: Dār al-Wafā.

Ibn Taymiyya, Aḥmad ibn ʿAbdel Ḥalīm. n.d. *Fatāwa al-ṣalah*, ed. ʿAlī al-Ṭahṭawī. Beirut: Dār al-Kutub al-ʿIlmiyya.

Ibn Taymiyya, Aḥmad ibn ʿAbdel Ḥalīm. n.d. *al-Jawāb al-ṣaḥīḥ li-man baddala dīn al-Masih*, vol. 1. Riyadh: Maṭābʿ al-Majd.

Ibn Taymiyya, Aḥmad ibn ʿAbdel Ḥalīm. n.d. *Kutub wa rasāʾil wa fatāwā Ibn Taymiyya fī al ʿaqīda*, vol. 3, ed. ʿAbd al-Raḥmān M. Q. al-Najdī. Riyadh: Maktabah Ibn Taymiyya.

al-Ījī, ʿAḍud al-Dīn. n.d. *Kitāb al-mawāqif*. Beirut: ʿĀlam al-Kutub.

ʿImāra, Muḥammad. 1993. *al-ʿAmāl al-kāmila lil-imām Muḥammad ʿAbduh*. Cairo: Dār al-Shurūq.

al-Isfarāyīnī, Abū al-Muẓaffar. 2010. *al-Tabṣīr fī al-dīn*, ed. Muḥammad Z. al-Kawtharī. Cairo: al-Maktaba al-Azhariyya.

al-Jābirī, Muḥammad Ā. 1990. *Bunyat al-ʿaql al-ʿarabī: dirāsah taḥlīliya naqdiyah lʾnuẓum al-maʿrifa fiʾl-thaqāfa al-arabiya*. Beirut: Markaz Dirāsāt al-Waḥda al-Arabiya.

al-Juwaynī, ʿAbd al-Malik. 1969. *al-Shāmil fī uṣūl al-dīn*, ed. Faiṣal ʿAwn, Suhair Mukhtār, and ʿAlī S. al-Nashshār. Alexandria: Minshaʿat al-Maʿārif.

al-Juwaynī, ʿAbd al-Malik. 1987. *Lumaʿ al-adilla*, 2nd ed., ed. Fawqiyya Ḥ. Ḥammūda. Beirut: ʿĀlam al-Kutub.

al-Juwaynī, ʿAbd al-Malik. 2009. *al-Irshād ilā qawāṭʿ al-adilla*, ed. Aḥmad al-Sāyiḥ and Tawfīq Wahba. Cairo: Maktabat al-Thaqāfa al-Dīniyya.

al-Kawtharī, Muḥammad Z. 1997. *Muqaddimāt*, 2nd ed. Damascus and Beirut: Dār al-Thurayya.

Maḥmūd, ʿAbd al-Ḥalīm. 1969. *al-ʿĀrif bi-llāh al-Mursī Abū al-ʿAbbās*. Cairo: Dār al-Kātib al-ʿArabī.

Maḥmūd, ʿAbd al-Ḥalīm. 1979. *Fatāwā*, 5th ed. Cairo: Dār al-Maʿārif.

Maḥmūd, ʿAbd al-Ḥalīm. 1985. *al-Ḥamdu li-llāh! hadhihi ḥayātī*, 3rd ed. Cairo: Dār al-Maʿārif.

Maḥmūd, ʿAbd al-Ḥalīm. 1989. *al-Tafkīr al-falsafī fī al-islām*, 2nd ed. Cairo: Dār al-Maʿārif.

al-Najdī, ʿAbd al-Raḥmān M. Q. n.d. *Kutub wa rasāʾil wa fatāwā Ibn Taymiyya fī al-ʿaqīda*, vol. 3. Riyadh: Maktabat Ibn Taymiyya.

al-Nawawī, Abū Zakariā Yakhyā. 1930. *Sharḥ Ṣaḥīḥ Muslim*, 2nd ed. Cairo: al-Maṭbaʿa al-Maṣriyya.

al-Nawawī, Abū Zakaria Yaḥyā. 2000. *al-Minhāj sharḥ Ṣaḥīḥ Muslim*. Amman and Riyadh: International Ideas Home.

al-Qarāfī, Shihāb al-Dīn. 1988. *al-Umniya fī idrāk al-niyya*, 1st ed., ed. Mūsāʿd Q. al-Fāliḥ. Riyadh: Maktabat al-Ḥaramayn.

al-Qarāfī, Shihāb al-Dīn. 2004. *Sharḥ tanqīḥ al-fuṣūl fī ikhtiṣār al-maḥṣūl fī al-uṣūl*. Beirut: Dār al-Fikr.

al-Qummī, Ibn Bābawayh. 2006. *ʿIlal al-Sharīʿa*, 1st ed. Beirut: Dār al-Murtaḍā.

al-Raysūnī, Aḥmad 2013. *Maqāṣid al-maqāṣid*. Beirut: al-Shabaka al-Arabiyya.

al-Rāzī, Fakhr al-Dīn. 1938. *Iʿtiqādāt firaq al-muslimīn wa-al-mushrikīn*, ed. Muṣtafa ʿAbdel Rāziq. Cairo: al-Nahḍa al-Maṣriyya.

al-Rāzī, Fakhr al-Dīn. 1981. *al-Tafsīr al-kabīr*, 1st ed. Cairo: Dār al-Fikr.

al-Rāzī, Fakhr al-Dīn. 1992. *al-Maḥṣūl fī ʿilm uṣūl al-fiqh*, 2nd ed., ed. Ṭāha J. al–ʿAlwānī. Beirut: Muʿssasat al-Risāla.

Riḍā, Rashīd. 1327/1910. *Majallat al-manār*, 2nd ed. Cairo: al-Manār.

Riḍā, Rashīd. 1986. *al-Waḥy al-Muḥammadī*, 3rd ed. Beirut: Maktabat ʿIzz al-Dīn.

Riḍā, Rashīd. 2006. *Tārīkh al-ustādh al-imām Muḥammad ʿAbduh*, 2nd ed. Cairo: Dār al-Faḍīla.

al-Shāfiʿī, Ḥassan. 2001. *Al-Madkhal lʿdrāsat ʿilm al-kalām*, 2nd ed. Karachi: Idārat al-Qurʿān waʾl-ʿUlūm al-Islāmiyya.

al-Shāfiʿī, Ḥassan. 2016. *Muqaddimah taʾsīsiya l-ʿilm al-qawāʿid al-ʿitiqādiyya*. Cairo: Dhakhāʿir al-Warrāqīn.

al-Shāfiʿī, Ḥassan. 2016. *Qawl fī al-tajdīd*. Cairo: Dār al-Quds al-ʿArabī.

al-Shahrastānī, Abū al-Fatḥ. 1975. *al-Milal wa-al-niḥal*, 2nd ed., ed. Muḥammad S. Kilānī. Beirut: Dār al-Maʿrifa.

Shaltūt, Maḥmūd. 2001. *al-Islām ʿaqīda wa Sharīʿa*, 18th ed. Cairo: Dār al-Shurūq.

Shaltūt, Maḥmūd. 2004. *Tafsīr al-qurān al-karīm*, 12th ed. Cairo: Dār al-Shurūq.

al-Shaʿrānī, ʿAbd al-Wahāb. 2018. *al-Yawāqīt wa-al-jawāhir fī bayān ʿaqāʾid al-akābir*, ed. ʿAbd al-Wārith M. ʿAlī. Beirut: Dār al-Kutub al-ʿIlmiyya.

al-Shāṭibī, Abū Isḥāq. 2004. *Al-Muwāfaqāt fī uṣūl al-Sharīʿa*, 1st ed., ed. ʿAbdullāh Dirāz. Beirut: Dār al-Kutub al-ʿlmyiyya.

al-Suyūṭī, Jalāl al-Dīn. 1987. *Miftāḥ al-janna fī al-iʿtiṣām bil-Sunna*. Cairo: Dār al-Kutub.

al-Ṭabarī, Ibn Jarīr. 1994. *Jāmiʿ al-bayān ʿan taʾwīl āy al-Qurʾān*, ed. Bashshār ʿAwwād and ʿIṣām F. al-Hiristānī. Beirut: al-Risāla.

Ṭaha, Abdurraḥmān. 2015. *Suʾāl al-manhaj*. Beirut: al-Muʾassasa al-ʿArabiyya.

al-Tirmidhī, Al-Ḥakīm. 1969. *al-Ḥajj wa asrāru*, 1st ed., ed. Ḥosny Zidān. Cairo: Matbaʿat al-Saʿāda.

al-Tirmidhī, Al-Ḥakīm. 1998. *Ithbāt al-ʿilal*, 1st ed., ed. Khalid Zahrī. Ribat: Kulliyat al-Ādāb wa al-Ulūm al-Insāniya.

Yābis, Abdullāh ibn. n.d. *Iʿlam al-Anām bi-mukhalāfāt shaykh al-Azhar Shaltūt lil-Islām*. Riyadh: Kālbānī Publications.

al-Zamakhsharī, Ibn ʿUmar. 2009. *al-Kashshāf ʿan ghawāmiḍ ḥaqā'iq al-tanzīl wa ʿuyūn al-aqāwīl fi wujūh al-ta'wīl*, ed. Khalil M. Shiḥa. Beirut: Dār al-Maʿrifa.

al-Zarkashī, Badr al-Dīn. 1992. *al-Baḥr al-muḥīṭ*, 2nd ed., ed. ʿAbd al-Sattār Abū Ghudda and ʿAbd al-Qādir al-ʿĀnī. Kuwait: Wazārat al-Awqāf wa-al-Shu'ūn al-Islāmiyya.

Al-Zuḥaylī, Muḥammad. 2003. *Maqāṣid al-Sharīʿa: Asās li-huqūq al-insān*. Doha: Ministry of Awqāf and Islamic Affairs of Qatar.

ENGLISH SOURCES

Abado, Geneive. 2016. *The New Sectarianism: The Arab Uprising and the Rebirth of Sunni-Shi'a Divide*. Oxford Scholarship Online.

Abdel Haleem, M. A. S. 2010. *The Qur'ān: A New Translation*. Oxford: Oxford University Press.

Abdel Haleem, M. A. S. 2018. "The Role of Context in Interpreting and Translating the Qur'ān." *Journal of Qur'ānic Studies* 22.2: 47–66.

Abdelnour, M. G. 2018. "Muhammad Abu Zahra's Muslim Theology of Religions," in *Religious Imaginations: How Narratives of Faith Are Shaping Today's World*, ed. James Walters, pp. 101–114. London: Gingko Library.

Abdelnour, M. G. 2021. *A Comparative History of Catholic and Ašʿarī Theologies of Truth and Salvation: Inclusive Minorities, Exclusive Majorities*. Leiden and Boston: Brill.

Abdelnour, M G. Forthcoming. "Muḥammad 'Abduh and the False Divorce between Tradition and Modernity," *The Oxford Handbook of Islam and Reform*, ed. Emad Hamdeh and Natana Delong-Bas. New York: Oxford University Press.

Abdul Rauf, Feisal, ed. 2015. *Defining Islamic Statehood: Measuring and Indexing Contemporary Muslim States*. London: Palgrave Macmillan.

Abou El Fadl, Khaled. 2001. *Speaking in God's Name: Islamic Law, Authority and Women*. Oxford: Oneworld.

Abou El Fadl, Khaled. 2005. *The Great Theft*. San Francisco, CA: Harper.

Abou El Fadl, Khaled. 2006. *The Search for Beauty in Islam: Conference of the Books*. Washington, DC: Rowman and Littlefield.

Abou El Fadl, Khaled. 2014. *Reasoning with God: Reclaiming Shari'ah in the Modern Age*. New York: Rowman and Littlefield.

Abou El Fadl, Khaled. 2015. "The Epistemology of the Truth in Modern Islam." *Philosophy and Social Criticism* 41.4–5: 473–486.

Abu Rabī', Ibrahim M. 2003. *Toward a Critical Arab Reason: The Contributions of the Moroccan Philosopher Muḥammad 'Ābid al-Jābirī*. Islamabad: Islamic Research Institute and International Islamic University.

Adamec, Ludwig W. 2017. *Historical Dictionary of Islam*, 3rd ed. London and New York: Rowman.

Adams, Charles. 1969. *Islam and Modernism in Egypt: A Study of the Modern Reform Movement Inaugurated by Muhammad ʿAbduh*. New York: Russell.

Ahmad, Abu Umar F. 2010. *Theory and Practice of Modern Islamic Finance: The Case Analysis from Australia*. Boca Raton, FL: Brown Walker Press.

Ahmed, Shahab. 2016. *What Is Islam? The Importance of Being Islamic*. Princeton, NJ, and Oxford: Princeton University Press.

Aishima, Hatsuki. 2009. "Doubt, Faith, and Knowledge: The Reconfiguration of the Intellectual Field in Post-Nasserist Cairo." *Journal of the Royal Anthropological Institute* 15: 41–56.

Anjum, Ovamir. 2016. "Salafis and Democracy: Doctrine and Context." *The Muslim World* 106.3: 448–473.

Arabi, Oussama. 2001. *Studies in Modern Islamic Law and Jurisprudence*. Leiden: Brill.

Arkoun, Mohammed. 1994. *Rethinking Islam: Common Questions and Uncommon Answers*, trans. Robert D. Lee. Oxford: Westview Press.

Arthur, Schmidt. 2000. *Biographical Dictionary of Modern Egypt*. Boulder, CO: Lynne Rienner.

Asad, Talal. 1986. *The Idea of an Anthropology of Islam*. Washington, DC: Centre for Contemporary Arab Studies.

Asad, Talal. 2003. *Formations of the Secular: Christianity, Islam, Modernity*. Stanford, CA: Stanford University Press.

Aslan, Adnan. 1998. *Religious Pluralism: Christian and Islamic Philosophy: The Thought of John Hick and Seyyed Hossein Nasr*. Richmond, UK: Curzon Press.

Atay, Rifat. 1999. "Religious Pluralism and Islam: A Critical Examination of John Hick's Pluralistic Hypothesis." PhD diss., University of St. Andrews.

Audi, Robert. 1999. *The Cambridge Dictionary of Philosophy*, 2nd edn. Cambridge: Cambridge University Press.

al-Awa, Salwa. 2006. *Textual Relations in the Qur'an: Relevance, Coherence and Structure*. London: Routledge.

Badawi, Elsaid M. and Abdel Haleem, Muhammad. 2008. *Arabic-English Dictionary of Qur'ānic Usage*. Leiden and Boston: Brill.

Badawi, M. A. Z. 1979. *The Reformers of Egypt*. London: Croom Helm.

al-Baghdādī, ʿAbd al-Qāhir. 1920. *al-Farq bayna al-firaq*, vol. 1, trans. Kate C. Seelye. New York: Columbia University Press.

Barlas, Asma. 2002. *"Believing Women" in Islam: Unreading Patriarchal Interpretations of the Qur'an*. Austin: University of Texas Press.

Belhaj, Abdessamad. 2013. "Legal Knowledge by Application: Sufism as Islamic Legal Hermeneutics in the 10th/12th Centuries." *Studia Islamica* 108.1: 82–107.

Berger, Peter. 1967. *The Sacred Canopy: Elements of a Sociological Theory of Religion*. Garden City, NY: Doubleday.

Berkey, Jonathan P. and Saleh, Marlis J., eds. 2010. "Al-Subkī and His Women." *Mamluk Studies Review* 14: 8.

Bora, Fozia. 2019. *Writing History in the Medieval Islamic World: The Value of Chronicles as Archives*. London: I. B. Tauris.

Brodersen, Angelika. 2013. "al-Bukhārī, ʿAlāʾ al-Dīn," *Encyclopaedia of Islam, THREE*, ed. Kate Fleet et al. Leiden: Brill.

Brown, Daniel W. 1999. *Rethinking Tradition in Modern Islamic Thought*. Cambridge: Cambridge University Press.

Brown, Jonathan A. C. 2007. *The Canonization of al-Bukhārī and Muslim: The Formation and Function of the Sunnī Ḥadīth Canon*. Leiden: Brill.

Brown, Jonathan A. C. 2012. "Faithful Dissenters: Sunni Skepticism about the Miracles of Saints." *Journal of Sufi Studies* 1: 123–168.

Brown, Jonathan A. C. 2014. *Misquoting Muhammad: The Challenge and Choices of Interpreting the Prophet's Legacy*. London: Oneworld.

Brunner, Rainer and Ende, Werner. 2001. *The Twelver Shia in Modern Times: Religious Culture and Political History*. Leiden: Brill.

Brunner, Rainer. 2004. *Islamic Ecumenism in the 20th Century: The Azhar and Shiism between Rapprochement and Restraint*. Leiden and Boston: Brill.

Burton, John. 1990. *The Sources of Islamic Law: Islamic Theories of Abrogation*. Edinburgh: Edinburgh University Press.

Chignell, Andrew. 2009. "As Kant Has Shown," *Analytic Theology: New Essays in the Philosophy of Theology*, ed. Oliver Crisp and Michael C. Rea, pp. 117–136. Oxford and New York: Oxford University Press.

Chowdhury, Safaruk. 2021. *Islamic Theology and the Problem of Evil*. Cairo: AUC Press.

Crisp, Oliver and Rea, Michael C., eds. 2009. *Analytic Theology: New Essays in the Philosophy of Theology*. Oxford and New York: Oxford University Press.

Daftary, Farhad. 1990. *The Ismaʿilis: Their History and Doctrines*. Cambridge: Cambridge University Press.

Dag, Esra Akay. 2017. *Christian and Islamic Theology of Religions: A Critical Appraisal*. Oxford: Routledge.

Dahlén, Ashk. 2003. *Islamic Law, Epistemology and Modernity: Legal Philosophy in Contemporary Iran*. New York: Routledge.

Davids, Nuraan and Yusef, Waghid. 2016. *Ethical Dimensions of Muslim Education*. London: Palgrave Macmillan.

D'Costa, Gavin. 1989. *Theology and Religious Pluralism*, 2nd ed. Oxford: Basil Blackwell.

DeLong-Bas, Natana J. 2008. *Wahhabi Islam: From Revival and Reform to Global Jihad*. New York: Oxford University Press.

Denny, Frederick M. 1994. "Islamic Theology in the New World: Some Issues and Prospects." Settled Issues and Neglected Questions in the Study of Religion. Special issue of *Journal of the American Academy of Religion* 62.4: 1069–1084.

Denny, Frederick M. 2005. *An Introduction to Islam*, 3rd ed. Cambridge, UK: Pearson.

Duderija, Adis, ed. 2014. *Maqāṣid al-Sharīʿa and Contemporary Reformist Muslim Thought: An Examination*. New York: Palgrave Macmillan.

Duderija, Adis. 2017. *The Imperatives of Progressive Islam*. New York: Routledge.

Dudoignon, Stephane A. et al. 2006. *Intellectuals in the Modern Islamic World: Transmission, Transformation, Communication*. London and New York: Routledge.

El-Awa, Mohamed S. 2016. *The Objective of Justice in the Noble Qurʾān*, 1st ed. London: al-Furqan Islamic Heritage Foundation.

Emon, Anver M. and Rumee, Ahmad. 2015. *The Oxford Handbook of Islamic Law*. Oxford: Oxford University Press.

Ende, Werner. 1990. "Sunni Polemical Writings on the Shiʿa and the Iranian Revolution," *The Iranian Revolution and the Muslim World*, ed. David Menashri, pp. 219–232. Boulder, CO: Westview.

Esack, Farid. 1996. *Qur'an, Liberation and Religious Pluralism*. Oxford: Oneworld.

Esack, Farid. 1997. *Qurʾānic Liberation and Pluralism: An Islamic Perspective of Interreligious Solidarity Against Oppression*. Oxford: Oxford University Press.

Esposito, John L. 1999. *The Oxford History of Islam*. New York: Oxford University Press.

Esposito, John L., ed. 2003. *The Oxford Dictionary of Islam*. New York: Oxford University Press.

Esposito, John L. 2004. *The Islamic World: Abbasid-Caliphate Historians*. Oxford: Oxford University Press.

Esposito, John L. 2009. *The Oxford Encyclopedia of the Islamic World*. Oxford: Oxford University Press.

Fakhry, Majid. 1983. *A History of Islamic Philosophy*, 2nd ed. New York: Columbia University Press.

Firro, Tarik K. 2013. "The Political Context of Early Wahhabi Discourse of Takfir." *Middle Eastern Studies* 49.5: 770–789.

Firro, Tarik K. 2019. *Wahhabism and the Rise of the House of Saud*. Sussex: Sussex Academic Press.

Fleet, Kate et al. 2013. *Encyclopaedia of Islam, THREE*. Leiden: Brill.

Foucault, Michel. 1972. *Archeology of Knowledge and the Discourse on Language*. New York: Pantheon.

Frank, Richard. 1994. *Al-Ghazālī and the Ashʿarite School*. London and Durham, NC: Duke University Press.

Freidman, Yohanan. 2003. *Tolerance and Coercion in Islam: Interfaith Relations in the Muslim Tradition*. New York: Cambridge University Press.

Gelpi, Donald L. 2007. *The Gracing of Human Experience: Rethinking the Relationship between Nature and Grace*. Eugene, OR: Wipf and Stock.

al-Ghazālī, Abū Ḥāmid. 1924. *Mishkāt al-anwār*, vol. 19, trans. W. H. T. Gairdner. London: Royal Asiatic Society.

al-Ghazālī, Abū Ḥāmid. 1980. *al-Mustaẓhirī*, trans. Richard J. McCarthy. Woodbridge, UK: Twayne.

al-Ghazālī, Abū Ḥāmid. 1999. *Qawā'd al-'aqā'd*, 2nd ed., trans. Nabih A. Faris. Lahore: Ashraf Printing Press.

al-Ghazālī, Abū Ḥāmid. 2004. *The Alchemy of Happiness*. Tehran: Elmi va Frahanji.

al-Ghazālī, Abū Ḥāmid. 2005. *Ayyuhā al-walad*, trans. Tobias Mayor. Cambridge, UK: Cambridge Islamic Texts Society.

al-Ghazālī, Abū Ḥāmid. 2005. *al-Iqtiṣād*, trans. Dennis Morgan Davis Jr. PhD diss., University of Utah.

al-Ghazālī, Abū Ḥāmid. 2007. *al-Maqṣad al- asnā fi sharḥ asmā' Allāh al- ḥusnā, 6th ed.*, trans. David B. Burrell and Nazih Daher. Cambridge, UK: Islamic Texts Society.

al-Ghazālī, Abū Ḥāmid. 2008. *Iljām al-'awām 'an ilm al-kalām*, trans. Abdullah H. Ali. Philadelphia, PA: Lamp Post.

al-Ghazālī, Abū Ḥāmid. 2010. *Kitāb sharḥ 'ajā'ib al-qalb*, trans. Walter J. Skellie. Louisville, KY: Fons Vitae.

Goddard, Hugh. 2000. *A History of Christian-Muslim Relations*. Edinburgh: Edinburgh University Press.

Griffel, Frank. 2009. *Al-Ghazali's Philosophical Theology*. New York: Oxford University Press.

Grzelak, Krzysztof. 2018. "A Historical Perspective on Inclusivism as the Prevailing Paradigm in the Christian Theology of Religions." *Sympozjum* 22: 161–192.

Haidar, Yahya. 2016. "The Debates between Ash'arism and Māturīdism in Ottoman Religious Scholarship: A Historical and Bibliographical Study." PhD diss., Australian National University.

Haj, Samira. 2009. *Reconfiguring Islamic Tradition: Reform, Rationality and Modernity*. Stanford, CA: Stanford University Press.

Hallaq, Wael B. 1984. "Caliphs, Jurists and the Saljuqs in the Political Thought of Juwayni." *The Muslim World* 74.1: 26–41.

Hallaq, Wael B. 1997. *A History of Islamic Legal Theories: An Introduction to Sunni Usul al-Fiqh*. Cambridge: Cambridge University Press.

Hallaq, Wael B. 2009. *An Introduction to Islamic Law*. Cambridge: Cambridge University Press.

Halliday, Fred. 1993. "Orientalism and Its Critics." *British Journal of Middle Eastern Studies* 20.2: 145–163.

Halverson, Jeffry. 2010. *Theology and Creed in Sunni Islam: The Muslim Brotherhood, Ash'arism, and Political Sunnism*. 1st ed. New York: Palgrave Macmillan.

Hartog, Paul A., ed. 2015. *Orthodoxy and Heresy in Early Christian Contexts: Reconsidering the Bauer Thesis*. Cambridge, UK: James and Clarke.

Hasan, Ahmad. 1976. "The Principle of Qiyās in Islamic Law: An Historical Perspective." *Islamic Studies* 15.3: 201–210.

Hasan, Ahmad. 1965. "The Theory of Naskh." *Islamic Studies* 4.2: 181–200.

Hawtung, G. R. 1999. *The Idea of Idolatry and the Emergence of Islam*. Cambridge: Cambridge University Press.

Heck, Paul L. 2006. "The Crisis of Knowledge in Islam (I): The Case of al-Amirī." *Philosophy East and West* 34.2: 253–286.

Heck, Paul L. 2007. Review of *Sufism and Theology*, ed. Ayman Shihadeh. *Journal of Qur'ānic Studies* 10.1: 129–133.

Hick, John. 1973. *God and the Universe of Faiths*. London: Fount/Collins.

Hick, John. 1980. *God Has Many Names: Britain's New Religious Pluralism*. London: Macmillan.

Hick, John. 1989. *An Interpretation of Religion*. New Haven, CT: Yale University Press.

Hick, John. 1993. *Disputed Questions in Theology and the Philosophy of Religion*. New Haven, CT: Yale University Press.

Hirji, Zulfikar, ed. 2010. *Diversity and Pluralism in Islam: Historical and Contemporary Discourses amongst Muslims*. London and New York: I. B. Tauris and Institute of Ismaili Studies.

Hodgson, Marshall. 1974. *The Venture of Islam: Conscience and History in a World Civilization*. Chicago: University of Chicago Press.

Hooper, Walter. 1980. *Selected Literary Essays*, 3rd ed. Cambridge: Cambridge University Press.

Hourani, Albert. 1962. *Arabic Thought in the Liberal Age 1798–1939*. Oxford: Oxford University Press.

Hourani, Albert. 2002. *A History of the Arab Peoples*. London: Faber and Faber.

Hourani, George. 1985. *Reason and Tradition in Islamic Ethics*. Cambridge: Cambridge University Press.

Ibn ʿĀshūr, Ṭāhir al. 2006. *Maqāṣid al-Sharīʿa al-islamiyya*, trans. Mohamed T. El-Mesawi. London and Washington, DC: III.

Iqbal, Muhammad. 2012. *The Reconstruction of Religious Thought in Islam*, ed. Javed Majeed. Stanford, CA: Stanford University Press.

Irwin, Robert. 2010. *The New Cambridge History of Islam*. Cambridge: Cambridge University Press.

Ismail, Raihan. 2016. *Saudi Clerics and Shīʿa Islam*. New York: Oxford University Press.

Izutsu, Toshihiko. 2011. *Concept of Belief in Islamic Theology*. New York: The Other Press.

Izzati, Abu al-Fzal. 2002. *Islam and Natural Law*. London: Islamic College for Advanced Studies.

Jackson, Sherman. 1996. *Islamic Law and the State: The Constitutional Jurisprudence of Shihab Al-Din Al-Qarafi*. Leiden: Brill.

Jackson, Sherman. 2002. *On the Boundaries of Theological Tolerance in Islam*. New York and Oxford: Oxford University Press.

Jackson, Sherman. 2009. *Islam and the Problem of Black Suffering*. Oxford: Oxford University Press.

Jaffer, Tareq. 2015. *al-Rāzī: Master of Qur'ānic Interpretation and Theological Reasoning*. Oxford and New York: Oxford University Press.

Johnston, David. 2004. "A Turn in the Epistemology and Hermeneutics of Twentieth Century Uṣūl al-Fiqh." *Islamic Law and Society* 11.2: 233–282.

Juergensmeyer, Mark. 2010. "2009 Presidential Address: Beyond Words and War: The Global Future of Religion." *Journal of the American Academy of Religion* 78.4: 882–895.

Kamali, Mohammed H. 1996. "Methodological Issues in Islamic Jurisprudence." *Arab Law Quarterly* 11.1: 3–33.

Kamali, Mohammed H. 2001. "Issues in the Legal Theory of Usul and Prospects for Reform." *Islamic Studies* 40: 5–23.

Kamali, Mohammed H. 2018 "Goals and Purposes Maqāṣid al-Sharīʿa: Methodological Perspectives," *The Objectives of Islamic Law: The Promises and Challenges of Maqāṣid al-Sharīʿa,* ed. Idris Nassery et al., pp. 7–35. London: Lexington.

Kant, Immanuel. 1999. *Critique of Pure Reason*. Cambridge: Cambridge University Press.

Karkkainen, Veli-Matti. 2003. *An Introduction to the Theology of Religions: Biblical, Historical and Contemporary Perspectives.* Westmont, IL: InterVarsity Press.

Kateman, Ammeke. 2019. *Muḥammad ʿAbduh and His Interlocutors: Conceptualizing Religion in a Globalizing World.* Leiden and Boston: Brill.

Kazemi, Reza S. 2006. *The Other in the Light of the One: The Universality of the Qur'an and Interfaith Dialogue*. Cambridge, UK: Islamic Texts Society.

Keller, Nuh. 1997. *Reliance of the Traveller: A Classic Manual of Islamic Sacred Law.* Beltsville, MD: Amana.

Khalil, Mohammad H. 2007. "Muslim Scholarly Discussions on Salvation and the Fate of Others." PhD diss., University of Michigan.

Khalil, Mohammad H. 2012. *Islam and the Fate of Others: The Salvation Question.* Oxford: Oxford University Press.

Khalil, Mohammad H. 2013. *Between Heaven and Hell: Islam, Salvation, and the Fate of Others.* Oxford: Oxford University Press.

Köchler, Hans, ed. 1982. *Concept of Monotheism in Islam and Christianity.* Vienna: International Progress Organization.

Krawietz, Birgit and Tamer, Georges. 2013. *Islamic Theology, Philosophy and Law: Debating Ibn Taymiyya and Ibn Qayyim al-Jawziyya*. Berlin: De Gruyter.

Laher, Suheil. 2014. "Twisted Threads: Genesis, Development and Application of the Term and Concept of Tawatur in Islamic Thought." PhD diss., Harvard University.

Lange, Christian. 2016. *Paradise and Hell in the Islamic Traditions.* Cambridge: Cambridge University Press.

Leaman, Oliver. 1985. *An Introduction to Classical Islamic Philosophy.* Cambridge: Cambridge University Press.

Leaman, Oliver. 2015. *The Biographical Encyclopedia of Islamic Philosophy.* London: Bloomsbury.

Litvak, Meir and Bengio, Ofra. 2011. *The Sunna and Shiʿa in History: Division and Ecumenism in the Muslim Middle East.* New York: Palgrave Macmillan.

Makdisi, George. 1962. *Ash'ari and the Ash'arites in Islamic Religious History I.* Paris: Maisonneuve and Larose.

Makdisi, George. 1962. "Ash'arī and the Ash'arites in Islamic Religious History I," *Studia Islamica* 17: 37–80.

Makdisi, George. 1971. "Law and Traditionalism in the Institutions of Learning of Medieval Islam," in *Theology and Law in Islam*, ed. G. von Grunebaum, pp. 75–88. Wiesbaden: Otto Harrassowitz.

Makdisi, George. 1990. *The Rise of Humanism in Classical Islam and the Christian West: With Special Reference to Scholasticism*. Edinburgh: Edinburgh University Press.

Malik, Fazlur Rahman. 1963. "The Post-Formative Developments in Islam—II:IV: The Philosophical Movement." *Islamic Studies* 2.3: 297–316.

Martin, Richard C. et al. 1997. *Defenders of Reason in Islam: Mu'tazililism: From Medieval School to Modern Symbol.* Oxford: Oneworld.

Masroori, Cyrus. 2010. *An Islamic Language of Toleration: Rumi's Criticism of Religious Persecution*. London: Sage.

Mayer, Toby. 2008. "Theology and Sufism," *The Cambridge Companion to Classical Islamic Theology*, ed. Tim Winter, pp. 258–288. Cambridge: Cambridge University Press.

McAuliffe, Jane. 1991. *Qur'ānic Christians: An Analysis of Classical and Modern Exegesis.* Cambridge: Cambridge University Press.

McCarthy, Richard J. S. 1980. *Freedom and Fulfillment: An Annotated Translation of al-Ghazali's al-Munqidh min al-dalāl.* Boston: Twayne.

McGrath, Alister. 2011. *Christian Theology: An Introduction,* 5th ed. Oxford: Wiley Blackwell.

McGrath, Alister. 2013. *Historical Theology: An Introduction to the History of Christian Thought,* 2nd ed. Oxford: Wiley Blackwell.

Melchert, Christopher. 2006. *Ahmad Ibn Hanbal.* Oxford: Oneworld.

Mitha, Farouk. 2001. *Al-Ghazālī and the Ismailis: A Debate on Reason and Authority in Medieval Islam*. London and New York: I. B. Tauris.

Moosa, Ebrahim. 2005. *Ghazālī and the Poetics of Imaginations.* London and Chapel Hill: University of North Carolina Press.

Muller, Max. 1889. *Introduction to the Science of Religion*. London: Longmans, Green.

Muller, Max. 1993. *The Need for a Sacred Science*. London: Curzon Press.

Nasr, Seyyed H. et al. 1996. *History of Islamic Philosophy.* London and New York: Routledge.

Nasr, Seyyed H. et al. 2015. *The Study Qur'ān: A New Translation and Commentary*, 1st ed. New York: HarperCollins.

Nassery, Idris et al. 2018. *The Objectives of Islamic Law: The Promises and Challenges of Maqāṣid al-Sharī'ā.* London: Lexington.

Nasution, Harun. 1968. "The Place of Reason in 'Abduh's Theology: Its Impact on His Theological System and Views." PhD diss., University of Montreal.

Nyazee, Imran A. K. 2007. *Theories of Islamic Law*. Islamabad: Federal Law House.

Opwis, Felicitas. 2005. "Maṣlaḥa in Contemporary Islamic Legal Theory." *Islamic Law and Society* 12.2: 182–223.

Petersen, Erling L. 1964. *ʿAlī and Muʿāwiya in Early Arabic Tradition: Studies on the Genesis and Growth of Islamic Historical Writing until the End of the Ninth Century*. Copenhagen: Scandinavian University Books.

Porpora, Douglas V. 2006. "Methodological Atheism, Methodological Agnosticism and Religious Experience." *Journal for the Theory of Social Behaviour* 36.1: 57–75.

Powers, Paul R. 2006. *Intent in Islamic Law*. Leiden and Boston: Brill.

al-Qarāfī, Shihāb al-Dīn. 2017. *Al-Iḥkām*, trans. Mohammad H. Fadel. New Haven, CT, and London: Yale University Press.

Qazi, M. A. 1979. *A Concise Dictionary of Islamic Terms*. Lahore: Kazi.

Radtke, Bernd. 1989. "A Forerunner of Ibn al-Arabi: Hakim Tirmidhi on Sainthood." *Journal of the Ibn Arabi Society* 8: 42–49.

Rahnema, Ali, ed. 1994. *Pioneers of Islamic Revival*. London: Zed Books.

Rapoport, Yossef. 2003. "Legal Diversity in the Age of *Taqlīd*: The Four Chief Qāḍīs under the Mamluks." *Islamic Law and Society* 10.2: 210–228.

Rapoport, Yossef and Ahmed, Shahab. 2010. *Introduction in Ibn Taymiyya and His Times*. Karachi: Oxford University Press.

al-Raysūnī, Aḥmad. 2006. *Naẓariyyat al-maqāṣid ʿind al-Imām al-Shāṭibī*, trans. Nancy Roberts. Herndon, VA: International Institute of Islamic Thought.

Rohman, Izza. 2012. "Salafi Tafsirs: Textualist and Authoritarian?" *Al-Bayan: Journal of Qur'an and Ḥadīth Studies* 1.2: 197–213.

Rosenthal, Franz. 2007. *Knowledge Triumph: The Concept of Knowledge in Medieval Islam*. Leiden and Boston: Brill.

al-Rouayheb, Khaled. 2015. *Islamic Intellectual History in the Seventeenth Century: Scholarly Currents in the Ottoman Empire and the Maghreb*. New York: Cambridge University Press.

Saeed, Abdullah. 2006. *Islamic Thought: An Introduction*, 1st ed. London and New York: Routledge.

Saeed, Abdullah. 2014. *Reading the Qur'an in the Twenty-First Century: A Contextualist Approach*. New York: Routledge.

Schacht, Joseph. 1959. *The Origins of Muhammadan Jurisprudence*. Oxford: Oxford University Press.

Shahin, Emad E. 1995. *The Oxford Encyclopedia of the Modern Islamic World*. Oxford: Oxford University Press.

Shaikh, Saʿdiyya. 2009. "In Search of al-Insān: Sufism, Islamic Law, and Gender." *Journal of the American Academy of Religion* 77.4: 781–822.

Shamsy, Ahmed El. 2020. *Rediscovering the Islamic Classics: How Editors and Print Culture Transformed an Intellectual Tradition*. Princeton, NJ, and Oxford: Princeton University Press.

al-Shāṭibī, Abū Isḥāq. 2014. *al-Muwāfaqāt fi uṣūl al-Sharīʿa* (The Reconciliation of the Fundamentals of Islamic Law), trans. Imran A. K. Nyazee, vols 1 and 2. Reading, UK: Garnet.

Shihadeh, Ayman. 2007. *Sufism and Theology*. Edinburgh: Edinburgh University Press.

Shihadeh, Ayman and Thiele, Jan. 2020. *Philosophical Theology in Islam: Later Ashʿarism East and West*. Leiden: Brill.

Siddiqi, Muḥammad Z. 1993. *Ḥadīth Literature*, ed. Abdal Hakim Murad. Cambridge, UK: Islamic Texts Society.

Smart, Ninian. 1989. *The World's Religions: Old Traditions and Modern Transformations*. Cambridge: Cambridge University Press.

Steinberg, Jonah. 2011. *Ismaʿili Modern: Globalization and Identity in a Muslim Community*. Chapel Hill: University of North Carolina Press.

al-Tabatba'i, Sayyid M. H. 1981. *A Shiʿite Anthology*, trans. William C. Chittick. Albany: State University of New York Press.

al-Tabatba'i, Sayyid M. H. n.d. *Glimpses of Shiism in the Musnad of Ibn Hanbal*, trans. Sayyid Shahbaz. Qom: Ahl al-Bayt World Assembly.

Van Ess, Josef. 2006. *The Flowering of Muslim Theology*, trans. Jane M. Todd. Cambridge, MA: Harvard University Press.

Van Ess, Josef. 2016. *Theology and Society in the Second and Third Centuries of the Hijra: A History of Religious Thought in Early Islam*. Leiden and Boston: Brill.

Verskin, Alan. 2015. *Islamic Law and the Crisis of the Reconquista: The Debate on the Status of Muslim Communities in Christendom*. Leiden: Brill.

Walters, James. 2018. *Religious Imaginations: How Narratives of Faith Are Shaping Today's World*, ed. James S. Walters. London: Gingko Library.

Watt, Montgomery. 1963. *Muslim Intellectual: A Study of al-Ghazālī*. Edinburgh: Edinburgh University Press.

Watt, Montgomery. 1974. *Muhammad: Prophet and Statesman*. Oxford: Oxford University Press.

Watt, Montgomery. 1985. *Islamic Philosophy and Theology: An Extended Survey*, 2nd ed. Edinburgh: Edinburgh University Press.

Watt, Montgomery. 1996. *The Faith and Practice of Al-Ghazali*. New Delhi: Kitab Behavan.

Wehr, Hans. 1976. *Arabic-English Dictionary*, 3rd ed., ed. J. M. Cowan. New York: Spoken Languages Services.

Wensinck, A. J. 1932. *The Muslim Creed*. Cambridge: Cambridge University Press.

White, R. Alan. 1969. "Coherence Theory of Truth." *Encyclopedia of Philosophy* 2: 131–133.

Winter, Tim. 1999. "The Last Trump Card: Islam and the Supersession of Other Faiths." *Studies in Interreligious Dialogue* 9: 133–155.

Wittingham, Martin. 2007. *Al-Ghazālī and the Qur'ān: One Book, Many Meanings*. New York: Routledge.

Zebiri, Kate. 1993. *Mahmud Shaltut and Islamic Modernism*. Oxford: Clarendon Press.

ONLINE SOURCES

Amin, Osman. n.d. "Influence of Muslim Philosophy on the West." *Renaissance Online Journal*, Pakistan, accessed 20 January 2021: http://www.monthly-renaissance.com/issue/content.aspx?id=25.

Ibn Al-Hashimi. n.d. "Are the Shia Considered Muslims? A Balanced Answer." *Le Chiisme Duodécimain*, accessed 11 February 2021: http://www.chiite.fr/en/islam_02.html.

Al-Beḥerī, Aḥmed. 2017. "Al-Azhar lā yamlik takfīr al-nās." *Al-Masry Al-Youm*, accessed 5 February 2021: https://www.almasryalyoum.com/news/details/1132163.

Shaltut, Mahmud. 1959. "Shaykh Mahmud Shaltut's Fatwa about Shia Madhab." *Digital Library*, accessed 2 February 2021: https://www.icit-digital.org/articles/shaykh-mahmud-shaltut-s-fatwa-about-shia-madhab-1959.

Index

For the benefit of digital users, indexed terms that span two pages (e.g., 52–53) may, on occasion, appear on only one of those pages.

ʿĀʾisha, 46
ʿAbduh, xvii, 1–2, 23, 26–28, 29–31, 76, 83–84, 86, 88, 89, 93–94, 95, 105–7, 113–14
al-ʿAdl, 56–57, 58
  Justice, xiii, 3–4, 17, 25, 38–39, 41–42, 54, 55–57, 58, 89, 110, 113
al-ʿĀmirī, xxiv–xxv, 5, 6
Abou El Fadl, xiii–, 45, 101, 114
Asad, xix
al-Ashʿarī, 10, 32, 33, 73, 77, 78, 90–91
  Ashʿarism, xxvi–xxvii, 8–9, 10, 31, 32, 39–40, 63, 76, 77, 80, 83, 84–85, 86, 88, 89–91, 93, 95–96, 111–12
  Ashʿarites, xvi, 8–9, 32, 33, 77–78, 80, 81–82, 83, 86, 93, 116–17n.19
Al-Azhar, 26–27, 84, 89, 96, 113–14, 126n.107

al-Baghdādī, 78, 90–91, 135–36n.34
al-Bāqillānī, 72–74, 78, 80, 135n.30
Bayānī, 51–52
Bennabi, xiv
Burhānī, 51–52

Ḍarūriyyāt, 77–96
  ḍarūriyyāt, xxiv, 68–69, 70, 71–72, 73–74, 75–76, 80–81, 83, 86–87, 88, 89–91, 93–94, 95–96, 111–12, 113–14
  primaries, xxiv, 75–76
al-Dehlawī, xxiv–xxv, 1, 23, 121n.71

El-Awa, 55–56

al-Farābī, xxii, 5, 119n.54
al-Fāsī, xvi, 55–56, 116n.13
Fazlur Rahman, xiii–xiv
Fiqh, xiii–xv, xvii–xviii, 23–24
Al-Firqa al-Nājiya, 77–86
  al-firqa al-nājiya, xxv–xxvi, 34, 76, 77, 78, 80, 83, 86, 95, 111–12
  saved denomination, xxv–xxvi, 70, 77, 80

Al-Ghazālī, 7–23, 46, 47, 50, 60–61, 73–74, 75, 80–82
  al-Ghazālī, xv–xvi, xvii, 1–26, 33, 34, 44, 47–48, 49–50, 51–52, 53, 59, 66, 72, 73–75, 80–82, 84–85, 86–87, 88, 89–90, 91, 92–93, 95, 103–4, 105

ḥadīth Jibrīl, 54, 57
Ḥājiyyāt, 68–69, 77–96
ḥājiyyāt, xxiv, 68–69, 70, 71–72, 74, 75–76, 83, 86–87, 88, 89–90, 91, 95–96, 111–12, 113
complementaries, xxiv, 68–69
al-Ḥakīm al-Tirmidhī, xxiv–xxv, 1, 2, 23, 120n.66
al-Tirmidhī, 2, 3–4
Ḥalīm, 84, 85, 137n.54
Ḥanbalism, 77
al-Ḥaqq, 56–57, 58, 59, 60, 78, 80, 110–11
Truth, xiii, 3, 5, 9, 15, 16–17, 34, 35, 42, 43–44, 47, 49–50, 54, 56–57, 58, 59–60, 62–63, 64, 65, 66–67, 73–74, 78–79, 80, 85, 90, 93, 104, 111
ḥifẓ, 55, 58
ḥudūd, xxv, 53, 54–56, 111, 113

ʿibādāt, 25, 38–39
ʿilla, xvi, 34, 36–37, 111
taʿlīl, 31, 32, 36–37, 39, 41, 111
ḥikma, 18, 34
wisdom, xvi, 4, 6, 14, 18, 27–28, 32, 34, 38–39, 41, 42, 60, 77–78, 79
thubūt, 58
ẓuhūr, 58
inḍibāṭ, 58
iṭṭirād, 58
istiqrāʾ, 45–46, 51–52, 111
istidlāl, 51–52
istinbāṭ, 51–52
ʿirfānī, 51–52
Ibn ʿAbbās, 60, 131n.31
Ibn ʿAbd al-Salām, xv–xvi, xxiv–xxv, 1, 23, 24–25, 115n.9
Ibn ʿAbd al-Wahhāb, 97–98, 100–1, 102–3, 105, 112–13, 140–41n.20
Ibn ʿAjība, 39–40, 43, 129–30n.5
Ibn ʿĀshūr, xvi, 58, 84–85, 116n.15
Ibn Ḥanbal, xxvi, 78, 97, 98–99, 102, 103, 112–13, 121n.75
Ibn Khaldūn, xxii, 118–19n.51
Ibn al-Qayyim, 38–39, 129n.1
Ibn Taymiyya, xvii–xviii, xix, 1, 23, 25, 75–76, 97, 98–100, 101, 103, 112–13, 117n.28
al-Ījī, xxii, 83, 119n.55
interfaith, 30, 64, 95–96, 113–14
intrafaith, 30, 95–96
Iqbāl, xxii, 32, 119n.56
al-Isfarāyīnī, 80
Islamic law, xiii, 3–4, 32, 53, 54, 55

al-Jamāl, 56–57, 58
Beauty, xiii, 12, 17, 54, 56–57, 58, 61, 110, 113
Josef van Ess, 32
al-Jubbāʾī, 32, 33
al-Juwaynī, 7–8, 53, 80, 86, 90–91, 124n.35

Kalām, xiii, 10, 21, 35–36, 77–78, 102–3
Kamali, 38–39
Kantian, xxv, 64–65, 66, 111
al-Khaṭīb al-Baghdādī, 77, 135n.27

Maqāṣid al-Sharīʿa, xiv–, 8, 23, 24–25, 31, 45–46, 53–56, 58, 60–61, 110, 111, 112, 113
legal objectives, xiv–xv, 2, 3
Moosa, xx
muʿāmalāt, 38–39
Muʿtazilism, xvii, 8–9, 84–85
Muʿtazilites, xvi, 27–28, 32, 35, 39–40, 72, 73–74, 77–78, 79–80, 81–82
mutawātir, 91

naskh, xxiii–xxiv, 70, 90–91, 93
abrogation, xxiii–, 63, 70
supersessionism, 90
supersessionist, 63
naẓar, 83–84

qiyās, 31, 127–28n.130
al-Qummī, xxiv–xxv, 1, 23

al-Raysūnī, xv–xvi, 55–56
al-Rāzī, xxiv–xxv, 1, 23–24, 39–40, 41, 43, 65, 82, 93, 121n.70
Riḍā, xxiv–xxv, 1, 23, 26, 27, 30–31, 93–94, 105–6, 121n.72
Rūmī, 66, 134n.40

Saeed, xx
Salafism, xix, 27, 84–85
Shaltūt, xxvi, 84–85, 103, 106–8, 121–22n.76
al-Shāṭibī, xv–xvi, 2, 22, 31, 45–46, 62–63, 69, 115–16n.10
Shiism, 4, 84, 97, 98–100, 101, 103, 105–8, 112–13
siyāq, 46, 111
Sufism, xiii, 35–37, 54, 56–57, 58, 83–84, 85, 110, 111

ta'wīl, 77–78
al-Ṭabarī, 40, 65, 130n.10
Taḥsīniyyāt, xxiv, 69, 77–90
supplementaries, xxiv, 75–76
taḥsīniyyāt, xxiv, 69, 70, 71–72, 74, 75–76, 83, 86–87, 88, 89–90, 91, 95–96, 111–12, 113
ṭalab, 55
ṭarīq al-ḥikma, 77–78
ṭarīq as-salāma, 77–78
Taṣawuf, xiii, 54
tashbīh, 77–78
theological objectives, 4, 8, 9, 24–25, 31, 32

Wahhabism, 100–1, 102, 107

al-Zāhid al-Bukhārī, xxiv–xxv, 1, 23, 121n.69
al-Zamakhsharī, 40, 41, 43, 130n.7
ẓannī, 44–46
Zaynab, 46
al-Zuḥaylī, xv–xvi